PROMISED LANDS

Growing Up Absurd
in the 1950s and '60s

DOUGLAS WILLIAMS

ABOUT THE AUTHOR

Doug Williams is an award-winning television director, writer and producer. He has written articles about the Canadian film industry for the Toronto Star and NOW Magazine, and film criticism for RELAY. He lives in Toronto, Canada, with his wife, the screenwriter Laura Phillips.

PROMISED LANDS Growing Up Absurd in the 1950s and '60s
© 2012 by Douglas Williams. All rights reserved.

Cover concept by Douglas Williams.
Front cover illustration by Danyel Baltus.
Back cover photo by Douglas Williams.
Pagination and graphic design by Pam Sloan - pamsloan.ca.
Publisher: Michael Grass House, Kingston Ontario

ISBN 978-0-9879725-4-5

TABLE OF CONTENTS

PART ONE   Let's Have Fun Instead

1   Kerouac's Children 11
2   Baggage 16
3   The Charm of Foreign Climes 19
4   Munich 23
5   A Brush with Hollywood 26
6   My Friend Gregg C. 28
7   Athens and the Greeks 31
8   Athens Underground 36
9   Life in Athens' Old City 40
10   Hashish 43
11   Takis Voglis 48
12   The Scene 50
13   Days and Nights in Athens 56
14   An Encounter with the Greek Police 60
15   Athens Adio 62
16   The Last Straw 64
17   Flash Forward 66

PART TWO   Me Of All People

18   Memories of My Father 75
19   Who Were My Parents? 92
20   Saint Tammy of the Mangers 96
21   Life with Mother 102
22   Country Life 107
23   Germans 110
24   Cousin Graham 113
25   The End of an Era 118
26   The Town of Kingsville 121
27   Meet the Keeles 126
28   I Am That I Am, So Fuck You 128
29   Kingsville Adolescence 130
30   Town and Country 136

PART THREE Condemned To Be Free

31   Istanbul, Constantinople and Byzantium 141
32   Shopping in Istanbul 147
33   The Samaritans 151
34   Further South 153
35   Slouching Towards Bethlehem 157
36   Do the Dead See? 159
37   Jerusalem 162
38   Socialed Farming and the Jews 164
39   Pipe Dreams 167
40   The Truth About Kibbutz Women 170
41   Ancient Evenings in Israel 175
42   Turkish, Lebanese or Afgani? 180
43   Eilat and The Red Sea 182
44   A Threat of War 186
45   Return to Givat Haim Me'uchad 188
46   Exodus 191
47   In Transit 194
48   Italy 199
49   La France 203
50   Pamplona, Sgt. Pepper and LSD 205
51   Encore une fois, la France 210
52   French Wine/Women/Song 214
53   Geneva and Mirjam 220
54   From Geneva to London 229
55   British Culture I 235
56   A Weekend in Nottingham 238
57   British Culture II 241
58   A Revealing Anecdote 244
59   An Unexpected Visitor 247
60   British Culture III 250
61   Film School and the Trots:
       Their Morals and Ours 254
62   Andrew Sarris, Auteurs and Hitchock 260
63   Triumph of the Dunes 266

DEDICATION

This book is dedicated to my patient and supportive wife, Laura Phillips, who generously tolerated my frequent unemployment and my excuse that I was busy writing a book.

FOREWORD

Special thanks to Danyel Baltus, a Belgian painter whom I met in Athens in 1966. He was a gifted and prolific artist – his drawing, that he declared was a portrait of me, graces the cover of this book. It is rumored that he died of a drug overdose in Tunisia in 1967.

Thanks to Gregg Connolly, Gildas Failler, Laura Phillips, Vasilis Pagonis, C. Seney, the Kingsville and Gosfield South Heritage Society, and the Southwestern Ontario Heritage Village and Transportation Museum, for permission to use their photographs.

I have changed the names of some of the young men I met during my travels – partly from a fear that they may retaliate in their current roles as high-ranking government figures, respected professionals or arch criminals. As for the young women mentioned, I have changed all names for reasons which may become obvious.

"*We was used to the balloon now, and not afraid any more, and didn't want to be anywheres else ... and always I had had hateful people around me, a-nagging at me, and pestering of me, and scolding, and finding fault, and fussing and bothering, and sticking to me, and keeping after me, and making me do this, that and t'other, and always selecting out the things I didn't want to do, and then giving me Sam Hill because I shirked and done something else, and just aggravating the life out of a body all the time; but up here in the sky, it was so still, sunshiney and lovely, and plenty to eat and plenty of sleep, and strange things to see, and no nagging and no pestering, and no good people and just holiday all the time. Land, I warn't in no hurry to get out and buck at civilization again...*"

— **Mark Twain,**
Tom Sawyer Abroad

PART ONE

LET'S HAVE FUN INSTEAD

Chapter 1

KEROUAC'S CHILDREN

I saw the best minds of my generation go off to university in the mid-Sixties. Some of the rest of us - wanderers, riffraff, bohemians, freaks, wayfarers, beatniks, hippies and the broken hearted, we who had decided to sidestep participation in becoming the most educated generation in history - saved up U$167.00 and flew Icelandic Airways to Luxembourg.

I think broken hearts were common to many of us. The choice to reject mainstream pursuits can be grounded in a mixture of ill fortune, sadness and pride. My habitual optimism had reached an all-time low by the time I flunked out of high school, and rejection of conventional life options now came naturally.

It was a frosty morning on November 6th, 1966. The day is best remembered for the launch of NASA's famous Lunar Orbiter, and news of its lift-off stole some thunder from my Kingsville departure. By home town standards, I may as well have been headed for the moon myself. While my friends (except Paul Keele, who joined me with knapsack and guitar) were heading towards sensible lives and dazzling careers, I was cutting all ties: my ticket to Europe was one-way.

In my limited financial experience, five hundred dollars in traveller's cheques and faint promises of a small tax refund from a year spent bolting transmissions to engine blocks at Chrysler's Windsor Assembly Plant seemed like a reasonable fortune to pit against the unknown. Paul and I were embarked on a poor man's

The author, November 6th, 1966. Photo by Irene Williams.

tour of the world (our copy of *Europe On $5 A Day* was discarded
as "frat-boy bullshit"). We had walked to the edge of town, braved
the taunts of the local "philistines" who paraded past in their new
Camaros and GTOs en route to the Ford and GM plants in Windsor
or the potash works in Sarnia, and stuck out our thumbs, holding
a sign saying *Athens, Greece!* Specificity about *which* Athens was
important. "Oh look - the other Athens," said some passers-by.
Ontario had its very own, perfectly good Athens, London and Paris,
and confident that the "other Athens" offered no *July Ploughing
Match and Tractor Pull*, no *August Cornfest*, no mercury-rich *Lake
Erie Fish Fry* popular among autistic kids hoping for careers as candy
thermometers, they gave our destination not another thought.

We felt no need to reveal that our first European stop would
be the tiny nation of Luxembourg – it was Icelandic Airways'
only destination. Brochure photos made it look like a storybook
theme park invented by Walt Disney: a mountaintop castle where

all its kings and royals lived, surrounded by quaint city and rolling farmland. As I was to discover, the Grand Duchy of Luxembourg is barely the size of a postage stamp (a fact which has often led to chaos in the European postal system) - too small for airline runways and duty free shops. North Americans, used to travelling thousands of miles in any direction without leaving their own back yards, will be shocked to find that to visit Luxembourg you first must land next door in France. You then pay a small fee and are ushered through a tiny gate into a miniature world of altitudinally-challenged people. Their diminutive size has led to bizarre confrontations with the outside world. The Grand Duchy has neither air force nor navy, a strange choice for a people who are – like their country – tiny and defenceless to begin with. Grand Duchess Charlotte's attempt to create a military in the post war era – she purchased miniature transistorized tanks and aircraft from eager Japanese suppliers - prompted gales of cross-border ridicule: diplomats and generals from Germany, France and Belgium gathered at checkpoints and laughingly offered to send their kids over for a play date.

But Luxembourg was not the First Act of my wanderings. My adventure had really started some four hours earlier, during a brief stopover in Iceland. Being there was the first heady proof that my life of angst and ennui in dreary North America had been left behind. I had just turned twenty. Standing on the icy tarmac at Reykjavik's Keflavik Airport, surveying the treeless terrain and the distant snow capped mountains, it occurred to me that I could end my journey here. I had read Sartre, who made the sobering pronouncement that *"Man is condemned to be free,"* so I frequently tormented myself with thoughts like this. Sartre's ominous words grabbed me in a way that (despite the millions of dollars spent on its creation by the geniuses of Madison Avenue) *"Come Alive! You're in the Pepsi Generation!"* completely failed to do. It was possible - in theory - to settle down with a fiercely pretty, ruddy-complexioned Icelandic girl (she was pictured on the government brochure that came with my ticket), her gaze permanently raised towards those snow capped mountains, a light breeze - even when indoors - moving the curls that garlanded her freckled face, and work in a fish processing plant.

But, despite her prim appeal, three hours out of New York seemed a little early to terminate a trip that I had been dreaming of for years - just for an imaginary girl and a lifetime supply of canned herring.

I was stretching my legs and gasping Iceland's frigid air. Peer pressure on the flight from New York required smoking countless American cigarettes until I had the wit and pallor of a mushroom. A November gale whipped across the landing strip and made me shiver; sleet began to sting my face. I remembered a picture from *LIFE* magazine of Sartre standing on an ice floe. Hoping I was invincible, I climbed back up towards the brief sanctuary of the plane.

I had a window seat. The atmosphere in the cabin was one of quiet excitement with intermittent bursts of revelry. Someone was playing a guitar, and Marlboros and Gauloises scented the air. Most of the passengers were young North American males like me, deep in the hippie-larval stage of development: longish hair, thin beards and moustaches, rumpled jeans. Icelandic Airways' turboprop hospitality was the last guarantee of warmth and security many of us had as we roared up into the North Atlantic sky towards *Europe, Land of Adventure*.

The flight brochure had trumpeted *FREE WINE WITH DINNER!* I had been looking forward to it for months. With the spectacular exception of Paul Keele's home made dandelion wine, it was very nearly my first wine (the United Church communion wine was grape juice served in tiny paper condiment cups – the limit was one thimble per customer, lest a Godless *bacchanal* be unleashed in the rectory). I shuddered as I savoured its acidic bouquet. The "drinking age" in Kingsville was twenty-one and I was having difficulty shaking the taboos of small town life. What was the drinking age over the Atlantic? My unease prompted a fantasy of startling intensity:

> *Nervously clutching my plastic cup of Beaujolais, I glance at the clouds outside my window - just as a Kingsville Constabulary Airborne Tactical Unit pulls up alongside our plane! I slam down the shade, but it's too late. Our co-pilot promptly patches the KCATU through the p.a. system:* "Douglas Williams - we know you're in there! Stand up and place your hands behind

14

your head! Do not attempt to hide the wine bottle!" *There's a crash and a furious whoosh of air as they board the plane. SWAT guys rush down the aisle towards me, as the squad leader's porcine features twist into a vicious grin:* "Sorry for the interruption everyone, but this kid's coming back to Kingsville with us! *(pulls Doug to his feet and whacks him with truncheon)* We'll teach you about the Devil's Beverage, sonny boy - now move!" *The guitars have fallen silent and everyone stares as I'm cuffed and led out. We cross a windswept footbridge to the other plane where I'm confronted by a judicial body of Kingsville's guardians of the moral order who have so generously given of their time to bring this wayward son to heel: my former algebra and chemistry teachers, a gaggle of Sunday school superintendents, three ageing farm wives from the Grundy clan, and of course, my mother. Across the way, I see my new pals resume their festivities. The footbridge is withdrawn and the Icelandic Airways Freedom Plane veers away into the clouds.*

In addition to the wine, the stunningly compact airline meal which lay before me – the rations of chicken, vegetables and dessert were cube-shaped - was possibly my last for days, weeks, maybe years to come: I actually believed I would attempt to eat once every two days in Europe. I considered keeping the tiny wine bottle as a souvenir, but realized that it was a little early to start hoarding mementos. I left it on my tray, lit up a Marlboro, settled into my seat and considered the blank pages of my new diary.

Chapter 2

BAGGAGE

My knapsack was loaded with books that I knew would be read by the kind of person I wanted to be, proving to me and anyone who might inquire, that my journey was a but a momentary glitch in my intellectual development, i.e. about a lot more than sex:

1. **Desolation Angels (Jack Kerouac)** :
   "From the International Underground of the Beatnik Empire!" said the blurb beneath the title. Kerouac wrote: *"All of life is a foreign country."*

2. **Film Form and the Film Sense (Sergei Eisenstein):**
   The Saturday matinee at Kingsville's Roxy Theatre was a cultural hybrid that combined juvenile detention with carnival fun house. Kids were thrust into the darkness, mid-film, by parents desperate for a break. In winter the smells of rancid butter, red licorice and steamy rubber galoshes filled the mischievous air. Unleashed, we ran up and down her gummy aisles, laughing, throwing popcorn, fighting, yelling, and chasing girls. This savage clientele cared little for the cinema's contrived beginnings and ends: we watched until a familiar scene reappeared - "This is where we came in!" - and soon Mom or Dad would return to take us home. But unlike most of Kingsville's townsfolk, I grew to love the movies. I saw *Forbidden Planet, Bridge on the River*

Roxy Theatre, Kingsville, Ontario.
Photo courtesy of Kingsville-Gosfield Heritage Society

Kwai and *West Side Story* there, *West Side Story* four nights in a row. The Roxy Theatre closed a few months after I left, I having been, on many memorable evenings, its only patron.

3. **Man Alone (various authors):**
    A popular anthology of really depressing essays about alienation, mental illness and existentialism. I seemed to have every symptom of every mental disorder mentioned.

4. **The Organization Man (William H. Whyte):**
    Being one was about as un-cool as you could get. How things have changed in corporate Canada.

5. **Growing Up Absurd (Paul Goodman):**
    It was what we would do before becoming part of the army of pipsqueaks that makes up the face of modern man - Organization Men. The title was both an inspiration and a provocation. In it, Paul Goodman wrote of youthful attitudes towards work:

"Good' jobs are frauds... it is intolerable to have one's style of life dictated by Personnel, the movies, TV, and Book of the Month Club, Life Magazine, Time Magazine, Fortune Magazine; the one-upping of the "typical" junior executive makes you sick to the stomach: it is the part of reason and honor to wash their hands of all of it."

6. **An Actor Prepares (Constantin Stanislavski):**
   The only career I had ever envisioned for myself was acting - if all else failed, I might be good at pretending to be an interesting person – i.e. from somewhere other than Kingsville.

In practical terms, however, becoming the kind of person who read those books took a back seat to my true aim. Yes, it's taken me all these pages to admit that it was the hope of getting laid that propelled me through the next few years - and through most of my life, come to think of it.

Chapter 3

THE CHARM OF FOREIGN CLIMES

Many great minds have addressed the allure and peril of male involvement with the (female) vagina. My early years were filled with rumours and speculation that, like their celebrated sisters around the world, Kingsville girls had been born nicely equipped. But Sunday sermons had warned that, outside the sparkling framework of God's approval, the consequences of having anything to do with that part of the anatomy - from the disgrace of "damaged goods", through the tragedies of syphilis, gonorrhoea and teen pregnancy, and onward to eternal hellfire and damnation - were horrific. Personally, I found the hellfire and damnation combo very effective and spent my adolescence in a perpetual fog of church-approved, thwarted desire.

From a faraway land, Playboy Magazine presented a vision of sexual liberation that was morally unthinkable in the Kingsville of the 1960s, and as such was relegated to the sordid lifestyles of guys who quit school and drove Camaros and GTOs. Consequently, my sole coital experience with Renate, my high school steady, was the culmination of years of foreplay. It was summer, 1966, and we had waited until her family left home on vacation. Just to complicate the excitement, Renate announced that she was enjoying her period that weekend. However, I had read that, with a girl's loss of virginity, some bloodletting was to be expected (as well as stoning in some remote countries I dreamed of visiting), and the anticipated messiness of the event would be obviated by its utility as cover story for her ruptured hymen and assurance that impregnation couldn't occur during menstruation. Still, as the fateful moment approached, our sudden freedom felt a little anti-climactic, our foreplay – always so exciting – now seemed déjà-vu, except for all the blood. The moment came, and, with my instantaneous ejaculation, the peace of a man who's fulfilled his biological destiny swept over me: resembling a lunatic brought down by a tranquilizer gun in an abattoir, I promptly fell asleep. When I awoke a few hours later, the bed was empty - Renate had fled to the guest room. I woke her tenderly, but she emitted a pathetic cry when she saw me and turned away. We drifted apart after that.

Three years of petting and one inconclusive fuck had not supplied me with a sure-fire method for getting laid. In lieu of widespread opportunities, elaborate sexual fantasies had become the dominant feature of my mental landscape. The growing horror of the U.S. invasion of Vietnam notwithstanding, the source of these fantasies was Hollywood war movies - ones which dealt with World War II, the "good war" in which only sixty-three million people died. From the movies I learned that Europe was a vast continent of artist-intellectuals, photogenic peasants, straw covered bottles of wine, crusty bread and Gauloises, quaint streets, and charming garrets drenched in picturesque poverty and scantily-dressed women. A sexual *Fantasia* of erotic possibilities was the result. For example: I am wandering along a country road in France or Scandinavia on a warm summer day, having parachuted in before dawn on a secret mission. No Nazis anywhere. I come to a quaint farm with a barn full of fragrant hay, where a buxom young farmer's daughter greets my arrival with the wordless enthusiasm common to such fantasies.

This blond, ridiculously generous agrarian goddess had an urban counterpart: a quiet, passionate brunette in silk scarf and beret. Our eyes would meet as she sat alone in a smoky French cafe, her shy smile welcoming the wandering, tumescent hero. We order red wine. In tense whispers, she relates her predicament: Vichy's French collaborators are closing in - it's only a matter of time. I promptly save the girl's ageing parents from being caught at their resistance duties by a group of Nazi SS, quickly dispatch the fascists - and reap the fruits of her boundless gratitude. This X-rated scenario drained much of the creative energy that I needed for hating my life, so I concluded that I had to go to Europe for real. That there were no longer significant numbers of Nazis threatening young European women mattered little to me.

The above misapprehensions notwithstanding, there is a clear human motive behind both war and travel. For the young men who are required to go to war and slaughter one another (sent by the old, who curiously seem to be exempt from such obligations), the underlying appeal, the implicit selling point of war (and certainly of travel) is the myth of sexual adventure: sex without any of the dreary rules of civilized society. Unfortunately, the main requirement of soldiers is that they kill rather than fuck - few taxpayers in these mean-spirited times would be willing to finance a mass sex education program in foreign lands (or at home) for the nation's young males (taxes for killing are no problem, however). So, an effort is made to blur the distinction between the reality and the myth. There was a popular T-shirt slogan during the Vietnam war that touched upon this facet of what we called The Big Lie:

Join the Army.
Travel to exciting, exotic places.
Meet fascinating, friendly people
... AND KILL THEM!

Kill them or fuck them, perhaps both. Military life is sold with a veiled promise of sex to the terminally repressed, the naive, the religious and the illiterate. Even in peace time, DND television commercials show sexy young women in uniform, erect and proud, able, apparently, to kill with their bare hands while wearing no underwear. Never mind that the recruitment of females is a tiny fraction of that of males and that sex, when experienced by soldiers, appears in three forms which, at best, may be acquired tastes: with each other, with prostitutes, or in murderous gang rapes of conquered peoples.

Through the churchy fog, I perceived that getting laid wasn't a sure fire result of enlistment. Kingsville pals who spent "character-building" all-male cadet-training summers at Camp Ipperwash or Camp Borden spoke about girls in a grotesque and mystified fashion. (While we're on the subject, "character" in this context appears to mean "avoids *over-thinking* things, willing to kill on command, and displays bum-sucking affection for the British Royal Family".) The romance of military life bore no appeal. Even then, I sensed that joiners were guys who were fleeing from women (or, as some authorities have speculated, fleeing from their own "womanly feelings"). Added to which, by 1965, you had to be a right-wing imbecile to feel romantic about the war in Vietnam.

Of course, Canadian youth weren't obliged to go to Vietnam, although close to sixty thousand young Canadian men *volunteered* - a statistic that doesn't fuel strong feelings of kinship with my countrymen. But an international anti-war movement that eventually grew to number many millions fought a war in the streets of the West against America's criminal slaughter in South East Asia. War, love, patriotism, freedom, pleasure: we, the Baby Boom's first wave, the hippie generation, had our own definitions. Drawing a distinction that was, apparently, beyond many of my countrymen, we said "*Make Love - Not War!*" We wandered, keened, protested, and marched in a tide of solidarity with the Viet Cong and with our American brothers who were thrust into that insupportable nightmare - a tide that eventually engulfed the whole culture.

Widespread draft evasion – via marriage, self-imposed exile, higher education, health deferment, conscientious objection or the destruction of draft records (thank you, kindly Weatherman, for pouring blood on those draft files!) ensured that many young Americans would never experience the horror of the Vietnam war at first hand. But there were parallels between the guys who were drafted and us hippies. They were expendable. We were outcasts. We didn't stay home, work in banks, sell life insurance or raise pigs and let conscripts do the government's dirty work. We refused to be part of the "straight" institutional world that we suspected was the foundation for wars of aggression and everything else that stank in contemporary society. We declared war on our parents' world – with complete justification. I am utterly unrepentant.

In other words, in spite of my sexual fantasies, I was a pacifist.

Chapter 4

MUNICH

On the plane, I sat beside Paul. He was one of Kingsville's few interesting persons (he would later marry young Jane Urquhart, the future celebrated Canadian novelist, an extremely interesting thing to do). We had been best friends since the age of six, but striking out on this life altering venture made everything from home, including our friendship, seem weary and stale. We were each in the process of redefining ourselves - perhaps I more than Paul - and it was a task that required new friends and a degree of solitude. On arriving in Luxembourg, we split up almost immediately over a minor irritation and rejoined the next day on the train to Munich. Luxembourg's minimal charms had quickly grown tedious (coincidentally, we had both committed crushing *faux pas* with our Kodiak boots in miniature cafes the night before, and had been chased by vengeful gangs of tiny people for hours through the dark streets of the Old City). But in Munich, we went our separate ways once more, and I didn't see Paul again until Athens.

I was really alone for the first time in Munich. I brought a mixed bag of expectations to my initial confrontations with the Germans - again, my preconceptions were largely movie-based, but I don't recall a kind face or friendly conversation with a native. Of course, money could buy civility and comfort - expensive commodities. But there were some friendly travellers around. After lurking in Munich's Englischer Garten the first night, I stayed in a youth hostel and fell in with some American and British hippies. The "scene" in

Munich was the bohemian Ludwig-Maximilians-Universität district of Schwabing, home to artists, writers, and students who I imagined spent their young lives attempting to make sense of the Nazi era. Reproduction of Hitler's image was banned at the time, but on a tour of the university's fine arts department, I saw a 3-metre-high portrait-in-progress of *der Führer* being rendered by a bespectacled, rather dishevelled young man. Some pictures require a thousand words: it was unclear whether this was a brave act of confrontation with Germany's past, or simple homage.

That afternoon, a group of us went to buy weapons. A cluster of Schwabing retailers offered an extraordinary arsenal of blackjacks, clubs, knives, brass knuckles, cattle prods, chemical sprays and hand guns of all kinds. German society stands ever ready to arm its street gangs, having had such marvellous experience with them in the past. We all bought giant switch blades - irresistible treasures after years of watching Hollywood's rebels slash each other to ribbons. And if you've ever tried it, you know that a flick-knife holds profound appeal, provoking powerful fantasies in both meek and mild.

Munich was the birthplace and headquarters of Hitler's National Socialist Party. After being appointed *Reichskanzler* in 1933, Adolph built many grandiose structures of the kind beloved by fascists, including a memorial hall for the party members who were killed in the failed Beer Hall Putsch of 1923. Later, eight miles away, his minions built Dachau concentration camp – completely (they claim) unbeknownst to the good burghers of München. It was revealed after the war that the German people excel at keeping secrets from one another. My God, imagine how different history would have been if word had got out to the German public that Jews and fascism's political opponents were being persecuted! Happily, the entire surviving population of München was required by the victorious Allied forces to tour Dachau and see evidence of a massive project of industrialized murder that had completely escaped their notice.

The predecessor of the Third Reich was the Weimar Republic. It was a liberal social democracy whose skepticism about the instruments of class and patriarchal rule and tolerance for leftist political formations, trade unions and personal and artistic freedom was a natural product of the bitter historical experience of the Great War and the twentieth century's advances in education, science and industrial production. But the war had produced other currents in Weimar as well, ones to which liberal democracy is fatally inclined to grant "equal time." In the midst of economic stagnation and outbreaks of class conflict, sinister myths of betrayal and subterfuge flourished. Union leaders and intellectuals were systematically murdered by bitter ex-WWI officers who believed that Germany's defeat in The Great War was the product of conspiracy by Jewish bankers and communists. They formed roving gangs called the *Freikorps* and murdered labour and socialist leaders such as Karl Liebknecht and Rosa Luxembourg. Many of these fascist vigilantes became founding members of Hitler's SS. Today, popular culture, to the degree that it bothers with history at all, carefully paints Weimar as a flowering of the destructive forces in humanity's soul. Weimar featured growing working class power, absence of censorship, freedom of speech and sexual expression, etc., an aggregate of the "anarchic" threats that God-fearing civilization has struggled against since its inception. Weimar stands as an example of *freedom gone too far* - surely its proponents got what was coming to them. As I wandered the rainy November streets of this infamous Bavarian city, the score from *Judgement at Nuremberg* pounding in my head, I searched each aged face for signs of a Nazi past. Invariably, the faces turned away - almost no one would meet a hippie's gaze. I imagined shame of fathomless depth here, mixed with furious contempt for those who would probe beneath the civilized veneer of contemporary German life. But I was fascinated to hear them speak: unlike those who regard German as an ugly language, I found it lyrical, almost enchanting (partly because I had no idea what they were saying). But I knew that in its beauty could be hidden the most pernicious ideas, that its gentle rhythms could conceal - as echoes of Hitler's diatribes still rang in the cacophony of Munich life - a core of religion-based madness.

Chapter 5

A BRUSH WITH HOLLYWOOD

I had heard that a Hollywood film production, shooting in Munich, needed extras and maybe production help. Working in films was one of the ways I thought I might survive in Europe (the very thought of my working in *movies* outraged Kingsville's elders - I would get my comeuppance!), so I made my way to the Bavaria Film Studios south of the city. The project was a little-remembered film about cat burglars called *Jack of Diamonds* (the very title telegraphed immense amounts of fun), starring George Hamilton. I met the director, Don Taylor, who offered me a one line part as a reporter.

Taylor showed me around the sets that were being built and pointed to a distant figure: on the far side of the studio, George Hamilton was swinging on a trapeze. He was dressed in a silken blue and white body stocking, and I watched him work out for a few minutes. He moved gracefully in an unhurried manner. I was struck by the fact that he was alone - have you ever imagined a movie star being alone? Of course, you're going to bring up Greta Garbo, but she only *vanted* to be alone, which proves my point. Taylor explained that George was to play the cat burglar who would pop in on guest stars Zsa Zsa Gabor, Carroll Baker and Lilli Palmer, and the star was presumably concerned about being in shape for the pleasant challenges which might confront him.

And George probably wanted to avoid German public gyms - although, with luck, he might have run into the young Arnold Schwarzenegger oiling himself in the locker room. Busy pumping pig iron and wedging himself into a tank turret as part of a philosophy course sponsored by his country's military, the Austrian bully-boy's likely reaction, back then, to the Hollywood star's famous tan and pretty

Cat burglar. Photo by Laura Phillips

pastel jumpsuit would have been to call George a pussy. No one was surprised when they nearly came to blows during the movie star's surprise appearance at the *Schwabing UberDeutschen IronPümmpenz unt Muscleboys Bümbenfuckenzie Finalz* a week before. Arnold was about to get really *Einsatzgruppe* on George's head when the Hollywood dandy saved his bacon by teaching him the popular American expression which would make Arnold's career: "Fuck you, asshole!" thereby expanding the Austrian ape's grasp of civility and justice, and affecting the world's notion of witty dialogue for decades to come.

However, Taylor said my movie scene would not be shot for another two weeks, and the production was unable to offer me interim employment. So I never went back. My route to celluloid immortality, and the personal interestingness which is its handmaiden, did not lie in the heart of Bavaria.

Chapter 6

MY FRIEND GREGG C.

In Munich I met Gregg Connolly, a third generation Irish Canadian, travelling alone on his way to Athens. Gregg looked like he'd just stepped off an album cover for The Band. Dressed in black and denim, he affected a scary, slightly criminal air - he reminded me of images of bank robbers from the Old West. You know those old photos: the subjects freshly killed, propped up for the camera in their rough wooden coffins, eyes still open but slightly crossed. Often, the box is too short and the body has a twisted, confined look. Gregg was one of the few guys I'd met who was taller than me - almost 6'5", so he looked confined everywhere - except under an open sky. There was a thinly-veiled air of discomfort, almost embarrassment about him - I had the impression of a clever child who has suddenly attained adult stature and has no idea how to handle the situation. He had messy hair, a scraggly beard and large hands that he never seemed to know what to do with - his gestures were those of one who must constantly suppress an urge to flamboyance, the result, no doubt, of having accidentally knocked over so many floor lamps, bookshelves and Christmas trees as a galumphing teenager. His size may have been the product of either the nutritional excesses of Canadian life in the "boom" years (each Canadian child consuming enough milk to create, say, three and a half Italians), or the little known fact that, prior to the potato famine, the Irish were among the tallest people in Europe. Sitting in cafes with Gregg, his spider-like appendages exceeding the normal boundaries of personal space, was to watch his constantly being bumped and stepped on by passersby. He would shrug wearily, stroke his young moustache and gaze scornfully out at this Luxembourgian world with his milky blue eyes, a giant in a land of impertinent dwarfs.

A voracious reader, Gregg was articulate, but, like many young people, he had honed his conversational skills to a few then-fashionable phrases. Some people have an urge towards versions of Orwellian "Newspeak" - especially if it's a key to membership in an exclusive group. The hippies of the 1960s were no exception, as this list of hippie quotations centring on the term "Wow!" and illustrating its broad application, reveals:

"Wow, is that marijuana?"
"Wow, they shot JFK!"
"Wow! I'm really stoned",
"Wow, they shot Bobby Kennedy!"
"Wow, look at that tree!"
"Wow, they shot Martin Luther King!"
"Wow, the music's in colour!"
"Wow, they shot hundreds of women and children at My Lai!"
"Wow, your face is beautiful!"
"Wow, they shot those students at Kent State!"
"Wow ... *wow* ..."

Gregg Connolly,
Istanbul, February, 1967.
Used by permission.

Although he said "Wow!" as often as any of us, Gregg's favourite expression was the more cryptic "Later." Something fundamentally dismissive in Gregg's attitude towards the world made the word "Later" an ideal term with which to respond to any request, demand or observation. I first encountered Gregg reading a copy of *Under the Volcano* on his bunk in Munich's *jugendherberge*. We had a tense, macho conversation in which we revealed our origins (Canadian), cultural tastes (sex, dope, jug band and books like *Under the Volcano*) and travel plans (Athens, Istanbul, Israel and points east). I decided not to take issue with the fact that Gregg had journeyed thousands of miles to spend his time reading a Canadian book in a German youth hostel. Instead, I opened my knapsack and showed him around the D. Williams Travelling Library, whereupon he seems to have concluded that I was an interesting person - an inexplicable reaction from a non-Kingsvillian (he subsequently revealed that he was from Don Mills, Ontario, which explained everything).

Gregg's father occupied a commanding position in the offices of the United Church of Canada (just my luck), and, as my childhood spiritual yearnings had been addressed in that peculiar, arid and joyless institution as well, we shared a good deal of common ground, particularly an interest in beer. Although the question of beer consumption is Protestantism's most compelling debate, the process of brewing the stuff is beer's least-interesting aspect. However we visited a Munich brewery, because of course, the tour culminated with free beer - all you could drink. The price of admission was attendance at an enthusiastic German brew master's lecture about the way the beverage is made, under the strict Bavarian Purity Laws of 1635. I now see these "purity laws" invoked in fine print on the labels of the products of Canadian microbreweries, as well as those of some of the major swill producers. In contemporary culture, historical memory has sunk to such a low, that the flaunting of Teutonic obsession with "purity" is regarded as an appropriate tool for the selling of beer. It's macho and part of the corporate "new world order" to be oblivious to the past and to identify with timeless values such as capital accumulation and Bavarian notions of perfection. Germans, as noted over a half century ago, are very concerned about purity of all kinds, and today, despite their "excesses" in the past, the corporate world admires their expertise in all things. Flaunting contempt for liberal concerns about "bad taste", this blatant promotion of Philistine values is ubiquitous.

In an important male rite of passage, Gregg and I went to Hofbräuhaus where we drank a dozen steins of the remarkably pure local beer and vomited into the urinals together. The moment cemented our friendship: we would travel together, by train, to Greece.

Chapter 7

ATHENS AND THE GREEKS

Gregg and I entered Greece on 24 November, 1966. For reasons which the Thessalonians kept to themselves, our train went only as far as Thessalonika. From there we hitched to Athens, and my European adventure began in earnest.

Athens was a major milestone for the road people of the 1960s. Back home, Paul and I had pored over travel articles and heard about this ancient Greek city from an ageing beatnik (he was in his late twenties, I believe) until it achieved, in our minds, the status of a Hippie Mecca. It wasn't Mecca - the Capital of the Beatnik Empire had shifted to Kathmandu - but we didn't know that then. Beside its obvious cultural and historic appeal, Athens was one of the cheapest places to live in Europe, and, like a town on the edge of a vast desert, it was the final outpost of Christian civilization for those travelling East. The "final outpost" idea may seem odd, especially for a generation of self-proclaimed internationalists, nonconformists, Zen Buddhists, quasi-Marxists, Yogis, anarchists, ersatz Hindus and assorted mystics. But there was a cultural ease in Greece that one missed only when one reached Turkey or the countries which lay across the top of North Africa. Of course, Greece was Christian as well as capitalist, and - in keeping with a series of authoritarian regimes – officially pro-American. And although few members of the social subgroup to which I belonged would have claimed allegiance to God or Mammon, you didn't need quite as much courage to live there as in the world outside Christendom - the

Moslem countries and beyond. In case of emergency, the spiritual sanctuary of American Express and the Athens Hilton were never far away.

Not that I felt at home with the Greeks. Although often generous and possessing a passion for life that I'd learned about while watching Anthony Quinn's celebrated *Zorba*, Greek men were, by and large, one of the most irritating groups I had ever met. This was 1966 and the young Greeks we encountered in the streets around the Acropolis affected the appearance of "playboys" or "James Bond" - caricatures of American media icons - the very role models we hipsters rejected. They strutted about in groups, their suit jackets worn over their shoulders like capes, twirled and caressed their worry beads, sang loudly, argued, smoked cigarettes and jeered at us hippies. I'd never heard people argue the way these men did - long, loud, and about who-knows-what? Are there that many things to argue about, so endlessly and so passionately? These verbal battles

Greek religious icons. Photo by author.

go on all the time and everywhere - even at work. An article in the *New York Times* a few years ago decried the appalling incompetence of Greek shipping and the experience of watching Greeks load and unload cars from a ferry in the port of Piraeus. The ceaseless arguing by everyone involved, as though the moving of some cars was a monumental task never before attempted, was simply astonishing to the *Times* correspondent. As the yelling and screaming goes on hour after hour, one gets the impression that Greeks actually don't understand *each other*. It's like suddenly being transported back to Old Testament days to watch proceedings around the Tower of Babel after God got pissed off. And, it gives new meaning to the old adage "It's Greek to me!" Evidently, it's Greek to them, too.

Having observed this chaos at first hand many times, and having slapped myself around guiltily for the feelings of contempt the spectacle aroused, the Times article was heartening. Almost any sojourn in Greece will provoke feelings of dismay and – if the observer is honest - contempt in the visitor. Voyage on Greek ships is hellish, even in the most costly class. Two ferries, Crete bound, sank during the months in 1966 when I was in Athens, with hundreds of lives lost. Greek shipping is regarded by seasoned travellers as among the worst in the world.

The following description of the sinking of Greek holiday ship Express Samina on the 26th of September, 2000, with the loss of 82 of the 550 passengers off the coast of Paros, from GreekIsland.com, a site devoted to promoting Greek island holidays, may confirm one's worst suspicions. The captain and first mate were arrested and charged with manslaughter amid allegations that at the time of the collision *"the crew had left the bridge to watch the replay on one of the ship's TVs of a goal in an important local soccer match."*

Of course, the Greek people, as a nation, are innocent here, and insults aimed at Greek workers in the media are entirely unfounded. Aside from immigrant populations, they are the most underpaid and exploited workers in Europe. The real culprits are the corporate and ruling class interests who place profits above human and environmental needs. But shady shipping companies, it should be noted, have a proclivity towards hiring Greeks to do the steering.

Numerous revelations regarding a Greek hand at the wheel in major marine disasters are available for researchers who indulge in such pursuits.

One enters similarly deep waters in attempting to make sense of the popular (in Greece) Greek wine called retsina, for the stuff has its defenders. My glass of Beaujolais over the Atlantic a few weeks before had hardly made me an expert, but the wave of revulsion that swept through me on tasting this "Hellenic house wine" confirmed my suspicion that Greek taste as a whole was out of synch with the rest of Europe. The ancient practice of flavouring wine with pine resin flowed from efforts to seal porous *amphorae* with the aromatic goo against the effects of oxidation. The resin inevitably tainted the wine, and ancient peoples were obliged to live with its unpalatable effect until the advent of glass bottles, whereupon everyone abandoned the practice except the Greeks. Thus, the Greek national drink is, like that of Ireland's Guinness, a taste that requires a determined effort on the part of the drinker to genuinely like. "You'll get used to it," people say, ignoring the fact that the process requires torturing one's palate into submission. And yes, I gamely order a glass of retsina – perhaps once a year – for nostalgia's sake, a masochist's "madeleine" – to acknowledge my days of freedom long ago.

In addition to all the arguing - in cafes, restaurants, tavernas, shops and in the street, and at a decibel level that makes the ears weep - the traffic noise in Athens is unbearable. With one of the highest accident rates in the world, the Greek driver, unable to carry on those endless arguments directly, has discovered an attractive substitute in the use of his car horn. The din of Athens city traffic has to be heard to be believed. Every conceivable reason for tooting is enthusiastically embraced - I believe Greek car horns actually honk more of the time than they are silent. I'd lay odds that the car horn is the most frequently replaced auto part in Greece. The country has been battered by the world economic crisis: I expect, any day now, to pick up the New York Times Magazine and read about *The Greek Economic Miracle*, fuelled to a great extent by a giant chain of Horn Replacement Outlets (Visit *NIKOS'S CORNUCOPIA*: "We got plenty horns, my friend!"), advertising "2-for-1" sales, bumper stickers that say "Honk if you're Greek!" and bulk rates for Christmas family gift giving.

The magnificent Acropolis is crumbling from pollution and neglect. The museums are in sad disrepair. The electorate happily supports the crassest authoritarian regimes, allowing the assassination of liberals, humanists and visionaries on a regular basis. Greece was thickly forested in antiquity, but the country is now as barren as the moon. And, in 1975, a Greek driver rammed Plato's Olive Tree, destroying a living relic of his country's glorious past - probably while busy serenading one of his countrymen with his car horn!

Chapter 8

ATHENS UNDERGROUND

Athens hosted a well established subculture of travellers and assorted exiles - mostly male, of course - people who had reached the end of their European sojourn, (like Paul, who talked daily of heading home - his travels having conferred sufficient additional interestingness upon him, he longed to return to Canada to show off) and people who were on their way to or from points further East. It was the ones returning from Asia - from Nepal, Afghanistan, India, and Pakistan - who were the true aristocrats of the road – the Illuminati of the hippies. Compared to them, we were dabblers. They radiated a peculiar calm, a sense of *Knowing*, which came with having braved the perils of hitching, often penniless, through landscapes as lonely and forbidden as the moon, from which one could easily disappear without a trace, at the whim of peoples who you could never really know or understand. These travellers had been about as far from home as you could get, and had suffered loneliness as profound as anyone's, except maybe astronauts.

Some of those who had journeyed the farthest were couples - English, frequently German or Dutch, sometimes American - who wore tattered Eastern garments and who were habitually silent or soft spoken. Conveying a sense of being shell-shocked or saintly, their demeanour was clearly a product of the rarefied path they trod. The men, usually a few years older than I, often had a vaguely oriental quality about which I wondered: was it something in the eyes that whispered, from deep in their past, of a tiny deviation from the

Northern European gene pool? Or were their facial characteristics the product of long immersion in the study of exotic and arcane religious texts? Perhaps it was the rigours of impoverished travel combined with long sojourns in distant lands that subtly altered their features. Or maybe their ponytails were just too tight (ponytails were a necessary concession to those eastern cultures that might mistake a full head of long hair as a signal of "availability" in milieux bereft of women). In any case, these were not Frat Boys slumming for six months before returning to school. Many had been travelling for years. Their genteel style was fashionable in those days, but life on the road made them lean, able, tough guys as well. They were workers and the sons of workers, with long hair, drooping moustache and goatee, often missing a tooth, or sporting a tattoo – a rarity in those days. Some were fleeing conscription to Vietnam; a few had already been there, done their killing, and were now on permanent vacation, fleeing memory. Told by the media that civilians back home hated them for serving in Vietnam, they were exiled and forever homeless.

Their women evinced an earthy, home-spun plainness, often with faint traces of the angelic. None of them had ever won a bathing suit contest back home, nor been the prom Queen, nor even taken a shot at it. Nor was there ever any hint from them of sexual availability, despite the reputation of the times. Marriage, formalized or not, was a necessity: they were in emotional bondage to their nomadic lovers (as Nadine Gordimer was to note some years later: "*What was love for a woman, but the decision to live inside one man's madness?*"), long-suffering, and childless - but not always.

Occasionally there would be a third member of the group. Usually four or five years old, they were invariably bright and precocious - products of constant parental attention and the changing stimuli of life on the road. No dull day care or nursery school for them! Their developmental lives somewhat paralleled those fostered by the progressive, free schools that emerged from the Sixties. They were fully-engaged with the adult agenda – books, exploration, bright conversation and creative leisure, un-intimidated, never shy, and curious - they were future citizens of the world. I encountered perhaps a dozen such children on the road, and have always wondered what became of them. The spectacle of these itinerant nuclear families fascinated me. I smoked their dope as they told travel tales or read aloud from sacred texts such as *The Tibetan Book of the Dead, The Hobbit*, or the novels of Hermann Hesse. I hung on their every word, enchanted at every story, for I was a very impressionable, naive, romantic and melancholy young man.

Invariably, these folks had treasures to sell. Some would succeed in becoming "hippie capitalists" and drift into the libertarian mindset that is antithetical to hippie communalism. The woman would spread a trove of flutes, trinkets, carved wooden boxes, paraphernalia for the smoking of cannabis, silver and brass jewellery, carpets, hats, mittens and oddments of exotic clothing across the bed, things they said they could sell for a fortune on Carnaby Street in London. Their eyes would shine as they revealed plans to return home, import native handcrafts and become rich. They were the vanguard of a trend that created chains of stores with packing-crate decor selling cheap Third World housewares to young marrieds. They often showed off big chunks of hashish with which they planned to finance their import business. From Turkish Red to Lebanese Blond, from scary Afghani Black (sometimes mixed with opium) to Moroccan kif (THC crystals and cannabis pollen mixed with hashish): each had distinctive characteristics. The Turkish and Lebanese rendered cerebral highs, light and full of laughter; the Afghani was an intense physical stone, regarded as the strongest and, by those in greatest need, the most desirable. Nepalese Mountain Kingdom Cream Hash invariably came with stories of its vendors' journeys to "the roof of the world," prompting heavenly visions of travel destinations that few of us actually pursued. (Thai Sticks and hash oil appeared later, in the 1970s, as Vietnam vets and CIA operatives made returning home a lucrative endeavour.) There was consensus among hippies that constantly being stoned was a wholly legitimate and desirable way of navigating existence – a form of rebellion that combined forbidden pleasure with easy concealment. My tendency towards dumbstruck despair when stoned was not universal. Feelings of superiority to "straight culture" - with its ambition, competition, wars, consumerism and "up-tightness" - were a given, and the drugged state was an approved framework for every activity. This attitude was bolstered by the emerging counter culture, whose most important contribution was sustained musical support for drug use from rich pop stars with whom even the most desperate and impoverished youth imagined affinity and rapport.

Bullshit.

Road culture produced unimpeachable "bullshit" about life on the road – stories that parallel urban myths of alligators in the sewers and alien abduction – although I'm convinced there was more than a grain of truth in them. In the countries to the East, they said travellers had their hands - or sometimes their genitals - cut off for smoking hashish. This didn't curtail the practice - it just made for giddier, more freaked-out highs. They told of desperate hippies who, trapped in some Middle Eastern hell hole, attempted to sell their blood for needed cash. Later, they were found in abandoned rooms, *all* their blood drained from their bodies! *"Never agree to sell your blood to a private buyer!"* were common words of wisdom spoken around a joint of Lebanese blond. But many naive Westerners - confronted with such a potentially lucrative opportunity in a hot, teeming street – apparently found such invitations impossible to resist. My friend, Dr. Waldo "The Needle" Plingehoffer, who travelled extensively in the Levant and beyond during his youth, and who sold eighty-seven gallons of his own bodily fluids over a period of twenty three years on the road, comments on the mysterious (sometimes fatal) allure of the black market blood trade in the introduction to his cautionary pamphlet, *"Easy Money: Selling Bodily Fluids for the Uninitiated"* (published posthumously):

> *"The wary traveller may be put off by the "friendly local" - who addresses him as "my friend", who promises a rate far in excess of that paid by the government clinic, who holds open his robe to show an alluring kit of needles, rubber tubes and bottles, and who ushers him towards a waiting car filled with sinister looking "family members" – but I'm frankly never able to resist the seductive charm and heady excitement of such encounters."*

Chapter 9

LIFE IN ATHENS' OLD CITY

Pursuing my clichéd expectations for life in Europe, I believed that I would make a living by drawing portraits in cafes. Greece was a vast life-drawing class waiting for me to capture it all in Conté crayon, and I earnestly unleashed this scheme in Athens. But, although I had attended art school in Detroit for a year and developed a modest drawing skill, it would wholly vanish in situations where it was most needed. And to my surprise, I found that European desire for portraiture was not as widespread as I had hoped. Paying customers were few. At least I had my film career to fall back on.

Gregg and I spent a couple of days at the Athens youth hostel getting our bearings, and then rented a second floor room on a winding street in the "old city". *Old city* was a generic term for an area that we searched out with arrival in each new town. The old city was where we wanted to be, for it invariably meant cheap living in a historical setting, bohemian atmosphere and lots of hippie travellers. The term *old city* is universal in Europe and unknown in North America for fairly obvious reasons – unless you count Disney World's Old European *Schnitzelhausen* in Orlando, Florida. In Athens, the old city was Plaka, a quaint and charming quarter located just below the Acropolis. Our landlady was a bitter-looking widowed asthmatic who summoned us into her dusty parlour to pay our rent. The room was illumined by a single bulb of wattage so low that its light, upon leaving the bulb, completely vanished into the shadows of the far reaches of the chamber. Our faces hovered like spirit masks in the darkness. Seated in the gloom, she motioned us to place the money on the sideboard. With appropriate deference, we did so, after which we stood, heads lowered, awaiting further instructions. She counted the money, swept it into her lap and held it there, wheezing loudly, regarding us with silent contempt, until it dawned upon us that we were dismissed.

Plaka, 1966, Athens, Greece. Photo by author.

Athens was warm and sunny in late November, 1966. In those first days we visited a mansion in the downtown area, minutes from Syntagma (Constitution) Square: 35 Vasilisis Sofias, where a special colony of hippie travellers was living - the guests, it was said, of a mad Greek millionaire named Takis Voglis. At that time, however, we had our hearts set on Plaka - our "scene" was there (we used Beatnik terminology almost exclusively then) - so we departed without giving the situation much thought.

In the winter of 1967, Plaka was indeed an atmospheric, magical place. It had its 007 Club (with unusually friendly Greek women whose overtures I took personally until I realized they were prostitutes) and its touristy *tavernas*, but these were charmingly naive in their attempts to cash in on the growing tourist trade. It still had narrow winding streets and Greek people living there. Little grocery stores and wine shops were tucked in among the ancient houses. It was quiet. In the evening, the music from the clubs was still genuinely Greek and just loud enough to be pleasant, the scents of real local cooking drifted out into the night air, small parties of revellers would pass by beneath our windows and the full moon painted the streets and the Acropolis above in its timeless silver light.

Despite my critical remarks about Greeks in the previous chapter, dear reader, their country was charming in the extreme - it fulfilled most of my exotic expectations - although there were never enough girls around. We lived on the periphery of Greek society, having little or no intercourse with the natives (a continuing disappointment to me, personally) beyond the rudiments of daily life. We ate in the cheapest restaurants, living on side dishes (how I longed to have a plate set directly in front of me!) of beans and vegetables, bread, feta and retsina, or bought simple foods in the little shops that could be found anywhere. I met Paul on the street one day. He claimed to have discovered a cafe where they offered free food. I followed him to a little shop with a few tables out front. We sat and were brought little plates of feta and olives. This seemed to be such a generous act on the owner's part that we gamely ordered some retsina. Strangely, the plates kept coming. Back home, you never got anything you didn't order and pay for, but here, snacks came with drinks! Enough snacks and you had, what was for us, a meal. But the proprietor's patience ran out as the snack-to-drink ratio widened, and he realized what we were doing. His comment introduced me to the popular Greek expression, "*Malaka!*", meaning *masturbator*, an insult in a land where "the Greek way" is said to be a popular alternative.

Chapter 10

HASHISH

Hashish smoking has deep roots in Greek life, despite official proscription regarding its use. It arrived with the tide of immigration from Turkey and the Middle East in the early 20th century, and, along with the drug-influenced *Rembetiko* music, became a mainstay of Greek urban culture. It was in Plaka that I smoked hashish for the first time (I never once encountered marijuana in my European and Middle Eastern travels). I had read lots of damning articles about drugs in wholesome magazines like LIFE and TIME, so I was well primed for the experience. Paul had scored a chunk of hash and we were wondering how best to test its effects. In the Milk Bar where we enjoyed vivid breakfasts of scrambled eggs, leather-skinned yogurt, thick slices of warm bread with sweet butter, Cretan mountain honey and strong Greek coffee, we met an

Greg Hildebrand, Athens, 1966.
Photo by Gregg Connolly.

American guy, Greg Hildebrand, who offered to *turn us on* (how archaic the term sounds now) to the charms of cannabis resin. Greg H. (no relation to Gregg C.) was about 27 years old, an American Harvard graduate, played guitar and was travelling with a flaxen haired girl of Vermeer-like beauty named Claudia. He was the perfect agent for the arcane protocols of the drug experience. It was a role savoured by the initiated in those days - one akin to the group leaders in the burgeoning Human Potential Movement, with its self-help and therapy circles. As our guide, he was required to ease us gently towards the doors of perception, to heaven rather than hell, to show us the path to ecstasy. And he proved to be very good at it. Gregg C. and I invited Greg and Claudia (and a small international delegation of novices) back to our room.

The ritual of hashish smoking was a source of pure fascination. Greg performed the rite with simple authority. First, in a candle flame, came the softening of the drug - a hickory nut sized chunk of matter resembling dried dung. Some authorities believe that it *was* largely dried dung, an apparently "classic" form of adulteration. Then came the careful crumbling of a portion of the dark, pungent resin into a quantity of tobacco which he had carefully laid out upon, not one but a grouping of three cigarette papers which he had joined together to provide the skin of a party-sized reefer (sometimes called a spliff), next the laborious rolling of the joint and the licking of the gummed edge of the paper, then the shellac-like sealing of the thing with his saliva. It's worth noting here that drug-taking, like sex, falls under the aegis of Herpes, the Greek God of The Exchange of Bodily Fluids. Then, the twisting shut of each end, and finally the careful drying of the illicit cheroot with the aid of a candle flame, during which Greg, with easy, homespun humour, his audience hushed with the kind of respect that elders of the United Church in Kingsville only wished they could garner, talked of the war, the police, the antics of the "straights" back home and the protests at the universities. Then, he lit the thing. I watched its fiery rocket trail as it made its way around the circle. The loopy cigar-sized joint stuffed with Turkish hash reminded me of Flash Gordon's silly, smoking space ship in the 1936 RKO movie serial. I must admit that almost any object moving along at eye-level secretly reminds me of Flash Gordon's flying machine, so profound was the conditioning power

Actual hippie reefer.
Used by permission of the International Underground of the Beatnik Empire.

of 1950s television. There was an air of quiet expectation - quiet because, as the joint was passed from hand to hand, the growing majority was holding its breath - punctuated by sudden exhalations, snorts and coughs from those who had reached the limits of their endurance. The room gradually came to sound like the terminal ward in a sanatorium. I toked deeply and waited for the rush. Even for a cigarette smoker, inhaling the hash fumes and holding them in was an act of disturbing recklessness - the vapour seemed to sear the lungs. The joint circled again - again I inhaled deeply. There was no effect beyond my initial nervous anticipation. This was a little disheartening, but I told myself to be patient. Someone else confessed disappointment. I looked around the room and saw a gathering of strangers, their faces made gaunt by the harsh light of a single bulb. I realized that the scene resembled grainy film footage of *an actual drug den* of the kind I had been warned about in Kingsville! Greg said nothing, but smiled as he fetched up his guitar. "It will begin to sound like bells," he said, picking a delicate tune. And it did. I was borne aloft on the purest music I had ever heard - it was almost as though I had never heard music before. Then he and Claudia sang a duet in a soft country twang and the sweetest of harmonies:

> *"Beautiful, beautiful brown eyes,*
> *Beautiful, beautiful brown eyes,*
> *Beautiful, beautiful brown eyes,*
> *I'll never love blue eyes no more!"*

Although I wasn't about to reject any blue-eyed romantic opportunities that came my way, its unexpected rural American flavour, rendered with an unswerving dignity and force, was a perfect foil for the pop and folk rock treacle that clogged my soul. The freshness and

45

audacity of the choice seemed perfect for my *entrée* into this new world. Getting high was wonderful. I realized suddenly, that I was in the company of interesting people. Everyone was beautiful and fascinating, every utterance was wildly funny or profound - often meaningful, it seemed to me, beyond the conscious intent of the speaker. It was as though everyone spoke in free verse with multiple subtexts. The superiority of the hashish experience to that of alcohol was irrefutable. Greg made another joint and passed it around.

But, with hash or grass, there was always a line, visible only in retrospect, over which I crossed at my peril. The official hippie term for it was "Oh-Deeing", but to modern science, it's known as "too much dope." After a rush of elation, I became overwhelmed, scared, or, more often, sad. The activities of the others were distanced and irrelevant. I checked in and out of what was going on - the music was extraordinary and the jokes insanely funny - but a kind of lonely depression always crept in. The enchanting complexity of people's talk became strange, then disturbingly ambiguous, uncomfortably revealing, then degenerated further into meaningless strings of words, and I lost touch with those around me. I fell silent and spiralled down into paranoia.

This first drug encounter set the tone for virtually all of them. I have often wondered why I was the only hippie in the world who didn't like dope.

- Years later, Woody Allen popularized the term "*anhedonia*" - the inability to experience sustained feelings of pleasure. Maybe that was my problem.

- The rumour that our words *assassin* and *hashish* derive from the Arabic word *haschishin* threatened the complacency of my "peace and love" beliefs regarding cannabis resin. In the absence of other negative stimuli, I envisioned crazy-eyed burnoosed stoners waving bloody scimitars, lopping off heads in every direction.

Maybe dope isn't really all that much fun. It exacerbates symptoms of short term memory loss, and ADHD which I suspect I had as a youth, even though it hadn't been invented yet.

Was dope just not for me? Would I be doomed to wander, un-stoned, through the labyrinth of the counter culture without this essential interpretive tool? Fearing being ostracized, I smoked cannabis frequently for the next fifteen years and had a very hard time giving it up, despite the counter culture's repeated claims that it's not addictive.

To his credit, Hildebrand noticed my symptoms and suggested we go out to get some air. I was really stoned. We walked for a while through the darkness, the familiar sights and sounds of the neighbourhood suddenly fractured like "Nude Descending a Staircase" without the nude. At a stone bridge we leaned on the railing. Greg was a generous, empathetic guy. He spoke quietly, cheerfully, about what a wonderful place Greece was - his voice was a lifeline. The moon shed a pitiless light all around - that light, it occurred to me then - which makes people feel like earth-bound ghosts. The cliffs of the Acropolis loomed above, the dark stream far below. Still very high, I was sick suddenly, and my supper, as it fell away into the blackness, shimmered like a ridiculous neon rainbow.

Chapter 11

TAKIS VOGLIS

Takis Voglis was an eccentric Greek millionaire, scion of a wealthy fishing family, who had thrown open the doors of his house to the hippies and road people of Athens. He seldom appeared there, leaving a changing roster of guests to fend for themselves. And fending they were. Like the scene in *Zorba the Greek*, in which Leila Kedrova's house is stripped bare by the local villagers as she lies on her death bed, the Voglis mansion was slowly being ransacked and emptied of its contents. By the time we got there, only major pieces of furniture were left in what, until recently, had been a functioning *haute bourgeois* household. What disaster had befallen the Voglis family, unleashing destructive forces of which we were a relatively innocent part, we would never learn.

Those who tried to spend time with Takis (out of curiosity or because they wanted money) soon gave up in frustration. I once met him in Kalanaki Square, a pleasant area in a wealthy section of Athens. His presence was always announced by an uproar. Here, he was making a scene in a wine shop,

Takis Voglis, Athens, December, 1966. Photo by Gregg Connolly.

buying champagne for everyone around. He seemed to recognize me and handed me a chilled bottle of Dom Perignon in greeting. Then he wandered off, singing and yelling, down the street. It was rumoured that Takis' family periodically took him to court to wrest his fortune and his house away from him, on the grounds that he was clearly insane. After all, who but a madman would show such disregard for his earthly wealth? To their outrage, Takis would appear in court, impeccably dressed, defend himself eloquently, see his cousins' case thrown out, and return to his life of madness and waste. Takis didn't live at the mansion – none of us knew where he lived. His visits to 35 Vasilisis Sophias were always tinged with absurdity. His shabby dress - he was bearded and dishevelled – resembled, of course, an aging hippie. He invariably made us cheer and laugh at his antics. Probably at the behest of his enraged cousins, the police raided the house - in search of drugs, of all things. They had herded us into the study and relieved us of our passports (as Greek police and their fellow assholes everywhere are wont to do), when Takis appeared, knight-like, on the doorstep. He was still, despite his notoriety, a powerful man in Athens: a few words to the police and they quietly relinquished our papers. Then, before they could slink away, Takis made an elaborate speech in the various languages of those assembled there, apologizing for any inconvenience to his guests, invoking the United Nations and addressing us as though we were visiting dignitaries. And there was a nutty sincerity about it all. We cheered and applauded our champion, flattered and charmed

by this wild man, and threw haughty glances at our erstwhile captors who stood looking sheepish and confused. With their departure, Takis bowed graciously and, a Greco-Bohemian super-hero, vanished into the bustling noon-time streets.

Takis's house, 35 Vasilisis Sofias, Athens, December, 1966. Photo by Gregg Connolly.

Chapter 12

THE SCENE

In the basement of the mansion, there lived a band of Italian heroin addicts who occasionally drifted up to the first and second floors. They had the appearance of incompetent vampires. Sometimes we stumbled upon them in the upper hallway, lurking and mumbling in the darkness near our rooms. We knew that they only wanted to steal money or things they could sell, so we tried to discourage them

Takis's house, 35 Vasilisis Sofias, Athens, December, 1966.
Photo by Gregg Connolly.

as humanely as possible (after all, heroin shooters were merely the braver fellow-travellers of hash smokers). Stamping our feet and clapping loudly, we forced them to flee, gibbering and squealing, to the caverns below.

On the main floor were large rooms filled with the remnants of a very wealthy lifestyle: a lot of Louis Quinze chairs and armoires, and at the front, the aforementioned study with a massive oaken desk. Upon it sat a telephone. If you had no scruples, you could phone anywhere you wanted, and talk for as long as you wished. Connolly and I left our scruples in Plaka and moved in at once. Paul had rented a room near mine in Plaka. He got involved with Greg H. and a group of musicians (he was a skilled guitar player) and I didn't see him often. But when word got around about the "big scene" on Vasilisis Sofias, Paul moved in with the rest of us. Shortly after, however, he went to Crete, missing the foundering ferries by only a week or so, and upon his return, I saw him only a few more times before he returned to Canada with a cache of hashish sewn into his jacket lining. Years later, Paul, with his new wife Jane, and I spent many evenings reminiscing about our days in Athens. Paul, who had become a promising painter at the Ontario College of Art, and was widely loved for his music and his humour, died in an auto crash on Hwy 401 on a rainy night in 1973.

It was mid-December when we arrived at Takis's house. The weather was still warm enough that we spent our days sunning on the roof and taking our meals on the front balcony overlooking the street, living the lives of impoverished aristocrats. In the beginning, there was a functioning kitchen, and some good mothering soul always cooked up pots of rice and vegetables for us ersatz nobility. We felt solidarity with those wealthy pop stars who bought Scottish castles and French chateaux and were photographed stoned and languishing in elegant dissipation amidst crumbling splendour, proletarian usurpers.

Two groups commandeered the second floor. Gregory Corso, the Beat poet, associate of Ginsberg, Kerouac and William Burroughs, occupied one room. Yes, my friends, the real Gregory Corso. He had a couple of beguiling British girls named Geraldine and Judi, who festooned him with their languid bodies while he held court on a big four poster bed (the note on the next page is evidence of betrayal

51

and broken hearts even among the hip cognoscenti). Two upper class British hippies, Jack Williams and Mandy Walker, and an American named Ted Worcester (who had a beautiful, BMW 1600cc motorcycle) made up his entourage. Only Ted was

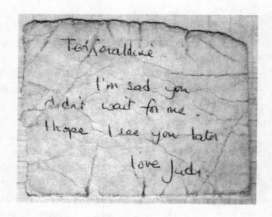

Another broken heart, Athens, Greece, 1966.

really friendly to us. Before he left, he gave me his beautiful grey rubber motorcycle coat. He was one of those Americans whom the evil tentacles of conscription tried to snare for Vietnam. I later learned that Ted motored to Kathmandu, began exporting Nepalese rugs, founded the Ted Worcester Yangdzom Healing Hands medical program in Eastern Tibet and died in 2004. I spoke to his father in 1996 in Cleveland. He said that Ted had never come home.

Our gang was more proletarian - but many had literary, musical or artistic aspirations: Gildas Failler, an obsessive journal keeper from Brittany, with whom I remained friends long after returning from Europe. He loved the sea, and often spoke about sailing around the world. We corresponded regularly until, in the early Nineties, our political differences became too sharp to warrant further dialogue; Danyel Baltus, a Belgian artist who produced a stream of drug induced drawings of faces and cityscapes which he sold regularly to astonished Greeks; a tall hail-fellow-well-met named Paul Z. whose family owned a chain of Land Rover dealerships in Kenya; and three Australians, John N., Peter P., and Tom V., who had the key to the Middle East - a Volkswagen van - and who planned to drive overland to Israel - land of milk, honey and Swedish girls hungry for adventure.

There was another Torontonian named Al Schiff, a hippie's hippie, a Dylanesque character - cool and aloof - who walked with us but stayed remote, often laughing at private jokes and spinning in circles. He had been around the psychedelic drug scene in Toronto's Yorkville since its inception, and claimed to have taken a great deal of LSD. No one doubted him. Al's head was the shape of an inverted egg, with a pointed chin, long, frizzy hair and lash-less eyes. Even compared to us, his dress was shabby. Waif-

Gildas Failler, 1967.
Used by permission.

thin, he reminded me of Huck Finn. Al constantly experimented with peculiar diets. I remember his sipping apple cider vinegar and eating charcoal granules purchased from a Greek apothecary, and speaking authoritatively about their effects on his already skewed perceptions. I was slightly in awe of Al because of his sharp critical tongue, the intensity of his opinions, his apparent intelligence and his unassailable hipness. In counter culture terms, Al had it all

figured out. "Oh wow man, you're so fucked up!" was his reply to almost anything anyone said. He'd then laugh cryptically and withdraw into himself. The effect on the rest of us was intense reexamination of what we'd just said, for signs of fucked-up-ness, because, of course, we knew his accusation was true. Self-interrogation is a worthy pursuit, but as the weeks passed, we began to suspect that Al was just playing head games, not only with us, but with himself. He alienated almost everyone. He often spoke of his desire to kill and eat a cannibal

Portrait of "my good friend, Doug" by Danyel Baltus, Athens, January, 1967.

if he ever got the chance. And when talking about an eventual return to Canada, he said he planned to start a charity that would help Japanese people grow bonsai trees really large.

Months later I encountered Al in Eilat. Al wasn't living on the beach - the "normal" beach community was a collection of tents and makeshift huts just past the only beach hotel - but far off alone, towards Aqaba, in the tall grass of the "no man's land" near the border, where, to pop up, gopher-style, from the long grass was proven to invite target practice from listless border guards. I found

Portrait of Alan Schiff,
Athens/Israel, 1966-67,
by Doug Williams.

him lying, emaciated, in a pool of sunlight, in a dilapidated shelter that the *fringes* people had built, staring at the sky through a hole in the roof. (Outsiders even among us, the fringes people were vagrant road people who'd settled in the Israeli border wilderness for years, living at the lowest levels of subsistence. I later encountered a similar community languishing in derelict houseboats on the Ganges River, during a trip to India. They were usually German, for reasons I now suspect may have had something to do with recent European history.) As usual, Al spoke little but told me he'd been fasting. He said that, living here, he'd returned to his natural home where he'd lived many lives before, stretching back to the wild days when Judea was overrun with prophets and self-proclaimed messiahs. He managed to mock me in his characteristic fashion, but I could see that it was he who was fucked up. Soon Eilat was evacuated and, except for a chance meeting in Haifa after the war, each of us en route to different destinations, I didn't see him again.

Years later, in Toronto, I reached his mother by phone. She sounded old and frantic and begged me to come and talk about her poor Al. I declined, but said I'd tell him to call her if I ever met him. I ran into him on Yonge street in the mid-Seventies. We had an uncomfortable talk in a Pizza Hut. He was with a guy who was similarly strange - they claimed to be Sufis or members of Subud, I think, and my lefty politics didn't interest them. I asked about his Reverse Bonsai business and told him to call his mother. If memory serves, I believe Al accused me of being fucked up. I saw him once more after that, some ten years later, on Bloor Street. He was standing in a doorway, shabbily dressed and appeared to be panhandling. Our eyes met, but I walked quickly by. Later, I felt bad for not speaking. No matter what I did, Al always made me feel fucked up.

Chapter 13

DAYS AND NIGHTS IN ATHENS

Back in Athens at the Voglis mansion ... Our group occupied three main rooms on the second floor - the centre of activities was Danyel's and Gildas's room: I spent a lot of time there smoking dope and listening to Bob Dylan sing *Sad-Eyed Lady of the Lowlands*, a beautiful song that paired perfectly with activities like watching a spider on LSD weave a three-dimensional web. And *Maggie's Farm* - a succinct reflection of my views concerning

Doug Williams,
Athens, December, 1966.
Photo by Gregg Connolly.

work and the older generation. When the record stopped, I would do my impression of Jerry Lewis's existentialist hit (no wonder the French love him), *(I'll Go My Way) By Myself*, to stoned and appreciative applause.

At any time of the day or night, you could find Danyel smoking hashish and painting and Gildas smoking hashish and writing his journals. Friends were always welcome. Danyel had a favourite "political" joke he would play on newcomers to the scene - politics in homage to Dali, Bunuel and Artaud. In the hallway near his room was a broken refrigerator which contained, predictably, a tub of rotting pork hocks. The house was large and airy, and windows were always open, so the smell was not obvious unless one opened the fridge door - it was then, however, overwhelming. Danyel took great pleasure in getting an unwary guest really stoned and then demand, in a loud and friendly voice, *"Oh, Charles, would you go to the hall fridge and get me a Coca Cola, please?"* The words "Coca Cola" would trip joyfully off his tongue, Coke symbolizing for everyone the hated onslaught of "Amerikan" culture. The guest - naive, eager to be accepted, perhaps relieved that this slightly scary, surrealist clown had made such an ordinary request - would jump up and run to the fridge, happily humming Coke's popular jingle *"It's The Real Thing"*, only to be confronted with the smell of Death: Lesson One in a crash course in hippie-radical enlightenment.

I spent a lot of time in Syntagma Square, in view of the Greek parliament building, at an outdoor cafe below American Express, drinking expensive lemonade from elegant frosted glasses and waiting for money or letters from home. Exotic people would come and go. From time to time, there were American girls who had jumped ship from one of the floating schools for rich kids that plied the Mediterranean. It was difficult to engage such jaded, cynical young women, but occasional conversations afforded me tantalizing insights into the strange lives of these richly pampered exiles. One very beautiful girl, named Melanie, told me she'd been in psychoanalysis and declared schizophrenic. She now used *schizo* as a verb, as in *"So I fucking schizo'd down the street."* AWOL for a day or two from their ship docked in Piraeus, she and her friends seemed to imagine they were slumming - going through the motions of rejecting Daddy's money - but you couldn't get near them if you weren't from the right class, even if you schizo'd earnestly alongside them for a while. To them, we were eccentric losers of little interest. Travelling on a shoestring (sometimes half a shoestring) was a lifestyle that they would never be required to contemplate.

One day an elegant young Greek woman came by and asked Gildas, Danyel, Gregg, Paul and me if we wanted to be extras in films being made near Athens. We were taken to studios filled with very impressive "city street" sets - I wondered why they couldn't shoot in Athens's picturesque streets until I realized that *THE HORNS! THE HORNS, MY FRIEND!* would make sound recording impossible. It transpired that what they really wanted was help with some sound effects for Michael Cacoyannis's followup to *Zorba The Greek*, a flop entitled *The Day The Fish Came Out*. With some satisfaction, I noted that my vagabondage had put me in touch with film production twice in the few weeks I'd been away from home. What did they know in Kingsville? I'd show the bastards what an interesting person was made of. After a long drive into the countryside, we were taken up to a windy mountainside and taught a tune by Cacoyannis himself, a song which he required us to whistle for a scene of some soldiers walking along a mountain pass. I was the best whistler in the group (one of my dozens of undervalued skills), but it was a peculiar moment for me, seeing a world renowned film maker coaxing a performance from a rag-tag bunch of hippies who would be paid a few drachmas from his own pocket. Two years later, I saw the film at the National Film Theatre in London, and heard our music - I resisted the temptation to jump up and scream "That's me whistling!" - but despite our efforts, the film's failure signalled the decline of Cacoyannis's reputation as an international cinema auteur.

I continued to hang around Plaka. Our gang from Takis's second floor - Gregg C., Al, Paul, the three Aussies, Gildas and Danyel - found cheap *tavernas* and enjoyed enormous, stoned, evening meals, bought with earnings from artistic endeavours, panhandling, borrowings from friends or money from home. Following a day of fasting, those evenings - filled with laughter, coloured with retsina,

hashish and an occasional bottle of Romilar - are some of my happiest memories. Romilar was a popular over-the-counter cough suppressant containing the drug dextromethorphan. Researchers have found that it can produce "distortions of the visual field, feelings of dissociation, distortions of bodily perception, excitement, loss of comprehension of time, out-of-body experiences, perceptions of contact with "superior" beings and miscellaneous delusions." Who wouldn't want that? Added to which, it afforded pleasant relief from the tyranny of hashish. Naturally, we took Romilar as often as possible. One such evening, while running, stoned and joyful, down a winding cobblestone street, I waved to the friendly girls at the 007 Club, stepped into a pot hole and felt my foot twist over on its side with such force that I was sure, for a moment, that I had broken it cleanly off. In that instant I saw stars and envisioned myself hobbling about Athens for the rest of my days with crutch and bloody stump, like a movie leper, the notorious "Lame Canadian of Plaka." But after a few minutes of frantic rubbing, the ankle seemed OK. Apparently, God had turned it to rubber for that one instant when needed, or had quickly rejoined it in the panic-stricken moments following the break, and I felt able to walk again, undiminished. It was a miracle.

Being careful was not high on my list of conscious concerns, but I was not a complete naif. The friendliest Greeks were smooth fellows who invited us, usually individually, to "visit Onassis's yacht - he is a friend of mine!" I always declined (I could kick myself now for not meeting Onassis). One rather fey character, Robert (pronounced as though he was French), whom, I suspected, had haunted doorways in Plaka for some time, had the air of an outsider – other local street people shunned him - although his origins were not clear. Robert latched on to me and, on subsequent occasions tried to entice me to travel to Budapest: "I have many friends there. We will have a fantastic time!" The line between us foreign hippies and Athens street people sometimes felt thinner than desirable. I toyed with the prospect, remembering that I was condemned to be free - plans for travel to Israel were still uncertain - but despite Robert's mild insistence, I was not tempted. I shudder to think, now, of who he might have been, and how easily I might have met an unpleasant end, in woods near a border somewhere, far from home.

Chapter 14

AN ENCOUNTER WITH
THE GREEK POLICE

It was the eve of the infamous Greek Colonels' Coup of April, 1967. In a few weeks, the Greek military would establish an extreme authoritarian regime that lasted until 1974, and, on the evening in question, some of her foot soldiers apparently needed to flex their muscles. As we approached the Milk Bar, we were asked to step into police vans and taken to jail - Gregg C., Paul Z., Al S., Paul K. and I - and were put in a holding tank with human wreckage who looked like they'd been supplied by the Zombie Unit at Central Casting. Our passports and switchblades were confiscated, and we were left for twenty-four hours to contemplate our social status and our future. We kept up a defiant front, showing that we were deeply insulted by this treatment, and yelled the words "Passport!" and "Embassy!" at our jailers whenever they appeared. We hoped they were intimidated and it helped keep our spirits up. Luckily, in a bizarre omission engineered by our guardian angels, none of us was carrying dope. Some others whom we knew only slightly were taken away that night, too. When we heard of them, months later, through the international grapevine of the beatnik underground, they were still in jail. Finally, a greying senior officer – we were told he was the Athens Chief of Police himself - appeared (introductions were perfunctory: I remember he looked like General Mapache from Peckinpah's *The Wild Bunch*). From his pocket he produced our switch blades. Glaring at us, his hands quivering, he spat on the floor to show his disgust. Then he laboriously – manually! So as not to have fun! - opened each one of the knives, stood them at an angle against the wall and, yelling curses at us in Greek, smashed them with his boot. Of course, we were at a loss to figure out what he was trying to say, but loud demands for a translator seemed ill-advised. Later, I wrote a letter to Chief Mapache, thanking him for his thoughtful intervention in my life. And I kept in touch with the old guy for years after in a stream of postcards from a dozen countries detailing my drug trips, sexual adventures, anti-war activities and contempt for the police. Athens jail had been a gruelling and humiliating experience, and I was eager to make clear its lack of success in my rehabilitation. But I never bought another switchblade.

Our passports were returned and, moments later, we were pushed out into the street, free men again. It was late afternoon and we decided on a purifying soak at the public baths (the water had long since been turned off at the Voglis mansion). I liked public baths. Although widely reputed to be a haven for homosexual activity, they also offered soap, hot water, complete privacy and clean towels for a few drachmas. Then to Plaka for a large celebratory supper, to relax, toast our freedom (we had been thoroughly terrified by our incarceration) and examine our options. It was a rather sombre affair. Overall, Greece was a safe, hospitable and friendly place, we mused as we headed back towards Vasilisis Sophias. But we had been there for nearly four months, and our welcome and our enchantment were wearing thin. I was running low on cash, the Athenian winter had been cold and damp, rainy afternoons were long since filled with talk of new adventures in warmer climes, and life at the Voglis mansion had taken an unpleasant turn. Takis regularly led parties of gawking Greeks through the house in the middle of the night to see the hippies. In addition, arrogant strangers, usurpers and thieves - new waves of road people with no respect for our fragile community - had invaded the increasingly chaotic scene. And who had the right to stop them? I suppose we might have assumed the right, but we were neither territorial nor violent. Gangs of armed hippies (or freshly disarmed, in our case) fighting an Athens turf war would not look good on the front of the *International Herald Tribune*. And we suspected that Generalissimo Mapache and his jailers might not go easy on us twice - not with full police state power finally within reach, only weeks away.

Chapter 15

ATHENS ADIO

The curtain had fallen on the opening act of my European exile: Winter, 1967. The travel photo guide, *A Poor Man's Tour of Athens*, features a morning walk to Plaka. With snapshots of winding narrow streets and sun-dappled stillness, it recalls tavernas in late morning as scents of lamb cooked on charcoal drift into the streets; and describes a mess of exotic culinary treasures: okra, zuccini, artichokes, lentils and aubergine, few of which I'd ever tasted before Athens.

It depicts the roaring chaos of Athens streets laced with diesel fumes and the smoke of chestnuts roasting in street vendors' stalls; meditates on the tastes of Greek mountain tea and thyme-scented honey; remembers the beauty of Athens' First Cemetery, where we placed blood-colored roses in the hands of white marble women; and climbs, at sunset, the endless stairs to the shrine at Lycabetto, to see the distant Acropolis bathed in ochre splendour.

There was the chilly comfort of Piraeus harbour cafes - the winter wind rattling the windows, and beyond, the waxen sea heaving and fuming in the grey light - where we spent many afternoons writing letters and plotting our next moves. We had begun to indulge in what would become a regular ritual in each country as the months passed: the scene had become "a drag". We disliked the natives, the food, and the police. Violence, poverty, boredom, theft, hostile, unsavoury people, and the lure of new adventures (and *warmth* - in this case Israel) - all conspired to push us on our way.

Plaka, Athens, Greece. Photo by author.

I was extremely excited about the approaching journey. A new chapter in my forbidden quest was ready to unfold. There had been a fashion for "Biblical spectaculars" (now referred to as "sword and sandal epics") in movie entertainment of the Fifties and early Sixties. Now that I was headed for The Land of the Bible, these images, combined with long, oppressive hours at Sunday school and Bible camp, created a heady cocktail of sexual anticipation, even without Nazis. I was eager to don a burnoose, pick up my staff and walk slowly through desert dust storms. The oasis straight ahead was sure to be full of dancing girls and large pillows. I was not to be disappointed.

Chapter 16

THE LAST STRAW

Frosty gloom hung over the mansion as we approached - Connolly, Gildas, Danyel and me – along Vasilisis Sofias. The crumbling Victorian edifice loomed up before us, dark and silent against the stars. It had become our custom to enter via the back doors, the front having been locked for security. As we passed along the side of the house, an ominous flickering light seeped from the basement windows - from the dungeon-like rooms where the Italian heroin addicts lived. Peering through the grimy glass, we could see orange flames and figures moving slowly about. I recalled having noticed a large pentagram drawn upon the floor of the formal dining room directly above. The interior of the house smelled of wood smoke. We went downstairs to investigate. In the middle of the basement room sat an ancient bathtub, filled with hot water and a nude, semi-conscious figure. A second vampire flitted around, wild-eyed, nervously tending a wood fire he had built under the tub to warm his lover's bones. He didn't seem to notice us - perhaps he thought we were just another hallucination. The scene looked like a wax museum tableau of the murder of Marat - this time by culinary-style execution. I wondered aloud if he was making vampire soup. The house electricity had been turned off - those mercenary Voglis cousins had inexplicably renewed their attempts to drive us out - firelight danced on the basement walls and the sepulchral room was filled with dank humours and evil spirits. And then I saw him - across the room in the flickering light, sat Gregory Corso against the wall, smoking a cigarette and peering fixedly through the shadows. As flames blackened the side of the tub, a murderous pillow of wood smoke descended slowly from the ceiling towards Marat's face. Connolly's head was already invisible and now his voice emanated from the toxic cloud, "Hey guys - later for this shit!" Lighting candles, we made our way to the dubious safety of the upper floors. Two days later, we left for Israel.

Chapter 17

FLASH FORWARD

We headed north from Athens, en route to Istanbul, on the morning of January 31st, 1967. There were eight of us in the VW van: the three Aussies - Tom, John and Peter - plus Gregg, Gildas, Al, Danyel and me. Befitting their ownership status, the three Aussies occupied the front seat, leaving the rest of us to sprawl in the seatless and windowless cargo area, propped up against sleeping bags and ruck sacks. It was a journey akin to steerage on a tramp steamer, or an extremely long voyage by submarine. An investigative team from Human Rights Watch or the Guinness Book of Records would have had a field day. Why?

The Aussies' van, April, 1967. Photo by Gregg Connolly.

Travelling in an airless, cramped, dimly-lit space offers no shortage of disadvantages, but chief among them is a lesser by-product of the digestive process. Scientific research has revealed the human daily per capita production of flatulence to be about one quart, or 13.6 "events" per day. 13.6 events multiplied by eight ordinary adults amounts to 108.8 instances of vented flatulence. However, young men, especially young men on the all-lentil-chickpea-fava bean diet so popular around the Mediterranean, make ordinary statistics laughable. At times, the Airborne Flatulence Level (AFL) in the van reached dangerous levels.

Under the circumstances, entering a new country was fraught with uncertainty. The night border crossing into Turkey was a floodlit clearing in deep woods. Loud speakers ordered us to halt; we waited for what seemed an eternity. Silence, blinding light. Then, swift as lightening, a dozen soldiers surround the van. One motioned with his Uzi: "Open!" Cautiously, we open the side door and, as the warm atmosphere of the interior merged with the night air, the Turk closest to the van fell back coughing, holding a handkerchief to his face and muttering curses. Confused, the other soldiers started yelling and pointing their weapons at us. We raised our hands, terrified. The first soldier laughed and said something to his comrades that roughly translated as: "Ain't smelt nuthin' like this since the Yuruk pig-jumping finals in Erzurum!" Wiping his eyes, he blew his nose and waved us through. As we passed, I heard him mumble something about Allah.

On a visit to my home town of Kingsville, in 1986, I watched the television show *60 Minutes* with my mother. Hugh Downs and Barbara Walters were weeping crocodile tears about the environment when I was astonished to realize that our tiny van was the subject of journalistic speculation (from the archival script):

HUGH DOWNS
Now scientists tell us that a major environmental blow may have been struck to the Earth's beleaguered ozone layer sometime in early 1967. We asked the U.S. Central Intelligence Agency if they

could shed any light on the mysterious occurrence, and they came up with this:

ARCHIVAL FILM: Grainy satellite surveillance footage - the shot ZOOMS down through the clouds and closes in on our little blue VAN bouncing along the road to Constantinople.

DOWNS (V.O.)(cont'd)
This satellite surveillance footage was taken in February, 1967, over western Turkey. It was part of a CIA program to combat suspected terrorists. Incidentally, Barbara, the funding for that effort was withdrawn by the Carter administration...

BARBARA WALTERS (V.O.)
Tsk, tsk. How could they, Hugh?!

Video enhancement shows toxic plumes of a GASEOUS SUBSTANCE intermittently wafting skyward from the roof vent.

DOWNS (V.O.)
The clouds of mystery gas that you see emanating from the vent in the roof have been analyzed as methane, perhaps the most actively hostile element threatening the ozone layer. Who knows what they were carrying aboard that van?

WALTERS
And who were they, Hugh - some kind of terrorist group?

Downs's voice, heavy with dismay and regret:

DOWNS (V.O.)
Unfortunately, the vehicle's licence plate is obscured, the culprits will never be found, although...

Sinister MUSIC as the video freezes frame and zooms in to a PEACE SYMBOL painted on the roof of the vehicle.

DOWNS (V.O.)(cont'd)
... this damning evidence was revealed by the CIA analysts - at least, now, we know what kind of people they were: itinerant hippies, unemployable parasites prey to left-wing propaganda, hashish smokers selling their blood for travel money, losers trying to get laid.

WALTERS
Surely, at moments like this, Hugh, one of our new Smart Bombs(TM) would be a lesser evil!

DOWNS
No, Barbara, while I might agree with you, and I do, we - er - the CIA was not allowed to deploy preventative retaliation - they could only sit helplessly by and watch, their hands tied by archaic laws designed to protect the guilty. Clearly a tragic moment in the eco-history of our planet...

My mother, tears streaming down her face in the flickering light from the TV, turned to me and said: "You didn't try to get laid when you were over there, did you, Dougie?"

Looking back, I think that, if there had been women with us in the van, the situation might not have reached a crisis. Women function the way canaries do, in mines, to detect poison gases: one whiff and they keel over, a warning to all that danger is near. Women, of course, don't fart, and their very presence usually keeps men from farting. I broached the subject with the Aussies. "Listen lads, we really appreciate you driving us to Israel and all, but why didn't you think to bring some women? It's getting pretty wretched back here." Our hosts' failure had deep cultural roots: the settling of Australia had occurred under similar circumstances to ours. Robert Hughes' *The Fatal Shore* describes the shocking conditions of England's prisoner transport system which delivered thousands of male "criminals" to Australia's penal colonies, providing the foundation of the country's population. Years later, when the settlements' first female settlers arrived, they were promptly subjected to mass rape in the streets and squares surrounding the harbour. Hughes quotes an observer: "It is beyond my abilities to give a just description of the scene of debauchery and riot that ensued..." The event set a cultural tone for much of Australian life for centuries to come, and I thought that my query would meet with a more sympathetic response, however, in its absence, alternative culturally-sensitive solutions were explored. A few days into the journey we established a Flatulence Early Warning System (FEWS), based on the Baader Meinhof Gang's *Farten Unt Signalachtung Einhalten* (FUSE), which was created to deal with potentially explosive situations. This plan, adapted for use in English, required the prospective farter to signal his intention by crying "Badger!" - a traditional term used successfully for centuries in the Australian Outback. But the Badger Rule was a mere bandaid, akin to those preposterous 1950's Civil Defense precautions to be taken in case of nuclear attack - *"Latch doors and windows securely"* ... *"Take shelter beneath a table or chair"* - and about equally effective. Consequently, considerable debate arose, among the van's passengers, as to whether knowing in advance served any useful purpose - after all, like nuclear holocaust, there was no escape and foreknowledge was torturous. Besides, if life in the Australian Outback was noted for anything, it was the airiness of its wide open spaces, where a cry of "Badger!" was little more than polite encouragement to stand up-wind.

PART TWO

ME OF ALL PEOPLE

Chapter 18

MEMORIES OF MY FATHER

Rural south-western Ontario made me: my first twelve years were lived in farmland a mile north of Lake Erie. Hot windy summer days with sighing conifers along our lane, smoke from burning autumn leaves, egg shell ice on morning puddles, silent snow storms muffling the world - these form the backdrop to my father's sudden death.

My education began in P.S. #1, a one-room clapboard school house (built A.D. 1895). It hosted four grades on a barren hill above Skunk Hollow, a marshy spot fully deserving of its elegant name.

The author, summer, 1949.
Photo by Cliff Williams.

The photograph (below) shows the classroom in which I spent four years learning to read and write: old hardwood desks, pot belly stove and high windows. Banishment to a broom closet was a frequent penalty and "the strap" was legal punishment. It was a harsh environment with pedagogical roots in pioneer days, but art appreciation had roots there too: the shelves at

Skunk Hollow School, 1952. Photo by Cliff Williams.

the back contained a set of encyclopedia which became popular among the boys when we discovered that they featured photos of sculptures of naked women.

My scholastic history is far from glowing. With her preference for Readers Digest Condensed Books and the Holy Bible, my mother (who taught high school English and French before marriage) established a respect for literature in the house, and I consequently

Skunk Hollow School classroom. Photo courtesy of Southwestern Ontario Heritage Village and Transportation Museum.

out-shone my rural classmates in mastery of *Fun With Dick and Jane*. But my father, who had been a boosterish businessman in the town of Kingsville, Ontario, died when I had just turned seven, and following his surprise departure, my all-A report cards show a downward trend. My faltering marks paralleled a decline in social status: in 1957, my mother resumed her teaching career and moved us into town. The stupefying silence of the countryside was left behind for the electrifying hurlyburly of Kingsville - a town boasting a population of nearly three thousand - and I tumbled from country squire to proletarian.

My father, Ivan Clifford Williams, was an immigrant, one of thousands of Englishmen who came to Canada in the 1920s to escape the doldrums of British life following the Great War. Although official history describes the post-war era as rejuvenated, optimistic and full of fun, the real history of Orwell's "upper lower middle" class is one of growing desperation – not unlike today. The photographs of Cliff's final years in England show a pleasant Birmingham home, named in that quaint romantic way preferred by people who've avoided council flats and row houses, "The Hawthornes." Another photo, taken ninety-one years ago, shows a tense looking group of young people, informally seated on the lawn. It's Easter Monday, 1921. There is my aunt Lorna, her future husband, Eric, and, in the

The Hawthornes," Birmingham, England, 1920. Photo by Cliff Williams.

77

Cliff Wiliams and friends, Easter Monday, 1921. Photo by Edward Williams.

foreground, holding a tennis racket, my boyish-looking father at 19, who stares intensely at the camera. His lips are frozen mid-word, the way newspaper photos frequently show politicians, and I imagine that he is trying to say something important to me. What could it be?

In photographs which document his early years in Canada, he is almost always pictured with an automobile, ranging from: "Sparky", an ancient vehicle resembling a Dadaist construction; a 1931 Model A in front of which he poses, frowning magisterially with cigarette; a 1939 Packard sedan; a fleet of Chrysler hearses and limousines which he sold to a Windsor funeral home (he eventually opened a Chrysler dealership, among other businesses); an elegant open car which had borne the King and Queen of England on their 1939 Canadian tour; numerous shots of him at the Indianapolis 500 race seated happily in the official pace car. The notes he wrote in fountain pen on the back are often phrased in the past tense: "My 1939 Packard sedan. One of the nicest cars I ever had ..." (ellipsis included) - eerily perfect for a voice which, even then, was clearly aware of its own mortality – it's as though he's already writing from beyond the grave. In embracing the motorcar so completely, my father was a perfect assimilationist, a man who hungered for and acquired exactly what the New World had to offer. Although family myth hints at royal blood and vast

Cliff in royal limousine, 1940.

wealth, people who make such claims are a dime a dozen in the
United Kingdom, and I suspect that life at The Hawthornes was,
at best, a springboard for getting out of the old country. I imagine
an air of faded gentility, the "cracked vases and failed rooms", the
financial humiliation and repressed rage that have been features
of lower middle class life throughout the twentieth century. Cliff
never returned to England. Nor did he write home during his first
ten years away. A series of photographs which he mailed to his sister
in England in the Thirties contains notations for which the subtext
is clear: *"We danced on the boat coming and going ...Oh boy, what
a life!"* (referring to a cruise across Lake St. Clair) ... *"We like a
good time in this country!"* (unlike you ne'er-do-wells who stayed
behind in England) ...and (sarcastically) *"Wish I'd stayed in the old*

1939 Packard Sedan: "One of the nicest cars I ever had..."

country - Oh yeah!" on the back of that proud photo of the Model "A". He clearly had something to prove to his family back home, something which, for my father, had a single, eloquent symbol. Returning now to that group picture on "The Hawthorns" lawn - the yearning that I see on

"... automobile."

Cliff Williams, Easter Monday, 1921

those faces, and the shame of deprivation, especially in the eyes of the men, has an obvious source: there are only people, trees and grass in the photograph. They are above all, carless, and from that dappled yard, across the years, my father is mouthing the word "automobile".

*****

My father died on Sunday, December 6th, 1953. He had become a noted figure in the town of Kingsville, Ontario. His obituary lists him as, among other things, past president of the Chamber of Commerce and past president of the Automobile Dealers of Essex County. In the Thirties, at a time when the auto industry was becoming notorious for its high pressure sales tactics and shoddy products, he won an award for being the best car salesman in North America. In the early Forties, he won contracts for rust-proofing military vehicles, and manufactured automotive parts and shell casings for the war.

But in the eyes of the citizens of mid-century Kingsville, Ontario, where he finally settled, he was decidedly eccentric, and eccentricity is seldom a social virtue. He retained his British accent and, like Toad of Toad Hall, he played the part of the country gentleman. He wore a bowler hat and spats on special occasions, and sported a monocle and cane. He sang solos in the church choir and was a black faced "end man" in the annual Minstrel Show at Epworth United Church in the era before the United Church of Canada embraced political correctness, feminism, gay liberation, anti-Zionism and the Palestinian revolution. He ate and drank and smoked excessively and was a leading spokesman for the "wet" faction who campaigned for legalization of liquor sales in the "dry" town of Kingsville. Even after his first heart attack, he often ate six orders of bacon and eggs in the diner across from Cliff Williams Motors, and then helped his men unload refrigerators for his household appliance store. A photo taken at the front of the business shows sixteen employees.

Although he was far from being a pariah, his flamboyance and his "otherness" gained him the resentment and suspicion of many humbler townsfolk. And the feelings may have been justified: prefiguring Richard Nixon's public image ("Would you buy a used car from this man?"), it was rumoured that he would drive a newly-acquired Chrysler or Plymouth around town for weeks, then wind back the speedometer and - victimizing poor unsuspecting farmers with his hard sell - pass it off as "new".

I can list 43 separate memories of my dad. Summer evenings he took me for rides on the back of his motorcycle. He had an Indian and a Triumph, the two names a succinct summary of the challenge and outcome of the polite British venture among the aboriginals north of the 49th parallel. Once we raced a steam-driven freight train for miles towards the setting sun. Often, he took me to Windsor in his yellow Plymouth convertible or his wine coloured De Soto sedan, to the Chrysler distributor Abbey Gray, where a man in the office amazed me by taking out his teeth. Our tires snapped rhythmically

Management and staff of Cliff Williams Motors, about 1950.

on the concrete roads as we drove along industrial corridors burnished black and copper by the afternoon sun. We passed soot-covered steam engines puffing black smoke, shunting box cars and tankers, pushing freight onto sidings. I was fascinated by the round house where he said all the trains went to sleep at night. We dined in the car on wagon wheel pastries and bottles of Vernor's Ginger Ale and drove home in the dark. The car was warm and cozy, our faces bathed in the yellow glow from the dashboard. I sat beside him, humming along with the gear changes and making clicking noises to imitate the sound of dipping the headlights. Sometimes I lay down and his hand caressed my hair. The world was good - I was with my Dad.

We frequently visited prospective customers near the lake in one of his new Fargo trucks. African-American families came from Detroit or Windsor to fish in the estuary where Cedar Creek emptied into Lake Erie, and one evening, a solemn crowd had gathered on the bridge that spanned murderous undertow. My father slowed the truck to a crawl, a man leaned in the window and said: "'Nuther kid from Detroit drowned ..." Someone had lost his eight-year-old daughter because *Danger! No Swimming!* signs were too costly for the local municipality to supply. Boats circled slowly, solemn men probed the depths with poles and hooks. An ambulance waited, its back door left open, but its red flasher turned off now, to save the battery. A warm summer rain began to fall and we stared at the water, wondering what heaven's welcome was like for a newly-dead child.

I loved my dad unreservedly and unconsciously, the way little boys do. He sold boats as well as cars, and of course, he had a boat of his own. We roared out onto Lake Erie's restless waters, sometimes to the abandoned Colchester lighthouse - a haunted, sunny place - sometimes crossing fifteen miles to Pelee Island to visit my parents' friends, the Hooper family. Lake Erie is prey to sudden storms and often, as we returned home in late afternoon, thunderheads billowed, the sky darkened, lightening flashed, mountainous waves rose around us, the wooden hull leapt and banged on the swells, the greasy outboard motor roared hot, crackling, churning fish spray and wind. My head ached and my glasses were blurred with wet. A dockside photograph of the end of one of those Pelee Island day trips shows a disgruntled group of my parents' friends, mostly women - furious, wet, shivering, still seated obediently in the stern - having just stared Death By Drowning squarely in the face. My Captain and his bespectacled first mate beam proudly from the cockpit.

A Short Film.

On January 1st, 1947, my father, Clifford Williams, announced to the family that he was going swimming. His sister, Lorna Parker, and her son and daughter, Graham and Caryl, who had recently emigrated from England, were staying at our house, and the coercive mix of politeness and family obligation made them captive audience for Cliff's improvised drama. The show would require them to dress warmly. He drove us to Lake Erie's frozen north shore and we watched as Cliff demonstrated his peculiar love-hate relationship with life, captured in an 8mm home movie:

> *The screen flickers to life and it's New Years Day - some of us are hungover, all of us are shivering, fragile - gloomy figures in a snowy seascape. My mother holds me, two months old, wrapped in blankets, in her arms. My retarded brother, Ivan, blind from birth, sleeps in the car. My father is proud of the car - a black Chrysler New Yorker. Cliff strips to his bathing trunks as it begins to snow ...*

A few months before, he had met Lorna and her kids at La Guardia Airport in New York in his shiny new Chrysler - they had finally arrived from the old country - he hadn't seen Lorna in over twenty years. It was a warm summer day. He took them to a cafeteria near the Hudson River, where after years of British war rations, they wept with joy at the limitless bounty of America.

> *Cliff poses briefly for the camera, snuggling up to the overcoats among whom he looks like an oversized, naked baby. He is forty-five years old, but his face*

retains a youthful quality. He strikes a muscleman pose, kisses his sister on the cheek and waves to posterity ...

I imagine that the family wooing that began (as German bombs began to fall) in the early Forties with hale letters of invitation, and that climaxed with their arrival in the world's greatest city, now suffered a sobering denouement on the nine hundred mile drive back to Kingsville, Ontario. As they crossed the border into Canada the roads got worse and the terrain became listless and flat. There were none of the rolling hills, comforting hedgerows and pleasant villages of old England. They passed through ugly anonymous towns surrounded by dusty fields that looked like pioneer photos of the Australian Outback. Life hadn't got better since the Depression - the war had seen to that.

Cliff wades into the iron waters, looking back to deliver a clever comment, and to make sure his audience is watching. Turning away from the camera, he pauses for a moment, knee deep, his nerve faltering. He looks out at the horizon, where slate sky meets ashen sea, at ice floes - piled like towering, white tectonic plates to a height of ten or fifteen feet – like shrouded statues of Illuminati glowing eerily in the winter light, gathered to watch this sad spectacle ...

Their first glimpse of the town of Kingsville was in keeping with the smashed expectations of their arrival in "the colonies". Though it would celebrate its centennial a few years later, Kingsville was now an arid place. The town council had a penchant for destroying its finest landmarks - the town hall and the public school, structures rich with history and an austere, gloomy majesty - and replacing them with the cheap, fashionable products of local boosterism whose minimalist post-war "modernity" is now an eyesore, ready again for demolition. Among them was Cliff Williams Motors.

The truth about Cliff was slowly becoming clear. That mysterious twenty year absence had led to this - a small business in a bankrupt town on the shore of North America's giant open sewer, Lake Erie.

> *The camera pans to see the group on shore. Despite the cold, they are briefly amused by this man whose very liveliness fueled his self-destruction. Thoroughly soured by a disappointing life, my mother laughs contemptuously at her husband.*

Even then, they feared for his heart. Perhaps it had been broken somewhere long ago, and a steady diet of British beef had done little for his arterial health. His favourite snack was cold toast and beef "dripping." Nevertheless with six years of life left, he would show them how strong he was. But he was to become the absent father, the deceased, the centre which didn't hold.

> *Pan back just in time to catch Cliff's dive; the grey water parts then closes over him. A jump cut: my father, smiling and waving, takes a second plunge (in the darkness beneath the waves he sees his mother's face). Before he can resurface, the film ends, the screen turns white...*

... and I realize that I am holding my breath.

The town of Kingsville celebrated its Centennial in 1952 - the year before my father died. In anticipation of the event, he had acquired two Model T Fords, one of which we rode in. I will never forget the peculiar excitement of riding in that open car, cool and breezy under the tonneau roof, on that warm July day. A band was playing and we led the parade through the streets of town. My mother and father wore costumes from the 1920's; my best friend Bradley Lewis and I rode in the back, dressed as cowboys. Behind us came new cars from my father's lot. The procession offered a vision of Kingsville history as an endless stream of automobiles.

My father stood me on a dining room chair and made me sing *The Lord's Prayer, Land of Hope and Glory*, or *Ol' Man River* for visitors. The despair of the latter's final lines - "I'm tired of livin', and 'fraid of dyin'" – must have sounded especially poignant from the lips of a six-year-old boy. He threatened to cut out my tongue for talking back to him, often remarking that "Children should be seen and not heard." He spanked me once for throwing sticks at passing cars and another time simply because I dared him to (but I think, in spite of the custom of the day, he treated me gently). He liked to hold me up and talk about the beautiful shape of my head. His first son, Ivan, born deformed and blind a year before me, had a head that was not beautifully shaped. As a parent, now, I imagine the heartbreak and anguish that my parents lived with - the sheer horror of Ivan's birth – as simply overwhelming, and judging them is an act from which I should refrain. Ivan's fate - institutionalization - has been over fifty years of rejection, loneliness and humiliation which he will never comprehend.

Cliff liked to tell me ghost stories. I remember a Sunday morning, snuggling in bed with him. He told me a prophetic tale:

> *A fine lady's husband went to sea. There was a great storm and his fleet sank with all hands lost. She spent the remainder of her days in madness, high up in a tower (*he slowly raised his arm with wide-eyed horror during the recitation*) pointing silently at the horizon at the ghost ship of her husband heading perpetually towards home.*

Cliff took me to see the film Titanic (1953) in the spring of the year he died. He was ten years old the year it sank - every boy in Britain must have relished the sinking as respite from the obligatory memorizing of train schedules – and he seemed to know all about it. I have always associated the sinking with my father's death. "Even God could not sink this ship!" they said at the time, shortly after this great, glittering shell struck the mother of all icebergs. But this most sacred of historic events is not immune to theories of conspiracy. In one legend, the Titanic leaves Southampton with coal fires raging out of control in its hold. She finally exploded 700 nautical miles east of Halifax. Her hull was torn in two, and she plunged some two and a half miles to the ocean floor. Surely, one of the greatest cover-ups of all time.

The last time I saw my father, I was playing alone on a construction site, standing on a pile of gravel behind the hospital. It's a cold bright December day. Hydro wires keen in the winter wind. I am waiting for my mother to finish visiting her husband and take me home; children are not allowed in the hospital to see their dying fathers. I look up and he is there in the window, smiling like the "Living God" I would later see in Kathmandu. I stand on my little mountain waving to the face high up behind the glass. He waves too, goodbye. And then he was gone.

Cliff Williams died at the age of fifty-one. My mother believed her decision that I not attend my father's funeral was "enlightened", that I consequently would be forced to remember him as he had been - alive - not as the dead man he now was. Enlightenment was a concept with which I was unable to grapple - much less refute - at the time. The sharpened memory of a clear goodbye, a new awareness of myself as *boy without father*, one who had a right to

hear what the living would say to me in the heightened atmosphere of the funeral ritual – these considerations were rejected. Instead, my two-year-old sister and I were left in the care of an anonymous babysitter. My mother had reasons for what she did. She admitted before her own death that she had grown to hate my father before he died. Like so many foot soldiers of the British patriarchy, he had "a sharp tongue" and could be very cruel. When she was twelve, her mother died, and her Bronx pharmacist father shipped her off to be raised by his dead wife's sister in

Cliff Williams, 1947.
Photo by T. Denhardt.

Canada – essentially abandoning her. Her husband had now abandoned her too.

Despite his pretensions, my father did not leave a vast fortune to his heirs. Canada's financial and legal systems are rightly deemed to be a product of natural laws rather than, say, the artificially-imposed strictures of socialism,

"A rich trove..." Photo by author.

and the dissolving of his business followed classic patterns which rendered unto Caesar all the dead man's dough. When the vultures had finished, there was nothing left except a few personal relics. In the vanishing world that had been his, I hoarded evidence of his brief existence. On his death bed, he had painted a picture of a sailboat for me, which my mother, who was not sentimental, discarded soon after. Gradually, my father's memory became muted, trivialized, and, aside from what could be saved in a few boxes, purged from household history. She sold his business suits right away - I remember a fat man who came to our house to buy my father's clothes. Thereafter, I would see him singing in the church choir, wearing my father's suits. My mother never mentioned her late husband, and no pictures of him graced the mantle. There was a bureau drawer containing a rich trove of his personal items: straight razor, binoculars, an oval tin of Brilliantine, monocle, gold pocket watch, tin bank of foreign coins, Boy Scout whistle, magnifying glass, a box of Gentlemen's Talcum, silver pocket flask trimmed in leather, a treasured pocket knife with can opener and corkscrew, and a black plastic comb with a little dandruff still clinging to the tines. I sometimes think of that vanished comb and the dandruff: how different history might have been if I had been able to master DNA cloning with my chemistry set and what would have happened if I had: "Look Ma!" says sullen little Dougie, smiling at last. He brandishes a test-tube containing a tiny figure dressed in bowler hat and spats: "Daddy's back!"

He had a framed joke that proclaimed: "Everything I like is illegal, immoral or fattening." In the hall closet, there were other things of his. I taught myself photography on his obsolete Rolleiflex and Kodak Six16 cameras, and made my first images on photo paper dated 1937 (then over twenty years old) on his old wooden contact printer. He kept an elaborate workshop in the basement of our home where he built and painted miniature railway stations and mountains for his electric trains, a display that was the envy of fathers and sons for miles around. He also built scale model steam ships. Alone now, I haunted the gloomy basement rooms, playing with the trains and building childish versions of the boats he had made. I remember angrily throwing half-finished model ships across the basement when I couldn't match his efforts. There was an open cistern in the basement - we were dependent on rainwater for all but drinking - it added a swampy element to the already crypt-like atmosphere of the cellar. I stood on a box and floated my boats in the dark water.

Sometimes a boat would sink down into the shadows, never to be seen again. Despite the loss, it was exciting when it happened. I imagined its lying on the bottom, listing to starboard, celestial choirs singing *Nearer My God To Thee*, as microscopic tubas, deck chairs and plates of canapés floated upwards towards the surface.

His American Flyer electric trains are packed away now in my attic. I want him to know I have saved them. For years I told myself that I'd restore them and set them up in a blaze of glory. But they're corroded and

Cliff Williams, 1951.
Photograph by Irene Williams.

rusting now, engines frozen. In vain, I hook up the old transformer to a length of track, set my favourite Union Pacific steam engine in place and push the power lever. There is an ominous buzzing, the tender sparks and smokes, and the house lights shiver a warning that there's no going home again ... In the years following his death, I played with them by staging tragic crashes: a toy car would "stall" on the tracks, a crowd of tiny plastic people (and farm animals) would gather, more cars and police would arrive, but no one could budge that stuck auto. Then "The 4:15" would come hurtling through and wreak indescribable carnage with people screaming and animals bawling. Often the train would be derailed as well - a loud crash followed by silence - as a wisp of chemical steam engine smoke drifted over the scene in a ghostly benediction.

In 2013, my father will have been dead for sixty years. There is a child inside me who, against all reason, believes that his daddy's absence isn't permanent – I get flashes of the belief when I'm not thinking about it. But hope for his return is fading. I catch myself looking for him in my rear-view mirror, as though he might be hovering behind me in rush hour. Not long ago, I dreamed that he hadn't died at all. "They" had weighted his coffin with a log, and he returned to England. My mother, who had planned to accompany him, decided to stay in Canada and take care of me. I went to England and tracked down a very old white-haired man named

My father, his Chrysler Windsor Sedan, and me, autumn 1952.
Photo by Irene Williams.

Clifford Williams who was living in a boarding house. There was suspense as I waited for him to come home, and I was attracted to his landlady. I awoke before he arrived.

For years, I believed that English people were the best and I told people that I had been born in England. I defended Chrysler's crummy cars, and felt a special claim to feelings for the sea, money and nobility. American Flyer made the best trains, and when they went out of business, survived by the inferior Lionel (the brand that all other kids had), the event took its place alongside the Chrysler Corporation's perpetually-dwindling fortunes, the sinking of the Titanic, the decline of the British Empire and the death of my father as signs of the incomprehensible and irretrievable degeneration of the world.

Chapter 19

WHO WERE MY PARENTS?

My father and mother, 1950.

By Kingsville standards, my parents married late in life. 1943: he was forty-one; she, thirty-one. What had he been doing all those years before? Were there other wives, other children? Are melancholy half-siblings, trapped in Napanee or Trois Rivières, writing bleak memoirs of abandonment and despair? If not, why had he waited so long? Maybe he was just having fun, instead. His letters to her are passionate, romantic and, given whom she appears to have been, oddly blind to her limitations. But that is part of the mysterious alchemy of attraction. Born in the Bronx, N.Y.C., to a Swedish father and French Canadian mother, she was an outsider like he (though a more assimilated outsider it would have been hard to find). In his eyes she was beautiful, highly educated (B.A. English and French, McMaster, 1934). She was teaching French and English at Kingsville high school when they met. Hers was an air of propriety and maturity which probably echoed the sensibilities of those Victorian ladies of his youth (including his own mother) for whom "The Hawthornes" wasn't quite good enough. He convinced himself that this small town school teacher was a key to his *arriviste* aims. On her he projected all his longings, all his feelings about who he could be if only ... Her presence would confer dignity; she would be the foil for his overly gregarious antics; she would be living proof that despite his passionate eccentricities, he could find a girl as fine as his own Mom.

It was here that Clifford Williams made his fatal mistake, for in marrying a small-minded ultraconservative, both a victim and an exemplar of the psycho-sexual repression of lower middle class Canada, he found, not a foil but an enemy of everything that he stood for. She hated gregariousness and flamboyance. It was a sin for people of her social class to do anything other than hide their meagre virtues under a bushel of modesty, lest they be accused of – God Forbid! - pride or social aspiration. The meek would inherit the earth if they were just patient. Showing off, which he did all his life, and which he encouraged me to do, was common and nasty in her view. It was unthinkable to draw attention in any but the most self-effacing or self-deprecating manner - with, perhaps, the exception of the correct recitation of French verbs.

But my mother was very class-conscious. Before marrying my father, her role as a high school teacher afforded her significant status in an era when university degrees for women were relatively rare. However, housewives were another category altogether – mere attachments to successful men like Clifford Williams - and she stopped teaching in order to furnish my father with three children. I remember her icy

My mother, Jean Irene Williams.

perfume and hurried goodnight when they'd go out for the evening: together, Cliff and Irene were at the centre of the Kingsville social whirl. However, widowed, she became a half-person, expected to take her place knitting among Kingsville society's periphery of crones, brutally ostracized at the age of forty from a milieu which never questioned its own values. Kingsville high school board compounded the difficulty by opportunistically imposing part-time status and reduced wages on her return, after a prior decade of distinguished teaching there. She was a bitter woman, as well as a woman of "character" who, *Mildred Pearce*-like, raised ungrateful children under gruelling circumstances, but her embrace of philosophical absurdities such as "A man shouldn't try to rise above his station" and respect for the British Royal Family, produced decisions that turned common sense on its head. By my sister Wendy's seventh birthday we had moved from the country house to Kingsville, into a shoe box-size bungalow with living room, kitchen and three tiny bedrooms. There wasn't room for all the kids at the kitchen table - some were put at little tables in the hallway. Among these outsiders, in the seat farthest away - placed there lest anyone accuse her of feeling too special or too important - was my sister. I don't recall who got the place of honour at the head table. Perhaps it was a child who did particularly well in school, one who already showed an aptitude for the scholarly virtues, one for whom my mother could feel some empathy. At any rate, there was no chance of offending any of the guests by making Wendy too special.

Although I'm disinclined to declare Kingsville society innocent of cliquish indifference to the plight of widows, my mother's lack of empathy may have encouraged her isolation following her popular husband's death. Although she was attentive in many ways to my needs – quick to apply a mustard plaster at the first sign of bronchial congestion, and unhesitant in administering an enema when nature required – true nurturing instinct was not the strongest current in her character. She never understood how appalling was her admission that bottle feeding me was unbearably tedious, and that her solution was to prop the baby bottle on a pile of books beside me in a clueless attempt to relieve herself of the task. She added, laughingly, how angry her flimsy grasp of the physics of parenting skills - and my seeming non-cooperation - made her. In sharp contrast, my wife breast-fed our daughter for three and a half years until, one morning, little Zoe said, "I think I'll have the bacon and eggs, instead."

My mother died from injuries sustained in an automobile accident at the age of seventy-four. It's emblematic of her status in the town that her memorial service was well-attended – she had taught high school to generations of Kingsville children – but she was not terribly well-liked and died lonely and isolated. Many of those who rose to pay tribute to her proceeded to reminisce about my father. From the world of spirit, she must have looked on with irritation as the event turned into a *de facto* memorial for her husband, thirty-three years after his death.

Chapter 20

SAINT TAMMY OF THE MANGERS

 At the age of six, I had a cosmic introduction to sex. My mother had purchased a supply of novelty paper placemats for the dinner table, printed with a brief character profile of each sign of the Zodiac. I flaunted my reading skills for guests with my own sign description: "*Scorpio*... (blah, blah, blah) ... *extremely attractive to the opposite sex!*" I didn't know exactly what it meant, but something in adult reaction to my recitation told me it was important, and none of those other boring signs mentioned sex at all. But I wasn't to enjoy first-hand experience until the summer before my father's death. On a neighbouring farm there was a little girl of seven named Tammy. She had a round face, straight brown hair, and, like me, wore little wire-rimmed spectacles. I remember exactly how it all started: she offered to show me "how to fuck".

Tammy and I had the run of the farm - she led me to a barn which had separate rooms where cows might be segregated for calving or quarantine. We believed we were alone. In the room, there was a wall-mounted feeding trough (a manger!) built of wood. Full of hay, its dusty sweetness filled the still air and straw covered the floor. It was a hot, silent summer afternoon. To this day, being in a barn on a warm summer day stirs me sexually. Besides the new word "fuck", Tammy referred to our "getting hot" together. She knew all about this, and, for one of the few times in my life, I was a willing student.

She said we should take off our clothes and "rub" while I lay on top of her. The manger would provide a comfy bed. I was nothing if not a gentleman, and not wanting to oppress her with my weight (I had been teased by emaciated rural kids for being "fat" although in photographs I look pretty normal), I suggested that she lie on top of me. She removed her panties, got into the trough on top of my naked-from-the-waste-down with pants-around-the-ankles self, pulled up her skirt, lay on top of me and "rubbed." It was intensely exciting. I remember masturbating for the first time some six or seven years later. The extraordinary sensations of that primal sexual encounter were echoed in my first ejaculation. I'm sure I've masturbated ten million times since that day (some authorities claim twenty million) - at times during my adolescence I got a sore on my member (as well as a condition known as "penis elbow") from flailing away so often and with such force - all in an effort to recapture the innocent magic of that summer afternoon over fifty years ago.

Tammy and I pursued our new-found pleasure on a number of occasions. As a teenager, I bragged to my friends that I first "got laid" when I was six, and although I am pretty sure I had an erection (having had one ever since), I doubt that penetration occurred. Nor do I think I had an orgasm. But I experienced an overall body thrill of indescribable intensity. It was my sexual awakening, and I have been intensely horny from that day forth. I was sexually "conscious" during those years between six and puberty when few of my peers seemed to be interested in anything but cowboys, hockey and skipping rope. Whether that's "healthy" or not, I don't know. But about the way in which the situation was handled by our parents, I have few doubts.

We were observed by the German hired hand. For how long, and exactly how, I will never know. Were our activities a source of shock and horror to the man who watched us, or a few moments of stolen entertainment? All we were told was that the hand observed us. It's like a dream: a giant hand floats in the air outside the barn window, seemingly observing two children fucking in a manger - kind of like if Baby Jesus had a friend in for a naughty sleep-over - but any historically conscious German would have known it was no dream. Where he came from, the sight of thousands of hands floating in the air had been, until recently, very familiar.

Tammy seemed to know all about "rubbing". Where had she learned it? Had she observed her parents during coitus? Were they exhibitionists? Had she been molested by her father or brother? All I know now is that Tammy told me that her father whipped her with a belt for our crime. I can see us there in the school yard, risking a furtive conversation, a children's version of Winston and Julia's *1984* conversation in a crowded street after their torturous "rehabilitation." We played together after that, no doubt closely supervised, but we knew better than to attempt actual "rubbing" again. I remember our confiding that we wished we could "do it". But brave Tammy was incorrigible: once, I was playing outside her house when she stood up in their bathroom window, pressed her naked body against the rippled glass, and waved. She looked like an impressionist painting. Saint Tammy of the Mangers was declared to have "problems" during her adolescence, and in her adult years, was rumoured to have joined a religious cult whose members dress in saintly white robes. They manufacture ice cream for the profit of a guru who has sex with his many female followers.

I wasn't beaten. My mother's reaction to the affair differed from my father's. She forced me to give her every detail and wept with renewed despair at each tiny revelation – comically preposterous when I think about it now. She invoked the Ten Commandments and the term "adultery", her face streaming with tears. I wept too, with shame and humiliation. The misery I caused coloured our relationship for the rest of her life. In fact, after years of therapy, during one of her visits to Toronto, I brought up her handling of the issue at dinner. She became livid with rage at the memory of the pain I caused her.

My interest in the opposite sex tormented my mother. During my early adolescence, she found a package of condoms that I had hidden in a drawer (I hadn't been lucky enough to use them yet except for scientific experiments involving masturbation – rigorous testing was needed to prepare me for future activities). But to her, it was one more indication that her son had made a pact with Satan. She confronted me, tearfully, with the evidence. She had long since chosen permanent withdrawal of affection as a disciplinary tool (I was always in need of discipline), and her effect on me was powerful. I was filled with self-hatred and unable to defend myself.

"My interest in the opposite sex tormented my mother."

It wasn't until years later, when my wife, Laura, pointed out that my mother might have chosen to be relieved that I had sense enough to use condoms, even for dangerous experiments in "self-pollution" as it was known by Jesus's followers, that I began to realize how arbitrary, irrational and soul-destroying her attitudes were. And all in fear of God's wrath.

I remember dreading the inevitable reckoning between my father and me, but he seemed less upset. His reaction was muted, calmer, more rational than hers. He invoked the Ten Commandments too, but I suspect the term "adultery" may have thrown him, since it apparently had nothing to do with children. And in piecing together an adult picture of who he was, I can't imagine that, except for the demands of propriety, he was very concerned at all. It was the weeping woman listening at the door who demanded punishment. Maybe he was proud of me. After all, it meant I was alive and healthy (although Mrs. Grundy and her minions might raise a howl - one that could be handled by a boy who had a father) and attractive to his female peers. Good lad! Good little Scorpio!

The sinful desire awakened in me by Saint Tammy apparently ran in the family – on my father's side, at least. He emigrated from England in 1924. The only record of his early days is a photo album which chronicles his voyage and arrival in Canada - a nearly-wordless account of his amorous adventures with some fifteen different women: here he is with two, arm in arm – a cat with two canaries - strolling the icy deck of the R.M.S. Antonia (on which he sailed from England), each feverish to taste the New World (and maybe each other); here are casual portraits of young women taken on spring picnics; here, a smiling "Miss. D.N. Smith of Brockville, Ontario", posing suggestively in a passenger train doorway, her hands pulling back her fox fur wrap to reveal an ample bosom swathed in silk ... Few of the photos have captions (perhaps to protect the guilty), but they're indicative of memorable activities with these female fellow-travellers, and unless he was a simpleton, he must have had good reason: in staterooms on the high seas and in sleeping cars between Halifax and Toronto, on the sunswept floors of forest glades and in the tall grass of late summer, my father wrote his amorous signature and kept a photographic record of the participants in a little black album that didn't surface until after my mother's death. I'm surprised that it survived her censorial wrath.

The death of this very lively man was a fatal blow to what might have been a legacy of optimism and accomplishment. As my biographer may someday write:

"... a cat with two canaries..." RMS Antonia, 1925.

"Had his father lived, Douglas might have been a very different boy: the crown prince, the successful businessman's heir apparent - handsome, bright, wild, charming - with a taste for rich girls and fast cars; a brilliant turn at law school, a right life borne aloft on clouds of confidence and ease. But a shadow had passed over the sun ..."

All my life, I've wondered what it's like to leave your family for realms unknown, what it's like to have had an identity that features bowler hats, big cars, and a mysterious past. What it's like to lose all identity and vanish, irretrievably. I'll find out what it's like soon enough, I guess.

"Miss D. N. Smith, of Brockville, Ontario"
Photo by Clifford Williams.

Chapter 21

LIFE WITH MOTHER

During summer vacation in the years following my father's death, I sometimes stayed with the Hooper family on Pelee Island. For Lake Erie's mainlanders, Pelee is a mildly unsettling, slightly spooky presence across the water. At fifteen miles distance from the north shore, its appearance is dependent on changing weather conditions.

My mother, about 1952. Photo by Cliff Williams.

Normally visible as a narrow grey smudge on the horizon, it sometimes seems to hover above the water, and sometimes disappears altogether. Few of us ever visited the island, but almost everybody in Kingsville dreams of Pelee occasionally: the island often appears to have moved closer to shore. The dreamer sees trees, houses, the abandoned lighthouse - even cars moving along its coastal road. In the town's beer parlours and cafes, discussion of Pelee dreams was a widely indulged pastime, perhaps linking us to the dream lives of local aboriginals who lived in the area thousands of years before.

Mac Hooper was captain of the ferry that ran between Kingsville and the island, and he kindly let me steer the ship on the way home. It was difficult keeping it aimed towards Kingsville Harbour, and men on the dock joked about its zig-zag course when they heard I'd been driving. Mac fascinated me with his belief in flying saucers. This hardly qualified him to be a substitute father, but the subject was the single sure-fire link between me and the mysterious adult male world. His faith was later echoed by Jack Nicholson in the "hippie movie" *Easy Rider*, when he confidently declares that aliens have infiltrated "all walks of life on Earth." Consequently, I read FATE Magazine and all the popular books on UFOs: George Adamski's *Flying Saucers Have Landed*, Edward J. Ruppelt's *Report on Unidentified Flying Objects*, and others. I saw the movie, *Earth Versus the Flying Saucers* and was exhilarated by Civil Defence announcements on TV. For days at a time I lay on our guest-house roof, the hot shingles burning through my T-shirt, scanning the skies with my Dad's binoculars, just like those alert Americans who stood ready to sound the alarm

at the sight of communist or alien invasion. Later, I would learn that Mac was near-fascist in his political views (as was Adamski). Island life may have taken a toll on his perceptions: on a hill overlooking Lake Erie, he built a full-size model cannon, pointed north by north west, with a big sign saying "Russia

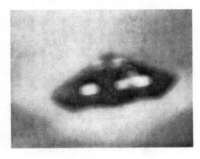

UFO. Photo by author.

Beware" attached to the barrel. At time of writing, he's still alive – in his nineties – living a few doors from Margaret Atwood's island retreat.

A boyhood friend recalls seeing me on my bike at age 12 or 13 - jeering at people coming out of Epworth United Church on a Sunday morning, church bells ringing – dressed in black cape and hood, and made-up as Death. I'm sure my mother had no idea what to do with me. I'm uneasy at the sad desperation of the act, especially since it appears to have been a function of a less-than-fully conscious impulse, but pride in its audacious and rather artful attack on believer complacency. The congregation was made up of people who, if they recognized me, were probably unaware that I'd heard of my father's death for the first time, nearly ten years before, on those very steps.

During this period, I developed allergies and severe asthma and spent what seemed an eternity in doctors' waiting rooms. I begged hypodermic needles and put together an impressive doctor's bag filled with bottles of coloured "serum". I had endured so many injections in my short life that I longed to inflict the experience on others. My sister Wendy's dolls were the best available patients - I pumped them full of green and yellow fluid, until every part of their anatomy bloomed with malignant patches of vegetable dye.

A Celebration.

On my tenth birthday, a year before we moved to Kingsville, my mother agreed to throw a party to celebrate the occasion in our crypt-like basement. I shudder when I think of it now - the dank, mouldy atmosphere, bare bulbs hanging from the ceiling, concrete floor, open cistern with its echoing drip - about as celebratory as the fruit cellar in Psycho. Why not hold the party upstairs in the spacious dining and living rooms - bright, airy, with carpets that could be rolled back? All these years I've accepted the notion that the "mess" would be too great to permit a party above ground. Perhaps it was really about sex, and the whole event belonged in a venue closer to hell. Rock 'n' Roll, courtesy of Elvis Presley, Fats Domino and the Everly Brothers, was a scourge upon the world of

Christian fundamentalism. I had requested dancing at my party and the "mess" that my mother feared may have been of another kind. You can never be too careful with ten-year-olds.

I have three distinct memories from the party. The first was a new record I had bought - a 78 rpm of *Come Go With Me* by The Del-Vikings; the three prettiest girls in my class at school each refused to dance with me; and, most of all, my mother's laughter - mocking as always - at my lively attempts to jitterbug. These were painful and confusing years. I began to answer my mother's proclivity for face-smacking by hitting back. I was a big boy (I remember being embarrassed by my weight during a "health inspection" at school - the toad in charge of the scales bellowed my unique statistic for all to hear: "*Wow! Eighty pounds!*"). My return blows hurt and angered my mother, and the fights escalated. They were the source of my first sustained feelings of anxiety and despair. It's disturbing to hit anyone, and it was nearly unbearable to strike my mother. And, although the physical confrontations subsided eventually, things only seemed to get worse between us as time passed.

We spent five more years in the country house. It was a bright, silent place with forty-one windows. I was deeply lonely - as only a boy without a father can be. My mother subscribed to LIFE magazine. Occasionally, it would feature hair-raising articles such as "Great Murders of the Twentieth Century" with lurid paintings of bodies locked in steamer trunks leaking blood in railway station baggage rooms, and stark grey photographs of bespectacled mid-western farmers who'd boiled their family's body parts on the stove and made lampshades from human skin. LIFE magazine. This was life on the planet on which I found myself.

I became a diffident, frightened child. Sometimes, when my mother left me alone at home, I saw doors move, heard inexplicable noises, and was frozen with fear. I believed that if I sat very still, nothing would hurt me. Fear became an addiction which made me feel more alive. Often I searched out my father's copy of Dickens's *A Christmas Carol*. The moral tale meant little to me, but the pure horror and the "Englishness" of John Leech's illustrations were irresistible: "Mr. Fezziwig's Ball", showing merry plump Victorians jigging grotesquely beneath sinister bouquets of mistletoe; scratchy pen and ink drawings of foggy London nights, with spirits drifting about in gas-lit shadows, pathetic street urchins cowering below in fear; and the illustrator's tour-de-force, poor Scrooge on his knees, hiding his face from an enormous black-shrouded figure which towers above him. I would return to that "horrid image (that) doth unfix my hair" again and again.

The Last of the Spirits.

"The Last of the Spirits" painting by John Leech, from A Christmas Carol by Charles Dickens, published by The Reprint Society London, 1951.

Chapter 22

COUNTRY LIFE

I had two dogs during my country years. The first was a stray of no pedigree who appeared at our back door one day. I called him "Boy" and I loved him – he was my constant companion for a year or two. He was gentle and sweet - obviously grateful for a good home. One heartbreaking August afternoon he was hit by a car. I remember weeping and seeing his crushed head by the side of the road. A few weeks later, my mother got me a yappy black and white replacement. "Boy" was a hard act to follow, but I barely had time to get close to the puppy - a few days after his arrival, he too was killed by a car driven by a distraught woman who seemed to have enough problems already. Blood spurted from his little head as he lay quivering by the side of the highway and I sat on the edge of the ditch and wept as the cicadas sang. There were no more dogs after that - the feminine cat became the pet of choice and the symbol of an impending era of reduced expectations.

Despair triggered unusual anxieties in me. An avid radio listener, I built crystal radio sets and hooked up earphones in my bedroom for late night listening to the American music industry's 100 most popular songs. But, by 1957 or '58, I was beginning to have doubts about the wisdom of churning out so many tunes. I had learned that music was structured on a rigid eight-note system - that any melody one heard used only those eight notes – there were no other choices. I calculated gloomily that a mere eight notes afforded song writers an extremely limited number of possible combinations, and concluded that - given the hundreds of popular songs, church hymns and tunes like John Brown's Body and others from the Civil War - most of the combinations had already been used. In short, with the daily appearance of new songs - with its Top 10, Top 30, Top 40 and Top 100 tallies framing our musical preferences as a contest with but one weekly winner - I feared that running out of songs was an imminent threat to our way of life. What would a world that had run out of songs be like? I shuddered at the implications.

Boys at school fell into two categories: kids from normal, functioning homes, who seemed dull and unimaginative, or toughs and bullies from unstable homes boasting alcoholic fathers and older brothers with prison records. Some of the farm kids were weirdly quiet and withdrawn - products of rural madness nurtured by cabin fever, incest, illiteracy, superstition and brutality - drifting like ghosts through the happy chaos of morning playground. A few were missing fingers, hands – one had only half a foot – the price of summer vacations spent poorly supervised, working with jerry-built harvesters, whirling tractor fly-wheels and snaggle-toothed silage cutters.

My best friends were two of the poorest kids in school: brothers, Roger and Doug B., who lived nearby with three other siblings, all of them as gaunt as concentration camp victims. Their father supported them with Ford factory earnings and lived in Windsor – they seldom saw him. Even by country standards, these kids lived difficult lives: home was a three room shack with no plumbing, no telephone; they hauled water from a well and ate margarine sandwiches, in the middle of a world where even the poor were vastly better off than they. I lived like a prince - albeit Hamlet - in comparison, but it was these two with whom I shared an imaginative world and a sense of humour. They knew more about TV, comic books and the world at large than all the other kids put together. The source of their erudition was their obese mother, who smoked cigarettes, read movie magazines and watched television all day.

Doug, Roger and I didn't play baseball, they perhaps because they were too weak with hunger, and I because I was the subject of a ban policed by a rotating squad of bullies. By famine standards I was indeed overweight, my family must have appeared wealthy to them, and I fear my demeanor combined weakness with evidence of

Stealer. Photo by Cliff Williams, 1953.

privilege, perhaps even a superior air. I was regularly harassed by schoolyard toughs, and didn't have the guts to oppose them. A kid nick-named Stealer because of his involvement in petty crime (no doubt egged-on by his prison-habitué older brother) threatened me until, in desperation, I asked my mother for advice. She gave me a pep-talk, convincing me that I had nothing to fear from Stealer if I stood up for myself – I was, after all, seven times his size. Fired up with new-found bravery, I went to school, daring Stealer in my mind to make a move. He said not a word - I don't think he ever spoke to me again except in friendly neutrality. Had he read my mind? Or had my demeanor substantially changed by virtue of my new-found courage? I would never be sure. Mother and I laughed often about the perverse interplay of expectation and disappointment.

Chapter 23

GERMANS

John Wiebe. Photo by Cliff Williams, 1953.

During the first summer after my father's death, I almost drowned on a school trip to Cedar Beach. I strayed too close to the undertow and found myself being pulled deeper into the urine coloured water when I was intercepted. "Are you drowning, Doug?" said a cheerful, accented voice as I was dragged into the shallows. I had been saved by John Wiebe, a German boy who had appeared at school the previous fall, dressed in lederhosen and stiff leather boots. He was barely a year older than me, but post-war Germany had trained John to look out for others' safety in a manner unknown to his Canadian classmates. There were many such "New Canadians" in the country around Kingsville during those years. My third and fourth grade teacher was Wolfgang Fieguth.

He was in his late twenties and almost certainly a veteran of the infamous youth groups of Germany in the 'Thirties and 'Forties. It was part of that tradition - those summer camps where they learned about racial purity and the heroic boyhood of the Führer - to which I now owed my life.

My mother invited Mr. Fieguth to dinner a few times. He was a fellow teacher, after all, and her son was a mildly promising student. Despite the war, she didn't seem to have a problem with Germans. She sometimes made anti-Semitic remarks and later had a friend, Charlotte, whose enthusiasm for her youthful membership in *Bund Deutscher Madel*, the girls' section of Hitler Youth, overflowed well into middle age. In my memory, Wolfgang was a little like Maximillian Schell in *Judgement at Nuremberg* - one of the many "good Germans" who came to Canada after the war. I liked him. He taught us multiplication by binding together coloured sticks with elastic bands - bundles of ten or five or three or six - little coloured fasces forever implanted in our consciousness, and moved them back and forth across his desk with his delicate white hands. He pulled up his shirt and showed us shrapnel scars on his back. He led the class on great nature hikes ("*I love to go a-wandering...*") and told us hair-raising fairy tales about the Devil's Grandmother, mixing a love of fresh air, blood history and myth for which Wolfgang's people are justifiably famous.

Our copy of LIFE's *Picture History of World War II*, published in 1950, contained not one mention of Jews or concentration camps where some ten million of fascism's enemies – real or imagined - were exterminated. In the years following 1945, Canadian Immigration was eager to show the Germans that there were no hard feelings about the war, criminally over-eager given Canada's record concerning Jewish immigrants (the infamous quote from a Canadian Immigration official, "None is too many!" succinctly describes Canada's Jewish immigration policy before and during WW2). After 1945, Canadian and American authorities threw open the doors to "ex-Nazis" in a way that is profoundly insulting to the men who gave their lives to the fight against fascism and scandalous by any humane measure. These acts must be taken at face value, not explained in complex apologies. It can only be because these government ministers were anti-Semites, and regarded fascists as temporary enemies at worst. However, the war had claimed the lives of many men from Essex County and the population tended not to forget as quickly as their government seemed to wish. When Wolfgang declined to hide his light under a bushel – he drove the county's first Volkswagen Beetle at a time when its German manufacturer was eager for North Americans to forget its origins as Hitler's "people's car" - a mounting chorus from the Kingsville area community labelled him a Nazi and drummed him from his teaching post. If I had entertained hopes that Wolfgang might become my new father, they were dashed when the platonic friendship between him and my mother failed to blossom into all-out *liebenslust*. Nazi Dad was not to be. She was a dozen years older than he, and perhaps disinclined to buck social convention by romancing a pariah. But she defended him, implying that Wolfgang's exit from the academic heights of S.S. No.1, the story of which she related to me in grave tones, was the product of a dark conspiracy. Wolfgang left town and became a distinguished university professor in Western Canada.

My mother worked very hard and was rewarded with a lot of bad luck (what other explanation than the arbitrariness of fate can there be?): a retarded first child, the early death of her husband, and total responsibility for three young children. I don't know how she stood it. Or, maybe I do. She was "a woman of character." She didn't indulge her own feelings – nor reveal them to her children. And she seemed to want to teach us the skill. My sister, Wendy, was two years old when my father died. Like most little girls, she had a battered first and favorite doll which she carried everywhere, and which she named "Nice-en-dary". One day, my mother was seized with the need to teach us to put the past behind us. Even then, the event felt to me like a scene from a movie, showing a sadistic parent tormenting her child. She burned Nicendary in the fireplace, saying she was old and no good any more - as my sister and I gazed obediently into the flames.

Chapter 24

COUSIN GRAHAM

My English cousin, Graham, was the closest I ever had to a mentor, but he left Kingsville for an acting career in Toronto before my father died. Educated in Stratford-on-Avon, he claimed to have attended the same public school as The Bard, and told me that his desk had the name "William Shakespeare" carved on its surface! He played the suave sophisticated Englishman for benefit of Kingsville locals and became an assistant director at Stratford's Festival Theatre for a few seasons; one of my earliest memories of Graham is his appearance on the stage in a play at the Crest Theatre in Toronto. He received an ovation when he appeared - I didn't realize that it was a tradition to applaud key performers when they first entered - I interpreted it as indicative of his fame and greatness for years after.

He generously returned to Kingsville in his Austin Healey sports car to live with us for a few months after my father died, to assist my mother in the closing of her husband's business. He had been acting, and working in advertising, in an era when many Torontonians were still impressed with a British accent. I remember not liking him much. He frequently wore a cravat. There was an air of formality and *politesse* about him which I associated with French aristocrats in old movies. After dinner, he would dab his mouth with a napkin and regard me with contempt. I remember mocking his hostility and his accent by formally pronouncing his name the way it was spelled:

My cousin, Graham Parker. Photo by Cliff Williams.

"Gray-Ham". The "Ham" may have been doubly insulting at the time, given his theatrical endeavors, though I was unaware of the added meaning.

However, for Christmas, 1954, Graham bought me the best pair of six-guns any kid ever had. Hard feelings towards him were thoroughly mitigated by his generosity with those guns. They were burnished silver and so heavy they seemed real; the holsters were black leather with silver studs. But the Holiday Season was an increasingly tense and miserable time of year after my father died – his gut-wrenching absence saturated every moment. Christmas would never be any good now that He was gone. And consciousness of that fact seemed to anger and embitter everyone, especially my mother, who could never make it all OK. As it dawned on me that Santa Claus was a myth, I trumpeted the news to my mother. Later, in childish retreat from the bleak realization, I asked her what Santa was bringing me this year. She bawled "There ain't no Santa Claus!" - her lips quivering with rage at my ambivalence.

In early adolescence, I visited Graham in Montreal. He picked me up at the airport in his 1952 Alvis Saloon, a classic British car that looked like a Rolls Royce, trimmed with wood paneling and red leather. Notorious in the city for his road rage, a little-known phenomenon at the time, he was mentioned frequently on Montreal morning radio: a celebrated British eccentric on the front lines of the Quebec language war, a rising young National Film Board director, and in my eyes, now a god. If someone behind him sounded his horn when Graham failed to speed away from an intersection quickly enough, he would switch off the engine, get out of the car, walk back to the exasperated driver and ask what the problem was - in his carefully-preserved English accent - the whole exercise designed to enrage the guy even more.

By the time I arrived, Graham had obviously had second thoughts about having to amuse me for a whole weekend. He was the one living male with whom I could identify, and, seeing him little more than once a year, I wanted to know what he thought about everything. I was bursting with questions and topics of conversation. He supported the newly-formed NDP and I asked him about it as we rode downtown. In a disapproving tone, he said we'd speak about the NDP later. The moment sounds trivial, perhaps, but I was devastated. I hated myself for being so stupid as to have asked him in the car!

When we reached his neighborhood, he turned down an alley lined with garages, to park his magnificent automobile. We wheeled up to a pair of doors and Graham got out to open them. I was in heaven - what an adventure! An exciting new city far from dreary Kingsville, my strange and fabulous cousin, a living exemplar of everything my father stood for - I was lost in the charm and exotica of it all. Suddenly angry, Graham turned and said through the windshield, "The least you could do is help!" I jumped out and "helped" open the doors. I felt horrible. When was I going to wake up? Could I possibly become worthy of this man?

We watched endless war footage on a Movieola at the NFB where Graham was making a training film for the Canadian Army. He was sixteen years older than me. Since then, I have met many other Englishmen like him – they share a nasty state of mind that is primarily a product of years of abuse in English boys' private schools and the British class system. Some people prefer to be mystified about the relentless brutality of such institutions and their continuing popularity, rather than recognizing that our ruling class requires their graduates as leaders. Military training will polish a man to a high sheen, arming him in the process with heady reserves of rage and cruelty. The stamping out of signs of "weakness" in a boy makes him a dependable and vicious stamper himself in adulthood. Such men make good captains of industry, fine military officers, preachers, teachers and leaders of all kinds and, like so many aspects of the dark side of life, they are an indispensable part of our civilization.

In addition to the six-guns, I got a pogo-stick that Christmas. Like the six-guns, it was The Best - heavy-gauge aluminum and an industrial-strength spring. There was deep snow outside, and my mother would not tolerate the stick's jackhammer-like effect on the dining room floor. The basement was the only place left, and Graham announced that he would show me how to use it. We descended into the gloomy stillness, home of my dead father's electric trains and his model boat-building, past the spot where I had stood in the shadows with Dad eating smoked smelt only months before (my mother wouldn't let him keep the odorous stuff upstairs) to a clear space in the centre of the floor. Gamely, Graham mounted the machine and began to bounce about with increasing confidence. But, in addition to under-estimating the strength of the spring, he had failed to take into account the lowness of the basement ceiling. Thick beams hacked from whole oaks stretched horizontally above us, lovingly placed there by a carpenter who adored the granite-like strength of the material to which he had devoted his life. Graham's head slammed with shocking force into a thick joist; with a small animal-like cry he fell to the floor clutching his skull. Breathing fast and moaning, he lay on the draughty concrete, growling and snapping when I approached, like a fatally injured dog. I sat on the steps, waiting for the lesson to resume, and listened to the soft swish of my mother's broom on the floor above.

In the late sixties, I worked for a Mr. Delbert Stiles in the picture wrapping department at Harrod's, in London. He was a senior man in the firm's middle management and typical of those trained for modest leadership: always filled with buoyant old school good humour, sporting a tatty blue suit and bow tie, with a light sprinkling of dandruff on his shoulders, and a copy of The Daily Telegraph tucked under his arm - a venerable aggregate of British clichés. However, I could barely stand to look at Mr. Stiles, because of the unusual shape of his large balding head. Fringed with auburn curls, it looked squashed-from-the-top, slightly lop-sided as though brimming with semi-liquid contents, like a warm fruit pie that has been set to cool on a tilted sill. I wrapped many minor examples of English pastoral art in brown paper while lost in speculation as to the cause of Mr. Stiles' phrenological peculiarity, because it inevitably drew me back to that terrible moment when Graham's head slammed into the beam years before. Happily in Graham's case, there were no verifiable long-term effects, although as the probable victim of an undiagnosed concussion, he was fond of muttered non-sequiturs about wearing a "corrective hat."

Chapter 25

THE END OF AN ERA

In 1957, a final blow to my father's world was struck - my mother sold our country home that he had bought some fourteen years earlier. We moved to Kingsville, into a shoebox-sized house on a subdivision at the edge of town. I wept openly with despair the first time I saw it.

Gone was the house whose beauty symbolized my father's world, gone the woods that lay to the north, the elm tree in which I had built a primitive fort, the solitude in which I had discovered books (I particularly liked Twain's *Tom Sawyer Abroad*, in which Tom, Huck and Jim escape dreary Mississippi life by sailing away in a balloon). There would be no more playing badminton on the lawn with my beautiful mother, in front of the porch where we drank ice cream floats and watched for tornadoes on hot summer evenings. No more sitting at night on dew-cold wood chaises longues, and no more making my mother laugh while we watched for shooting stars.

Gone was the one-room school house which is now a museum with my class picture in it at South Western Ontario Heritage Village. And gone the one-mile country walk I made each day, on which I gained intimate knowledge of rural life and the slow progress of the seasons. Never again would I spend silent hours collecting fossils - trilobites and brachiopods - from the limestone beds of the railroad tracks about half a mile from our house. That little boy, excited about dinosaurs on a hot day 200 million years later, was in the process of vanishing, too. I now wanted to be a palaeontologist, or maybe an

My father's house, about 1949. Photo by Cliff Williams.

archeologist who dug up dead kings. Occasionally, a diesel freight train would roar by - massive, dark, soulless and unimaginably powerful – its wake whipped the ragweed, almost tore me from my perch atop the fence, and I screamed as the world trembled.

I stand at my bedroom window listening to the callous trill of a robin - the last bird to call at dusk - as the summer sunset pulls light from the sky and color drains from the world. I imagine my father's red Chrysler arriving, the tires crunching softly on the gravel driveway. The wind dies, the earth lies motionless under heaven, the trees are silent and full of shadows, twilight fills my bedroom, and still the robin sings. I drove to my father's house a few years ago and sat in the car out front. From a distance, it looked large and elegant, built of brick on a landscaped dais, with a graceful veranda and a great sheltering roof. I returned at night, and saw the house ablaze with light, filled now with strangers. I imagined my father and mother, and my cousins and aunt, moving about within. All I had to do was join them. I wept, uselessly. The past hangs like a mirage, untouchable and irretrievable. My heart aches with the memories - an ache for which there is no salve.

Loss of my father at such an early age may furnish the analytical mind with an explanation for my preferences and life choices. As childhood tragedies go, it's fairly minor I suppose, but our sentient lives are the product of personal experience, not social consensus about the relative emotional impact of various events. However, fair or not, the world will judge me. While you may rightly perceive elements of accusation and self-pity in the preceding account, I should add that I also feel lucky to have lived so rich and painful a life.

Chapter 26

THE TOWN OF KINGSVILLE

Prohibition had ended in 1933, and the effect of America's renewed embrace of the Devil's Beverage was felt all the way across Lake Erie to the Canadian side. Since the 1880s, Kingsville had been a summer watering hole for thousands of Detroit vacationers seeking Canadian whiskey's blood-cooling effect. The Windsor distiller, Hiram Walker, built a private railway from the Detroit Tunnel to Kingsville's summer resort hotels, and, befitting its unique status as Canada's most southerly town, Kingsville became one of Lake Erie's busiest depots for running rum to Sandusky on the American side. Incredibly, following the Great War, Kingsville had briefly enjoyed status as the North American town with the highest per capita number of millionaires. Al Capone's gang was said to have rented a lakeside cottage a mile from town in the 1920s.

Despite such strong entrepreneurial currents, and the accompanying allure of big city sophistication, Kingsville's moral guardians had long seen fit to ban beer and liquor sales in the town – in all but the fancy hotels that lined Lake Erie's shore. Public morality is a powerful manipulator, and its primary target is the local working man. Fundamentalist temperance was to be seen to trump the needs of commerce – at least for ordinary people - and Kingsville's wealthier businessmen chose to garb themselves in robes of sobriety. The local saw mill owner, W.D. Conklin, and his clan lived in a cluster of mansions on the conveniently named Conklin Hill overlooking the town. He owned the Kingsville

Reporter and promoted temperance, rendering Kingsville a "dry town" for decades. He saved his workers from the ambition-sapping beverages until 1970, when, despite family fidelity to all things Tory and Christian, his lumber business collapsed and his little empire crumbled.

Conklin's role as a modern feudal lord combined moral and political leadership, the amassing of private capital and a distinctly Waspy tone in keeping with views disseminated by Maclean's Magazine and the CBC. These were days before Canada's present status as a "kick-ass nation". With its colonial ties, Canada was a noble country untainted by the crass commercialism of our southern neighbours. Our woollens were superior, our mountains more majestic; the British royal family guarded our democracy from republican excess and mob rule, and Christian folks didn't have sex outside the confines of marriage. This mingy-minded nationalism forbade realistic comparisons between us and "them" who dwelt south of Lake Erie. Apparently it was deemed imprudent to encourage discussion of such issues among those who lacked the financial ability to fully appreciate them.

While the word "genteel" might be used to describe Kingsville charitably, it was a town whose core values mindlessly duplicated some of the ugliest traditions of white American society. As rite of passage, many members of Kingsville's young male population tested their manhood in Detroit's black ghetto, where five dollars could buy a white boy "a suck and a fuck." With the growing radicalization of blacks in the 1960s, the Motor City's ghettoes became dangerous places for whites looking for drugs or sex with black women, and a number of Kingsville high school boys were killed in streets and tenements when race hatred triumphed over entrepreneurial considerations. Kingsville elders told us in hushed tones that black women could have white babies, but a white woman made pregnant by a black man would bear a black baby – and left us to draw our own terrifying conclusions. Consequently, it was said that no black man was allowed to stay in Kingsville over night, because you never knew what shenanigans ignorant poor people might get up to in the dark. This home truth was delivered with sage nods from those who stood on guard for thee. The two pamphlets (next page) were part of my father's collection. They typified the repertoire of racist

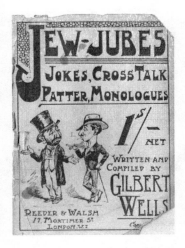 

Anti-semitism, racism and misogyny: inspiration for Epworth United Church minstrel show, Kingsville, Ontario.

propaganda which inspired Kingsville's Epworth United Church of Canada minstrel show with "humour." An ecumenical event in which the town's favourite sons appeared as comical figures in black face reflected what some thought of as the lighter side of traditional views (in the larger of the two photographs, my father is in white face, in the front row, fifth from the left. Note the spats.) Minstrelsy was rooted in seventeenth century America, and assumed its mature form in the slavery culture of the 1830s. It had all but died out by the end of the nineteenth century, except in places like Kingsville.

Cliff Williams on stage in Epworth United Church's Showboat Minstrels, Kingsville, Ontario, 1951. Used by permission of Kingsville-Gosfield Heritage Society.

Epworth United Church's Showboat Minstrels show, Kingsville, Ontario, about 1951. Photo courtesy of Kingsville-Gosfield Heritage Society

Until 1972 – nearly twenty years after Rosa Parks refused to sit at the back of an Alabama bus - Minstrel shows were presented at the United Church. It took letters of protest from the black community in nearby Chatham, Ontario, to liberate Kingsville's cultural mavens from their antebellum torpor.

Fear of human sexuality was not limited to my mother - it pervaded the town. Carefully fostered by the half-dozen churches, Christianity's pious proscriptions were upstaged - if not undermined - by touring "educational" shows such as *Mom And Dad*. These annual events featured a movie screened to sexually segregated audiences, and live lecture by "fearless sex hygiene commentator Elliot Forbes." Having flooded the town in advance with fake letters from churchmen and civic leaders both decrying and praising the event, its creators depended on building a level of near-hysteria for massive ticket sales. *Mom And Dad* was the fourth biggest Hollywood movie money-maker of the 1940s and '50s. It told the story of a teenage girl who got pregnant because her mother failed to supply the very "sex hygiene" literature conveniently sold at the back of the theatre. Women dressed as nurses patrolled the aisles selling pamphlets, ready to assist anyone who fainted from the graphic depictions of syphilis and gonorrhoea, and, most shocking of all, the birth of a baby. Some versions of *Mom and Dad* featured a punishing climax in which the illegitimate baby was born dead.

124

Crowds for film showing of Mom and Dad.
Photo courtesy of John Edwards.

Special late night screenings of altered versions (with somewhat more detailed depictions of un-hygienic sexual acts) admitted men only. Commentator Forbes, an actor hired to play the part, was noted by TIME Magazine to have appeared in 26 cities simultaneously on the same night. The screenings were never mentioned at my house, and I dared not show interest, lest hellfire be my fate.

Chapter 27

MEET THE KEELES

The Keele brothers, Tim and Paul, and I got acquainted towards the end of my country days. We met at Sunday school, at Tyros (the United Church boys' group) and later at the United Church summer bible concentration Camp Kenesserie. The Keeles had one foot in the mainstream - their parents were respectable church-goers and the boys did well in school - and one foot decidedly somewhere else. There were four sons and a daughter whose group energy verged on demonic. For example, they frequently set each other or their house on fire. The boys would manage to squelch the flames and cover the evidence until scorched blue jeans or charred siding was discovered days later. Their mother Pat, a practical woman, took it all in stride, apparently relieved that she had well-raised children capable of dousing fires.

Meeting them was the real beginning of my life. The Keeles had imagination, fought their enemies successfully, read MAD Magazine, rode bikes, dug Rock & Roll and jazz (I heard *Rhapsody In Blue* and *American In Paris* for the first time at their house), painted pictures, built go-carts, wished they could be beatniks, wrote the word Zen on walls, camped out, smoked cigarettes, and engaged in a tireless search for mischievous thrills. I entered grade six in Kingsville. By grade eight, the Keeles and I had embarked on a clandestine criminal career of startling dimensions. We established a custom of sleeping out in backyard tents on summer nights, and the unsupervised freedom of the wee hours afforded us many opportunities for nocturnal iniquity. None of us had a driver's license at age fourteen or fifteen, but we stole our parents' cars regularly, and went for hair-raising high speed joy rides on concession roads. Returning the cars near dawn was always the trickiest part. It required shutting off the motor and pushing the thing quietly up the driveway, exhilarated, giddy with laughter, sometimes accidentally hitting the horn and fleeing into the night. In later high school, we drove all the way to Montreal and back, eluding a nation-wide police manhunt initiated by my mother.

We made gunpowder by mixing drugstore saltpeter, sulphur and charcoal in proportions which I'm forbidden to divulge for reasons of national security, creating pipe bombs of astonishing power. Our success with blowing a tree house to smithereens prompted an unprecedented bombing campaign on a string of summer nights in 1964. We set off a series of explosions in fields and vacant lots which perplexed the local constabulary and begat rumors of alien invasion heard all the way to Pelee Island.

One July night we dared one another to go outside the tent naked. At first, if late-night drivers passed, we posed as lawn statuary (although anyone believing that naked statuary graced Kingsville's front lawns was surely demented). Emboldened by laughter and the wind in our testicles, one dare led to another, and I can now lay claim to be among the very few persons in Kingsville history to have paraded naked down the centre of Main Street (at 2am). We brewed dandelion wine, got drunk, dreamed of fucking girls, got kicked out of school, made a mockery of our compulsory high school cadet training and rattled the bars of our cages as relentlessly as we could.

Chapter 28

I AM THAT I AM,
SO FUCK YOU

In the words of the Sixties, I was destined to become "the kind of person our parents warned us about." I gradually became aware that I was part of a generation that dared to shake a fist in God's face, and perhaps more importantly, at his eager self-appointed bum-sucking minions as well. As I entered adolescence, my burgeoning outsider credentials took on momentum of their own. I hated sports and avoided competition, became an intellectual and embraced the arts – theatre, painting, photography, classical music, movies – a well-trodden path for those who are thought to want the "easy way out" in small towns. Unsurprisingly, none of Kingsville District High School's preparations for adult life - neither algebra, cadet training nor courses in animal husbandry - had the slightest appeal. Not that I was yet an ordained hippie, but the town barber and I were fast becoming strangers, and I was beguiled by Bob Dylan's first albums. With his strange, faux-elderly voice, he mixed rural wisdom with youthful moral indignation, and blazed exciting trails through the backwater culture of small town Canada. As the Vietnam war escalated, songs like *The Times They Are A-Changin'* promised a new era of human liberation, featuring free sexuality, anti-war and anti-racism, mind-expanding pharmaceuticals and a life that was worthy of my generation's talents and aspirations. But the real turning point came when my best friend, Paul Keele, who had worked in a lumber camp in the summer of '64, returned home transformed into a folk singer, complete with $12 guitar. His short repertoire included the usual beloved folk songs about hanging drunken men who had stabbed their women through the heart, but he also sang Buffy Saint-Marie's magnificent *Universal Soldier* (I urge you to Google Buffy's rendition of this song immediately).

In a world gone so preposterously wrong, *Universal Soldier* changed my life. With the exception of *Send In The Clowns*, it's the single most thrilling song I've ever heard. It signalled to my generation that we should take ourselves seriously, and that it was time to change the world. But despite the gathering storm of the youth rebellion, it was clear that ending war was not going to happen in Kingsville. Whatever else I achieved in life, I had to get out. Hopefully the rules would be different far away.

Chapter 29

KINGSVILLE ADOLESCENCE

In a movie of my youth, the Keeles and I would be found languishing on the Kingsville Post Office steps on a hot afternoon, nothin' to do, same boring people doing nothing all around. Then, in the distance through the shimmering heat, we see a Christ-like figure approaching. We watch in awe as a bearded, long-haired guy with shades, knapsack, sandals and guitar saunters up and blows our minds simply by existing. He asks where the scene is; we scramble to explain that there isn't one here. Can he score some grass anywhere? Nowhere we know of. He flatters us by asking where we're from and we sheepishly admit the truth. He's from somewhere exotic and far away like Toronto, headed west to San Francisco. He sits on the steps and sings a few verses of a Bob Dylan song that features a character named "Mister Jones" who is accused of failing to grasp the significance of things that are happening in his presence. Silently thanking God that we're not named Jones, we keep it to ourselves that there's nothin' happenin' anywhere near here, lest he lose interest. But he eventually does, and rising, he solemnly pulls a joint from his shirt and hands it over. His eyes twinkle: "Share this – it's Acapulco Gold. Don't waste it – smoke the roach on a pin." He saunters away, sticks out his thumb, and doesn't wave as he climbs into a truck that stops. Our lives are changed, forever.

Hippies owed everything to The Beatniks of the 1950s. They were the vanguard of a movement against the narrow prescriptions imposed on youth for a "normal" life. And while America's reaction to an iconoclastic current in her midst was – in some quarters – celebration, there was no room for such indulgence in small town Canada. *Howl, Catcher In The Rye, Naked Lunch, Catch-22*, even *MAD Magazine*: I was kicked out of Kingsville District High School for possessing these publications. Not only were they immoral, they were American. School felt like prison.

So, my vision didn't include the advanced tedium of university life and the smug future that academic achievement seemed to guarantee. I had artistic aspirations: my short stories were published in high school yearbooks, and by a strange confluence of circumstances, I directed a half-hour film drama – based on Frederich Durrenmatt's play, *The Visit* – in 1965 when I was 18. Believe it or not, it was quite rare to direct dramatic films in south western Ontario in the 1960s. But something convinced me that post-secondary academic life would not provide what I wanted. Higher learning looked to me like little more than high school's rote learning with pretensions.

The Visit.
Poster Design by Helen Chilas.

If I had learned anything useful in my first twenty years, it was the importance of surrounding oneself with interesting people – in the hope that one might become interesting oneself. Such people were rare in Kingsville, a shortage which, according to local historians, had been "a feature of local life since the little town's founding over a century before." Some experts point to a general lack of ambition in the populace. Others to the town's dull right-wing Christian fundamentalist atmosphere, to the Kiwanis-Rotary-Lions Club axis whose cultural dominance was nourished by Readers Digest and radio broadcasts of Garner Ted Armstrong's *The World Tomorrow*. Whatever its genesis, Kingsville was a repository of low expectation and thwarted hope.

Were it in Europe, Kingsville would be a quaint sea-faring town, with picturesque fishing boats, harbour cafes and a thriving tourist trade. But no such charming enclaves can be found on the north shore of Lake Erie in any of the utilitarian fishing ports devoted to the harvest of foodstuffs from her toxic waters. Her summer hotels were abandoned, derelict, by the late Thirties. In sharp contrast to the Lake Erie of two hundred years ago, which boasted fish in such thick profusion that (according to local legend) "a man could walk on the water's surface like Jesus himself", this inland sea now boasts vast dead zones, the causes of which are officially denied by various interested parties. Still, the lake provides a grand and mythic presence, easily riled, murderous when angry, and hides many secrets beneath her broad expanse.

The port of Kingsville's main feature is the "government dock" which juts straight south from the Lake Erie's north shore, and is open to public traffic. A blunt row of customs buildings and storage sheds graces its east side, a ragged flotilla of snub-nosed fishing boats its west, and an iron and cement breakwater, referred to as the "coal dock" by locals, curves around the front of the harbour in defiance of Erie's restless moods. Nestled at the inner shoreline of this haven is a rusting mess of cranes, dry docks and jetties, lapped by oily waters in which we swam as kids. On summer afternoons, this liquid cul-de-sac is blanketed by an undulating slurry of dead fish, plastic bottles and used condoms steeped in factory effluent from Detroit, lending credibility to the lake's reputation as the world's largest freshwater industrial dump site. But, the lake was "ours" and, as our sense of taste and decorum matured, we abandoned the jetties and chose to swim at the harbour's mouth, in the coal dock's cleaner waters.

The coal dock's chief feature was three mountainous piles of anthracite which were deposited each September by a visiting coal freighter. It's a sight, if you have the time. After midnight, a massive alien craft, slow as a minute hand against the stars, gradually fills the harbour. She empties her hold, and the clang of her conveyors echoes through Kingsville's sleeping streets, out across the moonlit farmland, flat and lonely as prairie.

In late spring, after lengthy gestation in Lake Erie's muddy floor, billions of mayflies burst to the water's surface and rise into the air in shimmering clouds. Those that escape being eaten by fish and birds descend on Kingsville. They cling to every surface, their glassy wings shiver in the breeze. They carpet the sidewalks and crackle under foot, their fishy odour fills the town, and drivers lose control as their wheels spin on pavement grumous with insect slime. Inquisitive children experience torture's first pleasures by pulling off their wings and tails.

Mayfly. Drawing by Karen J. Couch. Used by permission.

Attracted by lights along the shore, mayflies arrive at night in a silent storm. One year, Kingsville town council draped the street lamps in red cloths, bathing the darkness in a blood-stained glow. The bugs came anyway. In the morning, workers shovelled them from the gutters and pulled down the cloths. The reason for this massive demonstration of Lake Erie's fecundity remains a mystery. Once landed, the bugs never fly again and seem to have no purpose but to die, dry up and blow away.

By January, Lake Erie freezes almost solid, creating - in the minds of some - easy access to America, Land of Opportunity. In the Thirties, a jobless man named Aikman decided to drive his family the forty-three miles from Kingsville across the ice to Sandusky. A trio of sepia photographs from the Kingsville Reporter shows them on the morning they left: in the first, Aikman stands beside his rusty Dodge sedan in Sunday best; his unsmiling wife holds a newborn baby daughter and, by the hand, a bespectacled little boy who appears to be crying. A second shows the car stuck in the thin shoreline ice as thoughtless well-wishers push them free. In the final shot, the car is a black dot in the white-grey distance. The papers said that folks in Sandusky stayed up all night with their lights on. Men with flashlights patrolled the shoreline, watching, listening, but no trace of the Aikman family was ever found.

On snowy days, I liked to stand on the government dock looking west and pretend, through squinted eyes, that the piles of coal were mountains in some interesting far-away land, their peaks billowing trails of black dust in the winter wind. Once, I climbed down the ladder embedded in her side, tested the ice's strength, and walked out across the frozen lake. The mountains grew small and faded behind me, and I thought about Aikman's desperation long ago. Beneath my feet, lightning-fast cracks ricocheted and boomed for miles, as though angry sea creatures or ghosts in their Sunday best were trapped in the dark below. Finally I reached the ice's edge, the open water of the "sea lanes" where it was clear and deep. Looking down, just before a cloud crossed the sun, I saw rippling winter light on an old Dodge sedan. But the slippery shelf began to sink, water slid in around my shoes and I stepped back quickly from what I'd seen.

Essex County, in southwestern Ontario, is called by local boosters "The Sun Parlour of Canada," and Kingsville harbour is regarded by some as the jewel in the region's crown. Here, in the most southerly town in Canada, late September often masquerades as summer. The sun is hot, the water sparkles, but the lake's grey swells turn opaque and surly – impatient for winter - as they crash across the breakwater.

Eight of us are swimming near the end of the coal dock: four boys and four girls. It's a warm fall afternoon in 1963 and, looking back, I think I have just enjoyed my finest hour. My delightfully sardonic girlfriend, Karen, adores me: I am the guy who holds his breath the longest, who dives the deepest. But as the afternoon sun sinks behind the mountains, the pounding of the waves grows stronger, and the breeze turns cool. We towel off and have picked up our bikes when I hear a war-whoop from the government dock; a horn honks, gulls rise screeching as an old blue Chevrolet races among the boats past tie ropes and fish crates straight towards the end. An arm dangles a bottle from a passenger window. The car reaches the foot, bumps up over the curb, nose-dives into the water and disappears. Then, as though changing its mind, it heaves up to the surface like a blue metallic whale. But enlightenment has come too late: it rolls and sinks again, in a hissing whirl of foam. For the next seven seconds, life on the government dock continues pretty much as it always has. Crates of fish glisten, seagulls hover, hose-men scour decks with blasts of water. But some have noticed the speeding car, and a few have watched it disappear over the end of the wharf. A fishwife screams and people run towards the scene.

I sprint barefoot around the harbour to the Anthracitian foothills, where the distance between me and the end of the government dock narrows to a channel of fifty yards, dive in and race for the other side. The water is cold; I dread the dark below and swim harder. At the dock, I scramble up the iron ladder, unable get out fast enough, *unlike them.*

No sobered heads bob to the surface. The bubbles from the car have stopped, and the thick moss that beards the waterline waves rhythmically in the current. A silent crowd gathers; we avoid each others' eyes. I don't look at Karen across the channel, either, because I fear she's waiting for me to be heroic. But it's clear that no one's going down - not even the guy who can dive deep and hold his breath. I stare at the water, hug myself and shiver in the wind.

Ambulances flash, police swarm, and eventually an old Fargo truck-crane, belching clouds of black exhaust, backs up to the edge and waits with engine running. The excitement is over. As I swim back across the channel to my friends, the water feels warm again. We huddle together in the dying afternoon, and watch them pull three bodies up with a winch. The corpses are the same colour as the car, which comes up last. It hangs from the crane like a blue skull, plumes of water arcing slowly from its eyes and ears. The men leave it suspended for half an hour, while doing grown-up things with protocol and paper, making people stand away.

I turn and look at Karen, my lanky teenage goddess with burnished skin and sun-bleached curls, and feel a sudden rush of tenderness and desire. She sees me looking, comes close and takes my arm, the heat from her lips burns my ear as she leans in and whispers, "They were drunks, that's all," and in silence, casting undulating purple shadows on the water, we wheel our bikes along the quay, closing ranks against the dead.

Chapter 30

TOWN AND COUNTRY

It's my belief that the true source of Kingsville's intransigent dullness was revealed in a mysterious event that Paul Keele and I - and we, alone – actually witnessed one moonlit night in the spring of 1963. Ever since childhood, we had heard about a bizarre force that haunted Kingsville streets on spring nights. Variously described as a spirit, a demon, even a monster like Nessie of Loch Ness, it wielded powers that no one understood. But it explains Kingsville's fate - and that of small towns everywhere. We saw the whole thing from atop Conklin's water tower where we had climbed with Paul's guitar, packs of Camels and a bottle of dandelion wine liberated from Keele's basement. Paul strummed quietly as the town lay sleeping below us. Beyond its borders stretched the dark countryside. As tobacco smoke and the liquor's citrus balm began to take effect, Paul stopped playing and raised his arm. "Look," he said, and pointed to something that I strained to see. Emerging from the darkness at the edge of town, a thick dun-coloured mist crept in past the Lutheran, Baptist, Catholic, United, Anglican and Pentecostal churches, flowed down Main Street, gushed silently across the four corners, swirled around the Legion Hall and the darkened public school, engulfing the post office and Quick's Five and Dime. We gazed in awe at the bizarre sight as its murky tentacles roiled around the street lamps below. "Doug, I believe that what we're seeing here is the idiocy of rural life," said Paul, who was well-read. "I wish I had a camera."

Conklin's Lumber water tower. Photo by Irene Williams.

Whatever it was that seeped in from the countryside that night, its effect was to render the sleeping townsfolk wholly imbecilic. From our lofty perch, Paul and I were the first to hear the groans of stupefaction, the muffled cries of dullness, the sudden shouts of the dim-witted. We watched the gesticulations of the dumbstruck and saw the newly-moronic stagger into the moonlight in their jammies, clutching their heads and moaning happily. We alone had escaped the comforting fog this time, but our contemptuous laughter died quickly as we realized that this sudden wave of cretinism made the odds one in a million against anyone in Kingsville ever being interesting again.

Although Kingsville's adult population had always seemed brain-dead to us, telltale signs of the mist's effects appeared immediately among the brighter students in my grade 11 class. It had never occurred to a single one of them that small towns were small because no one wanted to live there. In discussions of future careers, these "A" students, faced with the alarming prospect of not being allowed to remain in their beloved high school forever, could think of no other future than *teaching high school* – and hopefully returning to

Kingsville to do it! This poverty of imagination confirmed beyond question the sad effects of – not only rote learning of Latin verbs, but - the event which Paul and I had witnessed that night.

I'm not saying that my urge to travel was unique. I watched others of my age struggle with invisible cages in which Fate had dumped them - young men who had quit high school for the excitement of the open road. But in Kingsville, visions of freedom ended at the town line: they got jobs at the automobile plants in Windsor, bought new cars with enormous engines capable of blinding speed and vast distance, and - prisoners of the murky calamity that had swept through the town the spring before John F. Kennedy was shot - drove up and down Kingsville streets playing loud music and gunning their engines in a repetitive cycle that is aptly described by the term *stir crazy*.

For these adventurous nomads, life's next task was to reproduce - a project on which they embarked with the foresight of blind fish in underground lakes. Playing their part in what the radio's Garner Ted Armstrong called "God's wonderful plan," they enriched the world with their progeny, and as the years passed, their debts multiplied, their wives got fat, and backyard weeds engulfed their Camaros, Corvettes and GTOs, giving the rusting hulks the sad appearance of crashed spaceships from long ago.

So it may not be difficult to grasp why I regarded being from Kingsville as tantamount to being from nowhere. The sheer inescapable awfulness of hailing from Nowhere, Ontario, is a predicament that has haunted me all my life. Everywhere else had culture, lust for life, art, passion, romance, adventure, beauty and, of course, interesting people. Kingsville had none of those things. Even I, who at least wanted to be interesting, was not yet, and I knew that, if I stayed anywhere near Kingsville, like falling asleep among the pod people in *Invasion of the Body Snatchers*, my fate would be sealed. I had concluded that there were two kinds of people in the world, ably represented in Kingsville's population of 3000: 2999 who liked it all just fine, thank you - and me ...

OK, and Paul Keele too, may he strum in peace.

PART THREE

CONDEMNED TO BE FREE

Chapter 31

ISTANBUL, CONSTANTINOPLE
AND BYZANTIUM

Minaret, Istanbul, Turkey, February, 1967.
Photo by C. Seney

We arrived in Istanbul on the evening of February 1st, 1967. If Athens was a quaint, agreeable sojourn in a still largely familiar culture, Istanbul was the dark swirling flip side of the coin. Compared to this ancient Turkish city, Athens seemed as homey as church suppers, drag races and county fairs. The worst denizens of the back alleys of Plaka appeared to form the majority of the population in Istanbul. Rags and poverty describe a people and culture in the midst of which our being young, strong, slightly better dressed and usually in a group made us stand out like visiting dignitaries.

We stayed in the Taxim area, sort of downtown, near Sultan Ahmet, the Blue Mosque, the Topkapi Museum and the famous Grand Bazaar. Unable to secure lodging in the infamous hippy-drug Hotel Gulani (which seems to have disappeared since), we stayed in a similarly downscale lodging whose name I've forgotten.

Chapter 31

ISTANBUL, CONSTANTINOPLE AND BYZANTIUM

Minaret, Istanbul, Turkey, February, 1967.
Photo by C. Seney

We arrived in Istanbul on the evening of February 1st, 1967. If Athens was a quaint, agreeable sojourn in a still largely familiar culture, Istanbul was the dark swirling flip side of the coin. Compared to this ancient Turkish city, Athens seemed as homey as church suppers, drag races and county fairs. The worst denizens of the back alleys of Plaka appeared to form the majority of the population in Istanbul. Rags and poverty describe a people and culture in the midst of which our being young, strong, slightly better dressed and usually in a group made us stand out like visiting dignitaries.

We stayed in the Taxim area, sort of downtown, near Sultan Ahmet, the Blue Mosque, the Topkapi Museum and the famous Grand Bazaar. Unable to secure lodging in the infamous hippy-drug Hotel Gulani (which seems to have disappeared since), we stayed in a similarly downscale lodging whose name I've forgotten.

The streets were ancient and the buildings dark and crumbling. I often found myself gazing up at windows, wondering what mysterious lives were lived behind those shutters. As I pushed my way through the crowds, I became aware of tall, wedge-shaped tombstones looming everywhere above the throng. Throughout the city, crammed in among the buildings, there were slightly elevated graveyards - an ominous presence in the downtown core - so jam-packed with monuments and sarcophagi that the dead seemed to outnumber the living (as indeed they do, if you think about it. In Death's Democracy, sooner or later we all change sides.). Their gloomy silence lent a dark current to the pulse of daily life and, if unheeded, they seemed to threaten to crack open and spill their dusty contents into the sunlight.

Istanbul streets, which made those of Athens seem tranquil by comparison, were a smoking roar of ancient Mercedes, Citroens and Fiats, endless "third world-style" permutations of motorcycle and delivery van, taxis and an ingenious Turkish invention called the *dolmesh*, whereby you are wedged into a derelict vehicle with a lot of strangers, not quite taken where you wish to go, delayed in reaching your destination (sometimes by hours) and required to pay only slightly less than a regular taxi. Their popularity is one of those idiotic money-saving mysteries which often obsess the budget traveller, subsequently leading to a desire to avoid foreign travel at any cost. Naturally, we dolmeshed everywhere. One evening we returned to Sultanahmet Square from a stoned boat trip on the Bosphorus. It was twilight as we dis-endolmeshed somewhere near (according to the driver) our hotel. From the minarets, the imams' spooky call to prayer echoed across the water. Suddenly, a gang of young Turks who should have been at vespers confronted us with their habitual taunt "Beat*nikis*! Beat*nikis*!" and "Beatles! Beatles!" (which they pronounced "*Bet*less! *Bet*less!"). They were dressed in rags and a year or two younger than we, but able, clearly, to cause us trouble. They appeared eager to fight. Finally their leader stepped forward and said, with determined elocution: "Beatnik people all together FUCK OFF!" There was no mistaking the sentiment, but any temptation to point out that 1) that we were hippies rather than *beatnik people*, and 2) that as individualists, we could probably not be counted on to *fuck off all together*, was

Hagia Sophia Mosque, Istanbul, Turkey. Photo by C. Seney.

drowned in the tense silence as both sides stood their ground. We reached for our switchblades and fondly recalled our encounter with the Athens Chief of Police. Then Gregg stepped forward and glaring down at them with deep malevolence, growled "*La-ter!*" I was never able to ascertain if "Later" meant something more than *manãna* in Turkish, but Gregg's intervention worked. Our tormentor, perhaps noting that each of us weighed twice as much as he, slowly backed away, showing - I thought - real leadership. Presently, they withdrew, jeering at us to save face. We had avoided what might have been a colourful and one-sided Turkish razor fight.

The above experience notwithstanding, the Turks usually just stared silently at us, and were mildly friendly if we approached them. Unlike the Greeks, who, at least, had James Bond to compare us to, the Turks - one step further removed from the West - didn't know what to make of us, their apparent familiarity with beatniks and Beatles notwithstanding. The only Turk who had any grasp of our life on the road was a man named *Yener* who owned the worst restaurant in all of Turkey, which was named, to avoid confusion, *Yener's*. Turkish food is generally quite good, similar to, but more lively than Greek, and they avoid the Hellenic custom of eating everything at room temperature. However, the food at Yener's was

Ad for Hotel Takis Voglis.
Drawing by author.

surprisingly bad - after one try, a yen for Yener's was rare, even if you were Japanese! Ha ha ha! But we patronized Yener several times, gamely ordering various dishes. *Imam bayeldi* - stuffed eggplant with tomato - was an Istanbul favourite. The name, translated variously as "The imam fainted!" or "The imam shrieked!" presumably indicated the priest's enthusiastic reaction when he tasted the dish, although I prefer to think that the image of shrieking, fainting imams reveals a thinly-veiled, popular hostility towards the Turkish clergy.

However, it was obvious that the pampered imam in question had never sampled Yener's bayeldi. Nor did anyone except foreigners: Turkish people never patronized Yener. His attraction, for those budget travellers headed east, lay in his unusual custom of keeping a day book in which diners were encouraged to write, at length, their comments on the food (he must never have read these mini-reviews, or he would have closed up shop) and whatever else occurred to them – which for my generation of psychotropic wanderers, could be anything. It was an unofficial Istanbul tradition to have at least one meal at Yener's and leave notes for posterity. Yener had an enormous collection of these books - he would point to them proudly on a shelf near the door - a unique record of our peculiar social subgroup and the era in which we lived. I drew a full page ad for "The Hotel Takis Voglis", titled *"When in Athens ..."*, listing the various amenities: vampires, heated bathtubs, lots of dope, interesting people, nightly police raids and free phone calls to anywhere in the world (we heard, some months later, that when the house was finally closed, Takis's phone bill was over half a million dollars - over a trillion in today's dollars). Perhaps Turks avoided Yener's because our host was a police informer, paid a small stipend to keep an unofficial watch on the itinerant hippie community, his grub an afterthought purloined from the dumpster behind the Taxim precinct house. Whatever its source, it didn't stop Yener from serving his culinary efforts with great ceremony as he darted in amongst our tables, dishes held high, in an unintentionally wacky spoof of fine service. Yener was a legendary name among the hippies, and fondly remembered. He died of cancer in Ankara in 2009. The fate of those piles of guest books is unknown, but they'll form the basis of a social anthropologist's Ph.D thesis, someday.

I had a brief romance with a pretty blond American girl with one of those made up-sounding names that free-living, all-surfing Californians seem to specialize in – "Clysta" – seemingly derived from combining "crystal," "clematis," "Christus" and "clitoris" in a spiritual, *everyone's-creativity-should-be-given-full-rein-especially-when-naming-children* hybrid. But fortunately I kept my suspicions to myself, and later discovered that Clysta is a Celtic name, meaning "*sea inlet.*" She was on vacation from the Institute of European Studies at the University of Vienna. A year or two younger than I, Clysta was attracted to my age and maturity. In my eyes, an American surfer girl was the perfect antidote to the culture shock of Istanbul. It was snowing outside, but Christmas was nowhere in sight. We slept together in my hotel but, when push came to shove, she wouldn't actually *do it* with me. I remember looking at Clysta's nakedness in bed by the window. I kissed her tenderly, lifted up the sheets and gazed at her soft blond sea inlet, lit faintly by a street light. She would begin to respond to my caress, and then, mysteriously, stop. Privacy may have been the issue for Clysta - there were seven others snorfeling away in the room at the time, Yener's restaurant had

Portrait of Clysta,
Istanbul, February, 1967.
Drawing by author.

145

featured an *All You Can Eat Mediterranean Diet Luncheon Special* that day, the FEWS system was on Full Alert and, as the night wore on, random male voices invoked, repeatedly, the name of a larger member of the weasel family, signalling an impending assault from which there was no refuge. As volley after volley was fired, and the shouts and sounds of battle filled the air, I realized that it mighn't be Clysta's idea of a romantic atmosphere. Over forty years later, I found Clysta on the internet, and she kindly supplied the Rapidograph portrait I drew of her in a cafe in the Grand Bazaar.

Chapter 32

SHOPPING IN ISTANBUL

Istanbul's Grand Bazaar was an astonishing spectacle to a kid from Kingsville - a labyrinth of mysterious but friendly shops and corridors, through which one found one's way purely, it seemed, by chance. It was a warm, adventurous, magical place - a warren of benign exotica, where we passed many hours in a strangely exciting atmosphere. I bought the obligatory Turkish puzzle ring, some of us purchased wretched smelling embroidered leather coats made of lamb or goat skin trimmed with a woolly fringe (*de rigueur* attire for London hippies) and, of course, we all bought Turkey's famous carved meerschaum pipes. We puffed happily away in the main cafe, sipped chai or hot orange from tiny glasses and tried to straighten out - laughing, shrieking, fainting and telling tales. Sometimes we shared a hookah: the waiter would bring a large communal water pipe loaded with tufts of mild tobacco and we bubbled, puffed and snorted contentedly, oblivious to the possibilities of contagion.

One of our favourite cafe pastimes was playing "Did You Know?" The game was inspired by the locally produced tourism booklets with titles like "*Istanbul - Yesterday, Today and Tomorrow*", or, for the more sophisticated, "*Istanbul - A Study in Contrasts*", which traded on the European and eastern influences in the city while suggesting tour itineraries and listing mildly interesting info about local sightseeing. On the back covers, under the provocative title "Did You Know?" were listed quaint, colourful and sometimes wildly silly facts about Turkish life and history, usually in hilariously skewed English. We created our own "stoned" versions, and found these witticisms considerably funnier than they now appear. Giddy with laughter, we made up similar "facts" about the locals, such as, *Did You Know*:

- that if the moustaches of all Turkish men were laid end for end, they would - stretch from Balekisir in Anatolia to Nikopol in Ukraine?
- that each year in eastern Turkey, sufficient *imam bayeldi* is consumed to fill the famous underground Basilica water reservoirs of Taxim *two and a half times over*?
- Since 1967, AFL (Airborne Flatulence Level) detection units have been installed at all Turkish border crossings?

We had heard that no visit to Istanbul was complete without a trip to the legendary Turkish Baths. Outside North America, public baths are frequented by very poor people who have nowhere else to bathe, and are not synonymous with homosexual activity (although on this occasion I had my suspicions about two guys in the next cubicle). For those of us on the road, a huge tub of hot water once a week was a great luxury. However, the famed Turkish Baths were in a category of their own. We went one afternoon, freezing and stoned, and were baked, steamed and pummelled by enormous, baldheaded Turks into a state of limp, quivering, thoroughly-humbled cleanliness. We laughed hysterically as Anatolian giants twisted and tore us, beating months of grime and cheap drugs from our pores, all the while growling "*Massage!*" They soaked us, shampooed us and sent us back out into the world ready for anything.

We met Patrick (Tex) McKeever at Yener's. He was an American on a last adventure before Vietnam, and, although I only spoke to him for a few minutes, he gave us a very important piece of information: the location of an Israeli kibbutz that had an "open door" policy towards tourists - *Givat Haim Me'uchad* (a Hebrew name, Tex said it meant "lots of Scandinavian girls and good dope") - and the names of two American visitors there - Daisy Myers and Joy Robson - whom we should seek out.

Once again we loaded up the van and headed south. Al, who was Jewish, decided to take a boat to Israel rather than travel overland through the Arab countries. He made a typical exit one morning near

Sultan Ahmet: hurling his customary accusations in our direction, he emitted a contemptuous cackle, spun like a dervish and faded from view.

Danyel had decided to split, too: Lured by the *Naked Lunch* reputation of the North African drug culture, Morocco and Tunisia - with their expat French communities, "stoned" art scene and inexpensive lifestyle - would inspire him to paint again. He intended to hitch over to Spain and then swim south across the Strait of Gibraltar. Despite his harelip, Danyel had a handsome face. He mixed an earthy absurdist outlook with iron artistic conviction and impressive productivity - especially considering how stoned he was all the time. He had been a good friend. We took him to a major crossroads outside the city. A warm springlike wind scudded across the road as we piled out of the van and hugged our wild Belgian friend. John wondered aloud if we'd ever see him again. Gregg's predictable response concerning linear time was augmented by farewell cries of "Badger!" as we pulled away. I heard of Danyel only once more. Months later in Pamplona, someone said he'd seen him in Morocco, acting, not surprisingly, like Takis Voglis, freaking out in the street, stoned and apparently truly insane. I've never been able to trace him in the decades since.

We had stayed less than a week in Istanbul. A sixth sense, or perhaps the hand of a guardian angel urged us on towards our ultimate destination - Israel. We were all more or less broke and semi-starving. I shiver when I think of the risks I took, stoned and freakish, in Islamic police states. We were lucky that an indifferent universe neglected to victimize us. Years later, the film, *Midnight Express*, perfectly captured the perils of drug use in West Asia.

Moroccan prayer rug. Photo by author.

Chapter 33

THE SAMARITANS

It would take us just over three weeks to get to Israel, a distance of 753 miles (1212 kilometers) as the crow flies. Not being crows, we were forced to use the roads through southern Turkey, Syria, Lebanon and Jordan, making the distance closer to 10000 kilometres. I remember seeing a camel standing in the snow just after leaving Istanbul. This image didn't quite mesh with my movie notions about The Middle East. I was intensely interested in the journey, but hampered by the absence of windows. So, during vast stretches of the trip, I relaxed in the gloom and got stoned with my friends.

We drove southeast to Ankara, and then southwest towards Izmir, a grey, rain-swept Mediterranean coastal city. Then, southeast, crossing vast, treeless, bush-less, even weedless plains that looked like photos of Mars or the moon - on a straight road that led towards the distant Taurus Mountains. Traced on a map today, this route looks odd, but my journal doesn't lie. If we'd had a map at the time, I might have noticed its meandering character and said something. The weather turned cold as we headed inland from Izmir. That afternoon, off to the east, we saw what appeared to be a settlement: beneath an ashen sky, low, earth-coloured buildings rose up from the dirt and gravel. On arriving, we were confronted with an astonishingly primitive scene: sod houses with tiny windows, no shops or cafes, streets of frozen mud, and no sign - such as telephone or power lines - of connection to the outside world. The winter wind waged a steady assault on the town and its inhabitants. Forlorn-looking children drifted barefoot out of doorways and stared at us with dull curiosity. No adults appeared - for a moment I wondered if these tiny people were, indeed, adults, the effects of malnutrition and the pitiless wind having worn them down. We wanted a restaurant and indicated that we were hungry, but soon realized the hopelessness of our demand. They were hungry and wanted a restaurant, too. It may interest you to know that the term *restaurant* (from the French *restaurer*, to restore) first appeared in the 16th century, meaning "a food which restores", and referred specifically to a rich, highly flavored soup. Everyone on earth wants a restaurant, and these sad creatures were prime candidates. We stood regarding one another, as dust and snow hissed over the frozen earth, feeling like time travellers who'd landed in the Dark Ages. Who were these people? I had heard rumours that the Samaritans of Biblical lore had been cast out and lived on the fringes of society, poverty stricken and hopelessly inbred. Was this the earthly fate of compassion? Were these the legendary Good Samaritans, ready to help those who "fell among thieves?" I had fallen among hippies, but my plight wasn't comparable, and by the look of them, the Samaritans were fresh out of charity. We were beginning to turn numb in the wintry wind, when Gregg, who had refused to leave the van, stuck his head out and said, "Later guys - much later for this." The Samaritans were in trouble and there was nothing we could do to help them.

Chapter 34

FURTHER SOUTH

Border crossings were stressful but generally uneventful. Being fond of our freedom, we didn't carry drugs. We had long since got used to armed guards - only rarely were the soldiers openly contemptuous. Rather, they usually just stared with an amused curiosity (or backed away slowly, handkerchiefs to noses, mumbling curses).

High in the Lebanese Mountains, we ran into a heavy snow storm. The steep roads were extremely narrow and lacking guard rails. If a truck or bus came from the opposite direction, one was obliged, through some strange Middle Eastern protocol, to pull off the road - frequently out into mid-air over a bottomless precipice - and wait for the opposing vehicle (usually full of soldiers or sheep) to pass. Straight or stoned, it was a very difficult manoeuvre. We had driven for hours at dizzying heights in the blinding snow, when presently the icy road began to descend in what we hoped was a safe route out of the storm. Rounding a steep corner, we almost ran into - brace yourself - a traffic jam(!) winding for miles into a little valley town far below. Tom swerved just in time to avoid ramming a truck full of shivering chickens, piled in rickety wooden cages. Despite his efforts with our locked brakes, our van suddenly headed towards the edge of the cliff. Gildas ripped open the side door and everyone jumped out into the gale. Staggering on the ice, I ran around to the front of the truck to try to stop its slide. Cold and resolute, our warm little van had become a dumb brute nudging me towards oblivion. I met Tom's eyes through the windshield. "Get ready to jump!" I yelled. Tom threw open the door but kept his foot on the brake. Then, three feet from the brink, the wheels hit some gravel thoughtfully kicked up by another vehicle as it plunged over the edge, and the van came to a stop. I turned and looked down over the precipice. Beside a fast moving stream hundreds of feet below, lay the wreckage of a bus and two trucks.

Hours later, we reached the little valley town where we found a hotel and restaurant. A cluster of one and two storey buildings surrounded a treeless square and a snarl of military vehicles. Parked in the middle was a mysteriously empty London double decker bus, painted with flowers and peace symbols. Peering through the windows, we saw beds, a kitchen, living quarters - whoever the owners were, they were travelling in hippie high style. We took a room at the hotel - our host shrugged when we asked about the people from the bus - and, in the gloomy and deserted dining room, we shared a cold supper consisting of humus, pita, pickled hot peppers and onions, and some leftover *imam bayeldi* (which was always good for a laugh). Then, in a typically reckless act of revelry, especially in light of that ominously empty hippie-mobile outside, John N. went out and scored some hashish. We were naturally tense when he returned to the room. It had been an excruciating three days since we'd been high. The stress added to the effects of the dope - almost before puffing the group meerschaum, anxiety was urging me towards a major O.D. I looked around the room. Peter was playing an interminable Indian raga on his guitar, and everyone was grooving. The hot peppers churned in my belly as gnawing fears about the London bus and its vanished owners welled up in my imagination and my throat. Aside from the obvious drug arrest scenario (culminating in public beheadings), I picture the red British beast, a few days earlier, as it winds its way along those icy mountain passes, through a silent winter storm, carrying a group of very cool, very superior British hippies, who, at this moment, float weightless around the interior like fish in an aquarium. A tape machine plays *Tomorrow Never Knows*, from the Beatles' *Revolver*.

Suddenly the driver, Geoffrey Stiles, having shared a particularly strong joint of Lebanese primo hash with his passengers on the way up the mountain, notices on the downside, that the bus is going faster than he intended... VERY, VERY FAST! The rock face on the left rushes past in a grey blur. On the right, hundreds of feet down, the valley floor yawns, an abyss. Geoffrey hits the brakes. Wheels locked, the bus swerves dangerously near the precipice. He grabs the microphone: "Jump! Get out! Everyone out!" Geoff's fun-loving brother, Nigel, stands at the rear door, conductor's cap at a jaunty angle, ready to punch tickets. "Tickets please! Have your tickets ready. You're quite safe, really. Even God could not sink this ship!" Gaining speed, the bus hits some naked gravel and lurches to starboard. Ashtrays of roaches crash to the floor, a copper canister of pee-pee careens and splashes down the aisle. Nigel pulls the bell cord - Ding! Ding! Ding! - as longhaired maidens and frizzy haired guys leap to safety, race along the side of the bus, bravely hoping to stem its descent. At the wheel, Geoffrey sees his passengers run into view between the front of the bus and the precipice. He pulls up the huge handbrake, "Brave work, chums! Hang on and I'll – " but with sudden cries of astonishment, they fall from sight, plunging backwards towards the valley floor. The front wheels breach the edge, the bus slams to a halt, Geoffrey dives out into the storm, slips, tumbles and joins his friends as the engine shudders, stalls and a great shroud of black oil bursts from the beast - a severed aorta loosing its contents in an inky gush down the cliff face. Silence. Only Nigel is left alive.

Peter's *raga* was reaching a prolonged climax now. The pipe came round again, and John held it to Peter's mouth so that he wouldn't stop playing. He stopped anyway for a moment when he exhaled, made a Tibetan Buddhist demon face to show us how stoned he was, and then resumed his funeral march to Nirvana. A delirious cheer rose from the crowd.

Nigel lets go of the bell cord, straightens his conductor's cap and steps off the bus. A recent incident flashes through his mind - making love with Lucy on that mobile bed at window height as they wound through the mountains - a three-second cunnilingus primer for a group of Turkish shepherds. Edging along beside the bus, he looks over the precipice and sees, far below, his friends - through falling snow like shaken blossoms - frozen dancers sprawled across the rocks in a crimson tableau. Then, distant shouts. Down the road, a group of Syrian soldiers, brandishing rifles, runs towards him, their shouts muffled in the storm. Nigel stands before the broken bus and awaits his fate ... This was known as "a bummer" - the kind of *bad trip* that happened often when I got stoned. As was my habit, I suddenly leapt to my feet and ran to the bathroom, to be sick. The hot peppers were electrifying, second time around. And the high after the storm was very pleasant, as Peter's *raga* drifted slowly to a close.

The next morning the hippie bus in the middle of town was still there, silent and empty. We asked around, but no one knew anything, and we couldn't escape the feeling that going to the police station, say, or to the local militia headquarters to make further inquiries, might not be a good idea. It was warmer in this valley town than it had been in the mountains - the sunny streets were filled with diesel fumes and slush. I tried to reassure myself that the fate of the bus's owners couldn't have been as bad as my imaginings. So, oblivious to the desperate hands making futile gestures and tossing notes pleading for help from tiny barred windows far across the square (the bummer was taking time to wear off) we climbed into the van and made our way south towards freedom.

Chapter 35

SLOUCHING TOWARDS
BETHLEHEM

A few days later, we reached Beirut. It was a wealthy, modern seaside town with lovely tree lined avenues, pretty women in western dress, fresh orange juice and sweet almond cakes by the harbour. We had a wonderful open air lunch on a cool, sunny afternoon at a terraced restaurant on a mountain side overlooking the city.

In Bethlehem, after a quick visit to the birth site of the supposed saviour of the world, J. Christ, we bought burnouses and I saw the Hammer horror film, *Frankenstein`70* (1958). It was an unappealing invention, filled with pointless talk and drenched in preposterous ideas, which pretty much parallels my attitude towards Bethlehem and its famous son as well. It occurred to me that faith is insistence on believing in something you know isn't true. The Church Of The Nativity was shoddy and decrepit. It featured a tacky crèche populated by mannequins apparently retrieved from a bombed Beirut department store, with stuck-on beards that would have shamed my high school drama club. But I'm glad I went, although I had second thoughts about carving a heart on The Manger: "Doug & Tammy, 1953". Lucky for me, my Mom decided not to join the Warriors for Christ Evangelical Holy Land Tour in her later years. Seeing her bad boy son's sexual history permanently etched on that holy headboard, she would have had a conniption.

This was living! I was convinced that the kids back home, if only they could see me, would be overwhelmingly envious ... or if they weren't impressed and filled with admiration, I believed that they should go fuck themselves and become actuaries or sell vacuum cleaners for all eternity. I wrote home very seldom.

Chapter 36

DO THE DEAD SEE?

Our last stop before Israel was the Dead Sea. We arrived on its bleak, treeless shores late on the warm afternoon of the 21st of February. The water was dead calm and gave the impression that there was never a ripple – if there were lakes on the moon, they would look like this. In the distance was a single, modern hotel, just built and deserted-looking. We drove down to the water's edge, stripped off and plunged in. The extremely high salt content made the act of swimming akin to being a beach ball floating on the surface - you couldn't submerge. The water seemed to eject you, forcing you back up to the surface. It reminded me of playing with a beaker of mercury in high school: you could stick your finger into the shimmering liquid and it would almost *squeeze* you out. This buoyancy rated as one of the coolest experiences we'd ever had.

Mountains rose to the west of us, and blue shadows crept across the water as the sun began to sink. It gets cold fast in the desert after sundown. We towelled off and noticed that the darkening hillsides were dotted with campfires. Then some Arabs, who had built a fire further down the beach, hailed us. There were three of them, one dressed in western style pants and wind breaker, the other two in traditional garb. We shook hands and they invited us to join them for something to eat. Over lamb kebabs, expertly cooked, we told them where we were from and where we were going. We had learned to refer to Israel with the popular Arab term "Disneyland". Despite Walt Disney's purported anti-Semitism, the name encapsulated

Arab contempt for American support of their formidable neighbour, with their flashy war toys supplied by the U.S. military-industrial complex. There was some slightly bitter joking about "Disneyland" and what a nice place it was. They had met many others like us - young North Americans and Europeans who embarked on "exciting and dangerous" tours through Arab lands before seeking refuge in the safety of the *kibbutzim*. At that time they were losing the anti-Israel propaganda war for the hearts and minds of the West – public opinion has become more favourable since. The June war would create new definitions: no longer was Israel's population "Jews" – with all the victim-connotations that accompanied the term – but *Israelis*, who defeated Arab armies with ease, with rumours of an atom bomb.

The sun had just dipped behind the mountains when they took out the hashish. It was strong and dark - like the faces and the eyes of the men who offered it. Many joints were passed and the scene was tranquil and relaxed. When I asked about the .45 automatic in his belt, the western-dressed confessed that he was a policeman from Egypt. Alarms went off in my hash-dimmed brain: was he just a cop on vacation - or something more sinister? Who took guns on vacation? We were too stoned to run, but he didn't seem about to arrest us anyway. I stretched out with my feet warming near the fire, and looked over my shoulder. Herds of black and brown goats were descending the hillside through the twilight, stopping intermittently to graze. Presently, they joined us by the fire. Their goatees and little revolving mouths made them look pensive, almost wise, as they stared into the flames with their alien eyes.

Then the goatherds joined the party. They talked quietly, taking long tokes from the joint and deep pulls of orange soda. One squatted by the fire across from me and told a long story to appreciative laughter from our hosts. The Egyptian shrugged with a twinkling smile in my direction: "Untranslatable," he said, politely. The evening was arid, windless and cool, and the smoke rose straight up into a cloudless sky and a new moon. Including the goats, there were now about seven hundred of us around the fire. I looked down at the traces of sea salt on my fingers. I hadn't washed for a week, but my body was dry and odourless. I thought of T. E. Lawrence's reply when asked what he liked about the desert: "It's clean," he said.

The stamps in our passport called it "The *Hashemite* Kingdom of Jordan", and they weren't kidding. We had heard all about how the primo stuff was made and told everyone we met: *In high summer the beautiful, blond (!), female virgins of the village were required to run naked through lush, flowering valleys of hemp. Their young bodies had been smeared beforehand with wild honey which caught up the pollen grains and viscous resins that coated the leaves and blossoms. At the edge of the field, the thick, sweet liquor was scraped gently from their panting breasts and silken thighs by gelded craftsmen with dull gold hashemars, then reduced over fragrant cedar fires and packed into cakes bound for Christmas stockings around the world...* Harvest time among The Hashemites! This was the kind of agricultural work I could really get into (gelding optional, of course). But "Disneyland" beckoned: naked cinnamon Danish girls had been seen running through the kibbutz orange groves, and I was needed for the harvest, no gelding required. Apparently, the Israelis didn't share the Arab penchant for cutting things off - heads, penises, testicles, hands - it would be a safe place to pursue my agrarian interests. And, if I'd learned anything in Sunday school, it was that, in this area of the world, it was not cool to cast your seed upon stones.

Everyone had fallen silent as darkness crept in among the goats. The policeman threw a log on the fire, and a plume of sparks roiled up towards the firmament. We rose, shook their hands and thanked our hosts, and drove away through the moonlight towards Jerusalem.

Chapter 37

JERUSALEM

In March, 1967, Jerusalem was still divided, Berlin-like, between Jordan and Israel. To reach the Israeli side, one drove across an urban no man's land filled with boarded up, empty buildings. We moved cautiously through the deserted streets, aware of the Arab-Israeli tensions and imagining ourselves through the sniper sights we feared were trained on us. The steerage passengers hunched low in the back, thankful, just this once, for the lack of windows ("Bet you wish you could sit back here with us now!" we taunted the Aussies up front - still bitter at having seen nearly nothing of the Middle East so far). Finally, the Mandelbaum Gate loomed up before us, and, in a few moments, we were "safe".

We had left the East behind - the Mandelbaum was strictly one-way. I had seen Damascus and Jericho, of which I remember nothing. Of course, there had been talk of Sodom and Gomorrah, though no one was quite sure how to get there or what activity tradition might demand. There was genuine doubt about Sodom, the local preoccupation holding little appeal for us - we who had barely experienced heterosexuality, much less all the other kinds. I pleaded the more ambiguous Gomorrah's case as strongly as I could (we had heard in Istanbul that in Aramaic, "Gomorrah" meant *place of many Swedish girls and good dope*") - but to no avail.

UNCLE MOUSTACHE

BADER BROTHERS
UNCLE MOUSTACHE
RESTAURANT AND TEA-ROOM

Inside Herod's Gate   Old City, Jerusalem

We stayed overnight in Jerusalem, naturally concentrating on the "old city". We visited the famous Whaling Wall, site of the Prophet Jonah's gustatory encounter with the Great Cetacean, and hung out at a hip/fashionable Palestinian cafe called Uncle Moustache. We stayed in a hotel and saw an infamous Swedish movie called *Dear John*. It had a very sexy reputation in TIME Magazine but turned out to be a simple film of adolescent relationships, drenched in earnest, pre-Ingmar Bergman *angst*, and pristine enough to be shown in Sunday School. It was an affront to everything I stood for.

Chapter 38

SOCIALIZED FARMING
AND THE JEWS

Kibbutz Givat Haim Meu'chad (founded 1953) was a well established enclave about midway between Haifa and Tel Aviv, close to the towns of Hadera and Netanya. Thickly treed and nearly as old as the country itself, it featured concrete one- and two-storey buildings. Some were small, housing individual couples, and some large with multiple units, including two tourist residences.

Our surprise arrival caused shockwaves of excitement in the tourist buildings, where females, by some strange, quasi-Biblical miracle, outnumbered males by at least ten to one. Staggering from the van, the FEWS Alert lights still flashing, we looked up to see a row of squealing, excited girls lining the balcony looking down at us throwing kisses. If a moment can be both electrifying and charming, this was it. They were like a delightful collection of exotic birds, a United Nations peacekeeping team, twittering and serenading our arrival, barely able to contain themselves. They bent over the rail, their sweet and varied buttocks clad in kibbutz shorts of green or blue, swaying and shuddering with anticipation and delight. We strutted around in the parking lot for a few moments, stretching and kibbitzing, smiling stupidly and saluting our welcoming committee - letting the effects of our magnificent maleness sink in. Tom switched the FEWS light off - impressive as the technology was, it wasn't the best advertising. Presently, in my finest, mid-Atlantic accent, I called up: was there a Daisy Myers or a Joy Robson there? There was, indeed! The two of them screamed and jumped up and

164

Gildas, Gregg and Daisy, Kibbutz Givat Haim MeUchad, May, 1967.
Photo courtesy of Gregg Connolly.

down as though they'd won the Miss Universe Pageant. So this was The Promised Land! I knew how Moses felt. Soon, I would raise my staff and the Red Sea would be parted.

Compared to most of the people in Israel, I had little business being there. I had only the vaguest idea of what Israel was to the world, and who the Jews were – my education was limited to the films, *Judgement at Nuremberg*, *The Pawnbroker*, *Exodus* and *Ben Hur*, and a lot of biblical movies. I especially liked the score from *Ben Hur*, by Miklos Rosza. This music provided a sensual entrée, but the films had painted an incomplete picture of the Jews and their place in the modern world. My levels of maturity, drug-induced ADD and testosterone precluded deeper grasp of the situation. In a Dizengoff cafe on a day trip to Tel Aviv, I noticed a series of numbers tattooed on the arm of an elderly woman. She had seen things that my generation could barely imagine.

The kibbutzniks were neither friendly nor unfriendly. They saw many of us come and go, and we had little impact on their lives. We gave back somewhat less than we took, I suppose. I wasted the opportunity to get to know some Israelis. It was possible to be "adopted" during the duration of one's kibbutz stay by adult Israelis who generously offered friendship and counsel to any of us who wished to partake. However, my record with parents and grownups in general was not a good one and I didn't consider the offer for a second. Why would I choose talking to grown-ups over smoking hash, having sex or going for a swim? Kibbutzniks our age were absent - they were all away on military service - and, I had no interest in getting to know anyone over thirty. I suspect they understood us better than we them. In spite of the fact that most of us were *goyish*, had little interest in the meaning of Israel in Jewish history, smoked dope and listened to pop music, engaged (theoretically) in promiscuous sexual relations, and didn't break our backs working (all habits which might lure their children away from the sanctuary of kibbutz and family life), they were very nice to us. I think if one can generalize about a people (and, with the exception of Greeks who stand to benefit hugely from my criticisms - I don't believe in promoting racial or ethnic stereotypes), Jews are the most personally tolerant people in the world. Directly or indirectly, nationhood makes oppressors of those who indulge in its protocols, as Palestinians and native Canadians (and scores of others) will attest, but the kibbutzniks' attitude to us essentially *lumpen* kids was benign and *live and let live*, in a situation where we must have been rather unattractive guests.

Chapter 39

PIPE DREAMS

I settled into a very pleasant two months at Givat Haim. The work was easy - mostly orange picking in the *pardess*, an occasional foray into the familiar realm of turkey husbandry to break the monotony (in keeping with my Scorpionic proclivities, I had taken a job involving the artificial insemination of turkeys during my high school years - the source, no doubt, of an obsession with feather-covered women's panties which haunts me to this day) and sporadic duties in the peanut and orange canning factory on a neighbouring kibbutz. The factory work was the easiest. In a warehouse, an indifferent foreman would tell us to pile a few boxes and then disappear, leaving us to lie low, or in our case, high, for the day.

One day, Gildas, Peter and I stretched out on crates among the rafters, cool and dreamy from some hashish. We knew that we wouldn't stay on the kibbutz forever, and visions of the future arose for the group's consideration. No one was interested in returning home to live lives as grocery clerks or furnace installation technicians, while reminiscing or repenting for youthful folly. Instead, we envisioned returning to our respective homes as super hippies. The best plan was to buy a fishing boat in Brittany or better still, a *dhow* in Madagascar. We would outfit our craft with stereo equipment for parties on the high seas (ever ready to rescue shipwrecked women from shark-infested waters), and motorcycles for quick forays inland (this still sounds like a really good idea to me). We would sail around the world and return in triumph to our respective home towns. I had accumulated significant feelings of bitterness towards Kingsville in the months since my departure, and my fantasy bore elements of revenge. I imagined drawing near to Kingsville harbour at sunset in high summer. To heighten anticipation among the townsfolk, we have slowed our pace a mile or so out, our *dhow*'s exotic profile mysterious against the horizon. We signal our approach with long, echoing trumpet blasts from giant horns of Ramadan, or Alpenhorns purchased during a layover in Switzerland. The boat's lateen, emblazoned with my portrait, luffs slightly in the breeze as our ancient vessel glides gracefully into Kingsville harbour. Crowds of gawking townsfolk arrive, dockside. I stand casually in the bow with my exotic fellow travellers, beautiful hippie women clinging to my thighs. A thousand eager hands reach for the ropes we toss carelessly towards the wharf. We invent busy tasks for ourselves on deck, feigning distraction, even irritation, or laughing and making cryptic comments sprinkled with foreign phrases. The locals stare in awe and never think of their Camaros rusting in the weeds. But I do. Then, grabbing a rope, I swing out over the crowd and land lightly on the dock, greet by name in a friendly manner someone I had never said two words to during my Kingsville years and ignoring more familiar faces, instantly thereby rewriting history and making everyone question their own perceptions. The harbourmaster appears and I invite him on board, my magnanimous gesture dwarfing any authority he might have in this regard. We laugh loudly as he stands among us, and I sign his little papers. A supreme moment of triumph comes when my high school algebra and chemistry teachers arrive, tweedy and moth-eaten, to stand sheepishly in the crowd, forced to ask themselves - faced with my splendiferous

Our dhow. ("Wouldn't a dhow go good, now?") 1967. Drawing by author.

presence - what the hell they had done with their lives. I would, of course, fail to notice them. We then withdraw to the centre of the harbour, drop anchor, lay the long table for a candlelit feast *al fresco*, and wait for those who dare to row out in little boats loaded with gifts and tribute. The town fathers, doffing their caps, would respectfully offer us their daughters. My historic aims would have been achieved ... We never actually did this, though. Hashish makes for splendid dreams and little action.

Thus went our kibbutz work day until about three o'clock. Then, still high, we dragged our work-weary bodies to the dining hall and stuffed ourselves on fresh bread, butter, peach jam and warm milk - a daily feast which, after months of cold and semi-starvation, was reminiscent of the *manna* of biblical lore. The kibbutz diet was lacto-vegetarian for the most part: avocados, peppers, avocados, tomatoes, cucumbers, oranges, avocados, cream cheese, weak coffee, thin soups, turkey in a myriad of flavourless forms (in a charitable custom that goes typically unacknowledged by an anti-Semitic world, Israeli cuisine extracts the turkey's flavour and sends it to other countries where it's needed) and, of course, avocados. Then, more dope, shower with a Scandinavian of your choice and a rest or a swim in the kibbutz pool. This demanding schedule was followed by a supper of avocados in the large noisy dining room, where the setting sun cast bright shafts of light and long shadows through the happy din.

Chapter 40

THE TRUTH ABOUT KIBBUTZ WOMEN

There weren't any. Not Israeli women, anyway. Every sabra our age was away doing military service. Consequently, we were left to fend as best we could with a small handful of female tourists from Sweden, Denmark, Holland, France, Germany, England, Scotland, Ireland, Australia, New Zealand, the U.S. and Canada (none from Iceland, regrettably). It was a hardship, but with war approaching, I think we all felt obligated to rise to the occasion. I had two affairs during those months, as well as a couple of shorter term flings. Daisy was a tall, athletic American girl from Allentown, Pennsylvania, a graduate of Goddard College (the notorious centre for free spirits in Plainfield, Vermont) who was enthusiastic about knowing me and very supportive of my feeble artistic efforts and ambitions. She loved to get stoned and eat, dance, listen to music, laugh and tell stories – the most optimistic person I've ever met. We bedded down soon after my arrival, but, for me, there emerged a conflict between friendship and Eros, and the sexual relationship faltered. I suspected that, after years of sexual repression in Kingsville, I preferred an unarticulated, unconsummated sexuality - thwarted, desperate, and distant. Regular sex with a real human being was more of a challenge than I had anticipated.

It was very common to make love in the presence of others at that age and in that milieu - not because we were exhibitionists (*au contraire* - we could barely admit to what we were doing with each other), but because, as for impoverished youth everywhere, there was a shortage of private space. Daisy shared a room with her friend, Joy, whose cot lay opposite, a few feet away. This made lovemaking a rather furtive and subdued experience, to which no reference would be made, then or later, by the third party lying awake, listening in the darkness. Nor was there ever any hint of a "threesome" possibility, despite Playboy Magazine's attempts to mold the sexual revolution in its own interests. We were very unjaded and innocent. But Daisy and I didn't last long as a couple - settling into an exclusive arrangement was not what I thought I was there for. I was convinced that happiness lay in quantity rather than quality. Instead, Daisy and I became genuine friends and remained so until I lost track of her years later in London.

I had a somewhat longer affair with a Canadian girl named Gail Carpenter – even though we were not suitable mates. Despite our having little in common, I couldn't resist her beauty. She claimed to be a fashion model, was conventionally pretty with the aid of a great deal of makeup - a surreal preoccupation in the hip/spartan atmosphere of the kibbutz, but - apparently necessary for her self esteem. If she had a brain, she hid it successfully and was decidedly not part of the rebellion of the Sixties. She was preoccupied with her fall wardrobe ("pink" as I recall - she would repeat the word *pink* over and over, in a mantra-like chant) in anticipation of her return to Canada - an event for which she yearned with increasing impatience. Beyond that, she had very little to say. Her reasons for travelling remained a mystery – although perhaps they were the same as mine. She would appear in my room in her sheer robin's egg nightie, quite lovely, and we would make rather uninspired love - she was dry and distant - of course I was a neophyte, too, and had little idea of how to arouse a woman. Our relationship limped along for a few weeks, pointless and dull, while I laughed and skylarked with Daisy and Joy, and the other guys.

Gregg began sleeping with Joy and they moved into more private quarters across the courtyard in the other residence. These were times of exhilaration, not because of love, exactly, but because of life itself surging through our bodies. Snapshot memories surface as I think of those days. I remember Gregg yelling war whoops from his balcony one spring morning. I went out and yelled back, making jokes as usual. Joy appeared beside him and they stood together, their arms around each other, temporary allies. Lonely joyful couplings, cool morning air, pale sunlight filtering through the leaves, a light breeze moving the treetops as we traded gleeful witticisms – these things made life beautiful.

The reader may recall that the 1960s was an era that revered hair, not just facial hair in men and longish hair for both sexes, but unregulated pubic hair as well. We all had lots of it. Shaving one's pubic hair never occurred to anyone unless they had crabs or were having a really bad trip. Shaved skin was a grim harbinger of hair loss in old age, or possibly an alienated fashion statement made by bipolar Zen assassins (which may explain its current widespread popularity). Consequently, I'm perplexed by the ubiquity of pubic shaving in today's porn videos and apparently among the young. Beholding a woman's hairless vulva is fascinating, to be sure, but its partial veiling has greater merit: sustained exploration of the pubic forest, its flora concealing - then revealing - the mysterious pool at its centre, ranks as value added by any measure. Not that I'm against shaving, exactly. But like lingerie, shaving's chief virtue is that it signifies a woman's interest in erotic activity, and thus is a turn-on. However, my research clearly shows that women are nearly always interested in erotic activity anyway - they're simply choosey about whom they tell. The successful continuance of the race since pre-historic times, unencumbered by vinyl corsets, ball gags, high heels, epidermal piercing, shaving and branding, puts these arcane practices in proper perspective. In contrast, we revered the "natural" in all its forms – hair especially. There's feral charm in a sweet and feminine woman with whom familiarity reveals to be hairy in areas of special interest - an animal excitement that's devalued, even lost, by shaving. A hairy woman is both wild and tender, an exciting contradiction sadly tamed and subdued by application of clipper, soap and blade. After all, from Delilah's barberous intentions with Samson, to the shaved heads of Vichy collaborators, to the military tradition of buzz cuts for cannon fodder, hair removal has overtones of disempowerment no matter how you cut it.

I had an unresolved affair with a Danish girl named Lene. She was slender and pretty, with slightly rusty blond hair, pale skin which showed blue veins, a soft vulnerable mouth and *the strangest eyes I had ever seen*: one crystal blue and the other an earthy green.

Lonely Danish refugees, Kibbutz Givat Haim MeUchad, Israel, April, 1967.
Photo courtesy Gildas Failler.

The hormonal steroid testosterone makes men like me view women like Lene as flower-like and delicate, and the discovery of their sexuality profoundly exciting as well as slightly forbidding. I was deeply attracted to Lene. And her eyes fascinated me. I loved her voice and her accent - I would make her say "rudgrud med flude" (the name of a Danish raspberry dessert with cream), over and over, and watch her lovely lips form the words. The "d's" in Danish aren't pronounced, but taper off in little whimpering sighs, the way people talk in dreams - the sexiest thing I'd ever heard. But Lene and I never made love. Around women I really desired, I became tongue-tied and paralysed. Lene and I went for walks in a kind of formal courtship - I didn't even get to the point of holding her hand. I remember a cool, rainy day with a free afternoon. We were tramping around an outlying region of the kibbutz. She wore a royal blue corduroy coat and those elfin, honey-coloured shoes from her perfectly designed life in Copenhagen. We had climbed up on a low stone wall, and now, like a gentleman, I lifted her down. She was light and sweet in my arms - a perfect opportunity for a kiss, and yet I hesitated, and the moment passed. Later we slept together under the heavens in Eilat, but by then I had contracted gonorrhoea (star-crossed lovers indeed!) and could only stare longingly at her hairy nakedness in the moonlight. She managed to get out of Israel before the war. I've read that Danes are the happiest people in the world. The Danish embassy repatriated her and scores of other Scandinavian women (showing a real sense of what national treasure is, and what foreign missions are there for), and I never saw her again.

Chapter 41

ANCIENT EVENINGS IN ISRAEL

I spent many stoned evenings, smoking hash and listening to the three seminal recordings of the period: *Aftermath* by the Rolling Stones, *Mellow Yellow* by Donovan and the immortal *Revolver* by a now defunct group called the Beatles. I drew pictures and tried in vain to write in my diary. It's difficult to argue that dope clarifies or deepens one's perceptions or the ability to express them. However, my son Sam claims that, in terms of potency, the cannabis we smoked back in the 'Sixties bears little resemblance to the current products of hippie (or mafia or police) agronomy: today's stuff is thirty to forty times stronger than ours was. I read in the paper that a recently seized batch was an amazing "twenty-nine percent THC"! We were babies sucking pabulum in comparison - in fact, it appears that, by today's standards, we were never stoned at all.

Ned Logan.

When I didn't feel like getting stoned, I spent kibbutz evenings with an Englishman named Ned Logan. He was an arrogant eccentric, contemptuous of the drug culture (according to Al S., Ned was "old school" – an unusually discreet way of calling him "fucked up"). Ned was a year or two older than me. He told me he'd worked in the theatre in London's West End, had written plays (his mother was a noted children's theatre writer) and would help me get a foot in the door of London theatre if I looked him up after Israel. Although

Ned Logan, Kibbutz Givat Haim Me'Uchad, Israel, March, 1967.
Photo by Gregg Connally.

I was having fun travelling, I was painfully aware that life was slipping by and that others of my generation were making purposeful career moves somewhere far away, so Ned felt like an important contact. He was indeed "old school" - he was literate, quite big (like me), dressed in khaki, smoked a pipe and had an imposing, faintly threatening air about him. In my eyes, he resembled a hybrid of the British actors Jack Hawkins and Nicol Williamson, if that clarifies things any. Ned had literary aspirations – he wanted to write plays – and a love of absurdity. He had a silly joke he liked to tell: he'd assume a tortured countenance and gravely mutter, *"To be, or not to be..."* and then interject a second character in a nerdy little voice, *"Would you pass the salt, please?"* which I found very funny.

Ned talked of Ethiopia and South Africa as potential destinations, and of selling diamonds on the black market. He was a refreshing change from the majority of drug sodden innocents I met on the

176

road, and I considered him my most interesting friend for a time. My diary entries about him are a little embarrassing - I idolized him, briefly. But his dark side was disturbing - he spoke of criminals he befriended in London (he grew up in Nottingham) and sometimes gave the impression that he was cut from similar cloth. He once held a knife to my throat - *in jest*, if that's possible - when I tried to act tough. A year later, during my film school days, Ned helped me get work as a stage hand at the Strand Theatre in London, and we remained friends there until my radical political and cinematic interests drew us in different directions. Ned was no left-winger.

On The Beach.

One hot day, a dozen of us "tourists" jumped into the van and headed for the beach. It was an hour's drive and we took plenty of hashish (rumoured to have been smuggled from Jordan in the bellies of itinerant camels) to fill the time. Soon the interior was filled with the resinous smoke (we kept the near useless vents closed in order inhale as much as possible) as we hurtled along. Suddenly, Tom yelled that we were being pursued by a motorcycle cop. Panic stricken, we tore open the windows (which, we knew from FEWS/Badger experience, were extremely limited as ventilators) and attempted to air out the van, visions of a sudden rescinding of the Knesset's Old Testament *"Thou Shalt Not Cut Off The Testicles"* Law dancing in our heads. Gregg cleverly opened the rear window and acrid smoke billowed out behind us, engulfing the policeman momentarily and

making him swerve slightly. The cop was waving his arms now, and we debated whether he was threatening to start shooting or, due to his sudden involuntary inhalations, experiencing some kind of fascist-psychedelic policing fantasy. Boy, were we in trouble. Tom stalled for as much housecleaning time as possible and then slowly pulled over. We waited, rigid with fear. The cop stepped up to the driver's window and cautiously looked in. Tom handed him his IDL and tried to shut the window but he motioned for him to keep it open. When he peered in towards the back of the van, his gaze was met by nine pairs of blinking, bloodshot, terrified eyes. He walked around to the side door and knocked. Reluctantly, we slid it open. A sharp gust of wind from the distant Negev scooped the remaining smoke from our lair and wrapped it around the officer in an illicit swirl. How could he possibly remain oblivious? He looked to be about our age. Maybe he'd led a sheltered life and didn't know what hashish was. After taking stock of the situation for what seemed an eternity, he stepped forward, stuck his head inside and said, "Here in Israel, we don't cram people into trucks like cattle." He paused for effect, then withdrew, slowly closed the side door and motioned to Tom that we could go.

At the beach, Israel, March, 1967. Photo courtesy Gregg Connolly.

There's a photographic record of the day. It's a carefully staged shot of us at the beach, leaping in unison off a meter high sand bank. Over forty years later, I imagine that each surviving link in this human chain would offer a different account of why she was there and where he was headed – but we were unique. The fragile beauty of our aspirations contrasts sharply with the conviction of our enemies, who have couched their every campaign in contempt for the meaning of the Sixties. Celebration of war, competition, status, celebrity and wealth needs constant tending in a world that survives only because of communal effort and good will.

Chapter 42

TURKISH, LEBANESE
OR AFGHANI?

In 1992, the Kingsville chapter of the Imperial Order of the Daughters of the Empire (IODE) held a series of summer afternoon lectures on the grounds of the Conklin Estate. On August 4th, Professor Wilmot Plingé was the last-minute replacement for Mrs. Marjorie Pearsall who was to speak on "Chrysanthemums: A Lively Overview of Their History and Cultivation." Professor Plingé was very aware that the ladies before whom he now stood were united in their wish to "strengthen the bonds of Empire." Whether they meant the British Empire or the American remains unclear. Still, it's a safe bet that Leon Trotsky's *Theory of Permanent Revolution* hadn't had a significant impact on their discussions.

Plingé had suggested that he speak on "The Tragedy of the 1960s", and the ladies were happily prepared for a denunciation - not of the assassinations of John Kennedy, Martin Luther King, Malcolm X, Bobby Kennedy nor the obscenity of the Vietnam war but - of the era's sexual, libertine and recreational outrages. However, Plingé's trademark bluntness had become pronounced in later years. He particularly enjoyed springing unsavoury anecdotes, provocative ideas and implicit accusations on conservative listeners. He began with brief reference to the inspiring example of Theatre of Cruelty founder, heroin addict and full-time psychotic Antonin Artaud and his impact on Sixties culture: "As for Artaud's writings, we read "hashish" for heroin and felt we were at the forefront of a movement of liberation. We were, indeed, the foot soldiers of an important trend, but, with hindsight (and attention paid to reports of Mafia and CIA drug running, as well as the American military's rumoured experimentation with hallucinogens and mind control), it's difficult not to think of even the so-called "recreational" drugs as anything but weapons in the arsenal of our enemies."

There is polite silence from the audience of ladies, broken only by the screech of a blue jay and the buzzing of cicadas. Plingé continues: "Every drug-induced revelation had its dark corollary in political confusion, apathy and stagnation. People on drugs don't learn anything - nothing except fear. Drugs, classically, are seen as ruinous factors in people's lives and the traditional view is correct, yet someone sold my generation on their liberating qualities. Who was that "someone" and who benefitted from drugs' proliferation?"

Plingé's voice rises steadily until a ripple of alarm passes through the assembly. Valium tablets are seen to be consumed by audience members. Some of the women make mental notes to question Felicity Webb about her choice of lecturers. Others voice suspicion that Felicity's new Zoloft prescription isn't working. Plinge: "Drugs involved leftist radicals in illegal and dangerous activities, making them vulnerable to police harassment. Drugs gave the media ample excuse to discredit political activists with smear campaigns aimed at the "silent majority". Drugs fuelled a provocative youth culture and drove monsters like Charles Manson and others to commit acts of hideous violence. In the Sixties, drugs were the Establishment's single biggest weapon against the political radicalization of young people. It's pretty clear who benefited from that!" An uneasy silence is followed by lemonade and biscuits.

Chapter 43

EILAT AND THE RED SEA

After a couple of months, kibbutz life became monotonous, and it occurred to me that there was more to Israel than communal farming. Eilat - a seaside city at the southern tip of the country – beckoned, offering the excitement of a "frontier town," possible employment in the beach hotel or the tin mines nearby (a source of money - we were paid only a small stipend on the kibbutz) and a community of hippies living on the shores of the Red Sea. It was a very long hitch to Eilat, south through the green midriff of the country, past the camel market at Bersheva and across the Negev Desert. If Omar Sharif, in *Lawrence of Arabia*, could describe the Sinai as "God's Anvil", the Negev certainly rated the name, "God's Hibachi", although no one but me ever called it that. Because of the heat, snakes and scorpions, cold nights and Arab infiltration, it was said to be highly dangerous to attempt a crossing. I caught a ride in an old truck that I feared would never make it, but, near dawn one night in early May we pulled into Eilat - the rough Israeli outpost only two miles west of downtown *Aqaba! Aqaba!*

The day rose in hot, blinding sunlight over the rolling surf as I walked along the beach looking for a place to stay. I came to a group of huts where some friendly looking people (Dutch and Swedish hippies) were breakfasting on hashish under a desert style canopy - a roof and open sides in the manner of the Bedouin *beyt* - perfect protection from the sun. A cool breeze blew in off the water. They invited me to join them. It emerged that the community was reeling from a murder two days before. A German hippie who had been living on the beach for some time had been shot, Peckinpah-style, in the no man's land at the border between Eilat and Aqaba. Forty-six bullet holes, they said. He had eaten a *finger* of hashish one day and walked slowly and suddenly into a hail of gunfire from the Arab side - although it was rumoured that many shots had come from the Israeli side as well. I suppose that, from a military standpoint, the event was a touching moment of rapprochement between the lunkheads on both sides whose job it was to guard the status quo - recognition of a common attitude towards anyone who might stand for peace. And gosh, just a really swell opportunity to kill someone! As far as I know, the event went unreported in the press.

Veterans of Givat Haim gathered at an abandoned Quonset hut about halfway along the beach towards the border. I found work scrubbing pots in the beach hotel, and later, as a short order cook in the cosmopolitan atmosphere of the Half Past Midnight Cafe, where the forbidden pork chop, euphemistically known as "white steak", was the most popular dish, and where I learned to operate a two thousand pound hummus machine that resembled Robbie the Robot from *Forbidden Planet*. I had contracted gonorrhoea during an encounter with two surprisingly generous Israeli girls named Ahuva and Rachel, who visited the kibbutz tourist residence one evening. Weeks later, a hint that they weren't really philosophy students from the University of Tel Aviv surfaced when I was handed an Egyptian porno magazine containing pictures of them engaged in the exact same activities we had shared. I had fucked two celebrities and didn't even know it: with their familiar female responses to my efforts – ill-concealed boredom and a desire to get away – they just felt like normal girls to me. I think they were taking time off from servicing the vast armies gathered on both sides of the border, and had come to the kibbutz for a rest. Luckily, my only symptoms were a dripping prick, brief periods of blindness and spells of dementia. Seeking a cure, I visited Eilat's famous Dr. Alkenna, a kindly old gentleman who gave me a shot of penicillin and some pills (the Red Sea Cure) that made my pee deep red - pissing was like turning on an ancient, rusty tap after years of disuse. He asked me what I wanted to do with my life and said I could pay him some other time. Later, I met other of Alkenna's beneficiaries with similar medical histories, the same debt and the same kind memory.

I bought a diving mask and flippers, smoked a lot of hash and dove in the Red Sea. Stoned to the point of speechlessness, and able to hold my breath for hours at a time, I explored the shimmering reefs near the Egyptian border. The mountains of Technicolor coral made diving akin to flying through another world – I felt immortal. I saw a hammerhead shark and we had jellyfish fights in the sparkling light. One day, John, the biggest of the Aussies, hit Ned in the side of the head with a jelly fish. The question of who was really the toughest of our group climaxed then, as Ned waded into the surf and struck John hard in the face. It was no contest - Ned was the tough guy as John crept away in humiliation. Ned's status as "old school" non-hippie now went unchallenged.

Al Schiff's saving grace was his ability to amuse us with surreal humour. Stoned one day on the beach, he declared that he had, with his special diet, succeeded in reversing evolution. He promptly crawled backwards down the sand, and "returned" to the sea. We laughed as he lolled about in the waves, eyeing us solemnly, as though he'd proven us fools yet again.

Living on the beach in Elat brought the mystery of night here on Earth into sharp relief. Sleeping under the stars, I had never seen the firmament so bright and gigantic. It's a unique experience to drift off beneath that immensity – an hour or two spent gazing upwards brings on a profound awe - a little like those guys in the Bible

who turned their gaze away, unable to look at God. Roofs shelter us from its truth. Of course, Al said the sight made him feel really big and powerful.

Life in the Quonset hut offered little privacy and few amenities (none, actually) and I decided to build a hut on the beach. There was lots of useful debris - sheets of corrugated siding, iron pipes and timber - and in a few hours I had fashioned a beautiful shelter facing the water. Hours later, when I returned from shopping for house wares – knick-knacks, doilies, ashtrays, coasters, paper placemats with astrological character descriptions – I was shocked to see that the pounding surf had reached up and pulled my hut to her bosom. Not to be deterred, I gathered more material and rebuilt, this time on a spectacular scale, higher up on the sand, sure that I had outsmarted the elements. When I returned from work that evening, I saw the debris from my new abode churning and rolling in the waves. There hadn't been a storm; the sea had simply taken a personal interest in thwarting my feeble efforts at an elegant lifestyle, and taught me the old Biblical lesson about building one's home on rock instead of sand. And to underline its laughing indifference, after sunset - it treated me to a blazing soft fireworks display, as billions of tiny glowing fish rolled in with the pounding surf.

Eilat nightlife was centred on a group of outdoor cafes in town. The traditional evening meal was a plate of eggs, French fries and salad, followed by extraordinary Italian ice cream, all of which was as wonderful as any food I have ever eaten. We watched the sunset's light on the mountains of Jordan to the east, their reflection turning the Sea Red. The crystal clean air made my heart leap with joy. The long cool evenings of Eilat cafe society were the supreme hippie road people's rendezvous. Everyone, Israelis and travellers alike, seemed *happy*. We had made it to somewhere very remote and wild and far away, a place so obscure and special that only we, the initiated, could understand its importance.

Chapter 44

A THREAT OF WAR

Arab armies were surrounding little Israel, with men and tanks numbering in the trillions. War fever and fear had reached a high pitch. A couple of days earlier, I, at last on the very verge of being an interesting person, had written:

> *"The Middle East is about to explode. Egypt is going to attack Israel ... Here I am on the Red Sea with $20 in my pocket ... stomach bad ... headache ... It's hard to imagine that I might be murdered by Arabs. I could be dead in a few hours - or any minute!"*

My mother clearly had no idea how cool it was to be in a war zone, or how interesting her son was becoming. Across the ocean, in an event that she would later claim was caused by worry about me, she suddenly lost most of her hair. I felt I had done her a favour in saving her the trouble of pulling it out because of existential doubt about Jesus. The world and my Mom wondered if Israel would survive - there was no certainty as far as we could tell - and I thought of stowing away on a ship, just to get out. I learned, then, that air and sea transport out of the country had been suspended.

The Negev's ceaseless north wind hammered the town. Cold at night and hot in the day, it shrieked around her low buildings and hissed along gutters on its way out to sea. The relentless blast made for tough going, despite my burnoose and staff. Then, one morning in late May, the wind shifted. The *khamsin*, Israel's *mistral*, brought war's pestilence: army battalions gathered outside town, jeeps and troop carriers roared through the streets, radios blared from open doorways, and weariness and fear haunted every face. That afternoon the wind died, traffic stopped, cafes fell silent, and I watched an ochre blanket creep across the sky. Shielding their eyes with hands and newspapers, people stood in the street, gazing upward. It was eerie and ominous, like the atmosphere in De Mille's film, *The Ten Commandments*, as Pharaoh waits to see if Moses can make good his threats of death and famine. I half expected to see evil green mist slide along the ground and hear wailings of bereavement in the twilight. Presently, the still air filled with fine yellow mist, the wind rose to a roar and the town disappeared before my eyes. The dust storm lasted about an hour. This parched baptism changed everything - it was time to leave Eilat. The army had begun to evacuate all nonessential personnel, and our beach community was high on their list. I decided to head back to Givat Haim. Gildas, Ned and I got tickets on the last bus out and left at 2 pm on the 27th of May, 1967.

Chapter 45

RETURN TO GIVAT HAIM
ME'UCHAD

Two hours into the Negev, the tires on the left side of the bus blew out. "Arabs have done this!" said the driver, discounting the possibility that the tires might simply have melted in the heat. We staggered out into the inferno, ready to be machine-gunned by Hashemites hidden in the rocks. The driver and the guard worked feverishly as we smoked cigarettes, circled the bus, and peered into the distance. The shimmering horizon held all manner of strange figures, appearing and disappearing in the waves of molten air. Finally, the tires fixed, we headed off, amazed that we were still alive. The image of an Arab with a rifle, drawing a bead on this Canadian naif, would haunt me for months to come.

We were welcomed back at the kibbutz (recall, if you will, the shortage of men), and immediately put to work digging trenches and filling sandbags, and at night – even though exhausted – ministering to the sexual needs of tourist women. People fuck a lot when war threatens. News reports of the growing crisis were broadcast (in Hebrew, of course) over the public address system. A giddy excitement seized us - I was having a great experience! It was hot, tense and exhilarating. War fever was a trip! If not also dead, I was sure to be an interesting person after this!

The photo, on the next page, shows Daisy departing for a hitch across North Africa, saying goodbye to Gregg Connolly. Little by little, most of the kibbutz tourists would leave the country: Gregg, Daisy, Joy, the Aussies, and Ned. Left behind were Gildas, some

Gregg and Daisy, May, 1967.
Photo courtesy Gregg Connolly.

others and me. There was a country-wide blackout after dark – on the kibbutz the electricity was turned off. Hash smoking had reached an all-time high and the long, silent nights were filled with paralyzing fear and bursts of hilarity.

One evening after singing "I'll Go My Way By Myself" to a crowd who probably were willing to take me at my word, I stumbled out onto the veranda and peered into the darkness. The "pre-1967" border was only a few miles away. To the northeast loomed the Golan Heights. Tension and fear transformed the darkest scenarios into easily imagined possibilities: any Arab guerrilla worth his salt could sneak up through the trees, pick off a few tourists with his infrared *Kalashnikov* and be home in time for his morning falafel. Armed guards patrolled the perimeter of the kibbutz – and it was all I could do to fight a sudden stoned urge to go for an evening stroll wearing my burnoose. As I stood weaving slightly in the dim light, I distinctly heard, from the bushes only a few yards away, what I was sure was the cocking of a rifle (did Kalashnikovs cock?). I imagined the Hashemite panning his gun site along the veranda, past a window where candlelit figures laughed and gestured, to another where a young girl bent over a table writing a letter home, and then to me, silhouetted in the doorway, alert to the intruder but paralysed with fear. Lightning quick, I dropped down behind the rail and frantically considered my options. But before I could arrive at a plan, Gildas emerged, gloriously stoned and content as usual, loudly singing Ringo Starr's hit, *Act Naturally*.

Frantically, I shushed him, pulled him down beside me, pointed to the bushes, urgently explained our plight and insisted that he help me warn the others: we would crawl from room to room, douse the lights, send someone we didn't like out into the dark for help and grab whatever makeshift weapons we could muster! When I had finished speaking, Gildas looked at me dully, said "OK, man," rose to his  feet, burst into song and wandered inside. He was so stoned that the sniper could have killed him and he wouldn't have noticed. The night remained still. Eventually, I rose from behind the rail, braving a sudden spray of bullets which didn't come. Moments later, my glazed perceptions were dazzled as reconnaissance flares silently turned midnight into day. In the distance, a dog barked.

The June War of 1967 was one of the shortest in history (it's often called The Six Day War), and I didn't see fighting, much less participate. However, the kibbutz beside ours was shelled repeatedly from the Golan (the hoped for influx of lonely female Swedish refugees never materialized) and, from the top of the water tower, I could see the smoke of battle. The constant flybys (Passovers?) of Mirage jets at treetop height (with a roar designed to scare people to death), the sight of convoys of young Israelis in bloody burnouses racing from front to front, and a panicky feeling which never left, were all part of the extraordinary tensions of a country at war. And, although I was a pacifist, I knew where my immediate personal interests lay: I wanted Israel to win. Caught digging trenches on kibbutzim by victorious Hashemites, self-proclaimed "pacifists" might have their credentials questioned, with resulting jeopardy to balls, hands, penises, heads, etc. "Choose sides, idiot!" roars the cosmos. This fundamental truth destroys ideals and informs all the machinations of the world.

Chapter 46

EXODUS

The June War had ended with a decisive Israeli victory. It was also the climax of my Israeli sojourn. Efforts devoted to ageing my mother twenty years during my six days in a war zone had been realized, and it was now time to seek out even greater adventures. Peace now reigned around the Mediterranean, and further outrages would have to be confined to sex and drugs, but I was confident that my determination and commitment would again triumph. A grand road people's reunion was planned for Pamplona, Spain, on the 7th of July, 1967 ("777!"), for the Running of the Bulls. "7-7-7" was invoked by everyone who mentioned Pamplona, the numerological significance of the date was both unquestioned and unexplained. In spite of being raised in a technologically advanced society where science seems destined to answer every question, most people cling to some form of mystification as a source of pleasure, if not religious belief. It would have been spoiling the fun to call "7-7-7" nonsense. But for us, the real meaning of Pamplona was re-affirmation of the fragile itinerant community we had established – our chosen family would reunite at the Feast of San Fermin, where men flaunted their mortality in the face of stupid angry beasts (and I don't just mean the Spanish police). For the spiritually hungry, the trinity of sevens gave our odyssey a mystical glaze. But none of this provided much comfort for me. I haven't mentioned it much, but there was always something wrong, gnawing at my guts. I felt aimless and anxious about my place in the world - perhaps I was wrong about selling insurance or raising pigs. In an unusually urgent diary entry on 12th June, I wrote:

"Will life always be this struggle? Most people bury the struggle. Does anyone resolve it? Do real artists not bury the struggle? Is dealing every minute with the struggle what life is about? What the hell is the struggle?"

*****

My final days in Israel were spent in Tel Aviv and Haifa. In the ancient seaside city of Acco, I met a stunningly beautiful ballet student, whose charm, self possession and precocity were unforgettable. She said her name was Eva and we sat together in a seaside cafe. She gazed sadly at the horizon from time to time - her lean young face, dark hair and green eyes, framed in the dazzling Mediterranean light, are vivid in my mind to this day. I was completely in her thrall. As I walked her home towards her school, she suddenly stopped in the narrow street and looked at me – an angel was standing before me, waiting for me to reach out. But what would happen if I touched her? She couldn't have been more than fourteen. A peal of laughter burst from a roof top, a mo-ped buzzed past. She turned, walked away and suddenly I was an old man. Eva.

At a corner sidewalk cafe near the port of Haifa, I became addicted to hummus and the bar's blindingly cold beer. In Tel Aviv I had a two-day romance with a Jewish Londoner named Leah. We slept on the beach under the Hilton Hotel the first night and in a nice hotel room (not the Hilton) the second. The desk clerk stared at us glumly, from the sexless misery of advancing age. Leah was very attractive with a strong, tanned, athletic body, dark curly hair, ice blue eyes and a deep reservoir of desire. We didn't sleep at all.

For many months following the war, Lloyd's of London refused to insure ships coming to Israel. Fair weather friends: this was seen, in Israel, as another example of the world's indifference to her survival. It's the sort of telling detail seldom mentioned in history books, the politics of insurance companies being regarded as of little consequence. But we had heard that some air transport was available. We decided that from whatever neutral territory we could reach, we would sail to Italy and then hitch to Spain.

My foray into exotic lands had ended - I would go no further East until a trip to India in the early 1980s. For now, I would withdraw to safer climes and enjoy more civilized pursuits, such as LSD and women. My mother had sent me $400, an enormous sum by my impoverished standards - enough, it occurs to me now, to fly home with, though such a thing never occurred to me then, and such notions always remained unspoken with her. It was a season later to be described in the lore of the Sixties, as "The Summer of Love", and although I wasn't in San Francisco, as Gildas so often wished he was, it was to be a lovely summer, indeed.

Chapter 47

IN TRANSIT

Gildas and I caught a military flight out of Ben Gurion on 22 June, 1967, to Nicosia, Cyprus, whence we had booked passage on a Greek ship, Venus, bound for Ancona, Italy. We had trepidations about choosing "the Greek way", but in the aftermath of the war, travel choices were very limited at the eastern end of the Mediterranean. After a grimy bus ride to the coast, we waited around in Famagusta (the most pertinent translation for which is "absence of Swedish girls and good dope") for a day, renewing our tepid romance with Greek life and gazing out across the stormy waters, searching for signs of our ship. Finally, in the dead of night, the S.S. Venus appeared and, with typical Greek aplomb, dropped anchor about a half mile from the pier. We saw a portal open in the hull, Greeks on board and dockside began yelling and waving at each other through the gale, and, after a couple of hours, we lucky ticket holders were invited to embark in a small motor launch which would take us out to the ship. Borne like a peanut shell on the dark waves, our boat churned through the storm. It was like a scene from *The Guns of Navarone*: I began to suspect that, at any moment, our dinghy would change course and head towards a rocky coast where we would blacken our faces, scale rain swept cliffs and slit the throats of German sentries. But soon, we pulled alongside the battered hull and were hauled, like sacks of potatoes, into the womb of the ship by shouting, gesticulating Greeks. Typically, our arrival occasioned not the slightest interruption in their conversation. We picked our way across the hold, through a welcoming maze of hundreds of cars held in place by taut iron chains. I had heard that sometimes, in stormy seas, the chains would snap and become lethal whipping snakes, tearing arms and pieces of heads from onlookers, and the unfettered cars would roll, crashing and bashing with every heaving wave, and destroy vast sections of the hold. Despite the danger, heroic Greeks would try to corral the cars, to stop their maddening to-and-fro, lest they burst through the brittle hull and plunge into the sea. Sailors would be crushed, bloody and screaming, under their relentless, metronomic movement. Often, steerage passengers, because of the low fares they had paid, and especially if they were hippies, were ordered to run among the cars to try to tie the chains together. At other times, the Greeks would completely forget to use the chains, or sometimes, perhaps misunderstanding instructions from another Greek, they would actually remove them from the vehicles at the beginning of a voyage (this inspired the movie *Hercules Unchained*, 1959) with catastrophic results.

Photo by author.

There was a piercing metallic shudder as the ship weighed anchor. We were shown to our quarters, or, more precisely, quarter - a grey, windowless, iron room filled with seventy or eighty airline-type seats bolted closely together. The other passengers were mostly Greek (some of whom were accompanied by live goats), with a few ill-looking backpackers sprinkled among them. Whether the goats were cherished pets or gifts for relatives in Toronto, their presence in the hold with us was romantic at first. But sitting beside a goat in an airline seat, watching it swaying slightly with the sea as a feta-laced *mal de mer* rises slowly in your gorge, can become irritating. There was a sudden explosion of squawking feathers as a flock of stowaway chickens burst forth from a nest of crones. I took refuge topside and stood in the storm, mused about what life must have been like in Noah's Ark and watched the lights of Famagusta disappear into the blackness.

We passed a hideous night stuck bolt upright in those airline seats - floor space for stretching out had been carefully eliminated by the ship's designers - in our brightly lit and airless steerage. The heat from the ships engines booming only inches away gave the atmosphere a timeless, hellish quality. Morning came. It must have been morning, because a rooster, armed with a sixth sense for these things, let go with an ear-splitting *cock-a-doodle-doo!* in Greek right next to me. I opened my eyes in time to catch a crone scrabbling for an egg rolling lazily among our feet. Looking up, I met the gaze of a goat which had leaned over the back of the seat in front of me. To this day I will swear it asked me for a cigarette. Fending off the waiters who had just arrived with steaming trays of free coffee, croissants and hot towels (yes, I'm joking!), I once again made my way to the open deck. The day was warm and clear, the sea exactly like rippled green glass, which is why writers often describe it that way. The Greeks were maintaining a steady pace and life looked hopeful again. I stretched and filled my lungs with the sweet Aegean air. Leaning on the rail, I reminded myself that with genuine adventures both behind and ahead of me, I was in the very throes of becoming an interesting person. I had travelled thousands of miles in a windowless van, made love to a dozen women, cooked pork chops in Israel, survived a war, smoked a lot of hashish, and tormented my mother with some eight months of titillating non-communication. I felt seasoned.

*****

Pig iron and rape seed quotas had held little appeal for me in high school: despite my desire to travel, geography and its concerns had not been among my greatest achievements. For example, I was only vaguely aware of the Greek city of Corinth, its famous newspapers filled with Corinthian columns, and only slightly familiar with the perpetual bestsellers, the Biblical I & II Corinthians. But the greatest of these marvels, my brethren, is the amazing Strait (or Canal) of Corinth, which the 19th Century Greeks cut through the Isthmus of Corinth to avoid having to sail all the way around The Peloponnese on their way to Toronto. It is the one area of the world where Greek shipping has to follow the straight and narrow, and the whole

Photo by author.

waterway is kept free of derelict ships and excessive discussion. But there is something disturbing about this rigid geometric slash through the ancient landscape. In early times, the Greeks often incurred the wrath of the gods, and the Canal's severing of the southern half of the country seems to be a conscious effort to incite The Powers to further measures. Shortly after lunch, the engines slowed and our ship entered the narrow, four mile corridor. The ochre cliffs moved slowly past on either side - we could almost reach out and run our fingers along Neolithic layers, exposed to the sun after zillions of years. Corinthian children ran above, waving and crying out to us from the weedy, windblown summit until their parents snatched them away from the edge - it was both unnerving and *charmant*, if that's possible.

The Strait of Corinth provided a startling location for the climax of French cineaste Claude Chabrol's *La Route à Corinthe*, an undistinguished potboiler, with but one memorable shot: a very large, very fat man in a black suit running down an extremely narrow, low-ceilinged passage in a tomb. It is a classic "perspective shot", and the viewer has the impression that the fat man, as he huffs and puffs away down the tiny hallway, will inevitably get stuck at the far end. Looking west from the bow of the ship, along the perfect symmetry of the Strait, the same feeling arose - that the vanishing point in the distance was in fact *an end*, some kind of maniacal Greek joke, that this was their revenge for all the negative feelings that I had experienced about them, or, indeed, revenge by the gods for this brutal cleaving of the land, and that eventually we would grind to a halt, our boat wedged between the two walls. But we scraped through, emerged into the Ionian Sea, headed towards the Adriatic and arrived in time for supper at one of Italy's finest coastal cities.

Chapter 48

ITALY

Ancona boasts a trading history that harkens back to ancient times. There is a shipyard, a sugar refinery, many excellent examples of Romanesque, Gothic and early Renaissance architecture, and it's all I can do to resist writing an exhaustive essay on the town and surrounding region. But suffice it to say that it also features a small dockside restaurant where I enjoyed my first lasagne. I am happy to report that it was quite good, though lacking the *besciamella* sauce of the Bolognese lasagne that is essential for those of us on the 40,000 Calorie-a-Day Diet.

Two hundred kilometres to the southwest of Ancona lay Rome. We couldn't miss it although we were unprepared to spend the time or money for a thorough exploration. I remember sitting in a rococo funk at the bottom of the Spanish Steps. It's the only rococo funk I've ever encountered: I'll be devoting an entire chapter to the experience in a sequel to this book. But Rome was a hot noisy circus, and being a penniless pantheist, I was eager to get on the road again. Gildas agreed. Cities were anathema to us - they represented everything we were against - police, pollution, crowds, conformity, schools, subways, work, worry, adults and alliteration. Ironically, in the face of street life in some of Europe's major cities, the idiocy of rural life had become more appealing. However, after hours and hours of the most unsuccessful hitching we'd ever experienced - we had made little progress and had been abused by the Italian motorists - it seemed pointless to keep trying. Drivers would swerve at us, make "haircut" gestures, sound their Vivaldi *Trumpet Concerto-From-Hell* horns (there is intense horn rivalry between Italians and Greeks), or stop and speed away just as we were about to climb aboard. After many hours in the same spot, with hundreds of empty cars racing past, many mocking signs and gesticulations made for our benefit, we began to answer in kind. It became easy to assume that an approaching car wouldn't stop, and that it might, in fact, try to nick us as it flew past, so we decided to offer preemptive signals. The universal middle finger salute was our chosen response until a furious fat man in a black Mercedes screeched to a stop, jumped out and hurled curses at us. He looked like a classic Mafia thug, fresh from a Luca Brasi memorial luncheon, and his level of rage was astonishing. We feared, for a moment, that he would pull out a gun or that a group of similarly enraged friends might suddenly emerge from the trees to interrogate us. This was the most hostile populace we had encountered. However, we bravely pointed at our genitals, bit our thumbs like the Capulets and the Montagues, yelled "*Fungula tu puta madre!*" (the phrase approximates an Italian curse) and walked menacingly towards his car. He retreated and sped away.

The encounter shook us. Sitting in the hot sun by the side of the road, I got to thinking about our predicament as outsiders, secular misfits with what is now known as "attitude". In response to whatever Gildas and I were thought to represent, the Italians were just the nice side of murderous. Further east, the Greeks were hostile in an imbecilic way, but too busy arguing among themselves to be a genuine threat. The Turks were perplexed by us, but generally unaggressive. The Syrians, Lebanese and Jordanians (not to mention the Samaritans) were, at worst, indifferent and at best, moderately friendly. The Israelis welcomed us to their mildly socialist land and provided work, food and lodging. But here in Italy, there was no doubt that we were striking a nerve - street life is an important barometer of social attitudes. (The leftist filmmaker, Pier Paolo Pasolini, was to be beaten to death on a suburban roadway by Catholic fascist thugs a few years later.) It was apparent that many citizens of modern, western, industrial states hated us for our youth, freedom, and individualism, even though, by counter culture standards, our hair was relatively short and our dress conservative. What did this say about Christian culture? And, if there was a tendency towards

The author, summer, 1967.

less hostility as we moved east, what would Spain, our western destination, home of pal-of-der-Führer General Franco, hold in store? We had noted that the Spanish police were required to wear nonsensical-looking plastic tricorn hats, the absurd design of which had no apparent function except to humiliate and infuriate the wearer. And confronting a mobile force of identically dressed, armed and enraged men in silly hats on the lookout for anyone who might have the reputation of critical nonconformity - we, whose very appearance said "*Your hat looks stupid!*" - was a disturbing prospect. Add to that our intention to ascend to the Krishna Godhead by way of psychedelic potions while wandering among the bloodthirsty revellers at the Feast of San Fermin in Pamplona, a celebration that centred around the torture and murder of helpless cattle in front of drunken, screaming crowds ... one could not escape a feeling of, well, *anticipation*. We knew that Pamplona would be a watershed. The Running of the Bulls would do more than hurl a few Spaniards into the air. Letters from the Aussies, who had retreated to England before the war, assured us that LSD was coming. From that point onwards, we, the wandering tribunes of the Beatnik Empire, would make a subtle but meaningful stand in the midst of the straight world.

Western society was in a deep crisis. Detroit was still smouldering and Watts was exploding. Vietnam was a sickening, imperialist catastrophe. The media were filled with hostile accounts of the youth movement - condemnations of our open expressions of sexuality, rebellion and "anarchy". What was wrong with the older generation? Why couldn't they see that life was a beautiful adventure? Was there anything to respect about bourgeois culture? Did straight adult society have anything to teach us other than conformity and greed?

After Rome, we spent two nights in rural Italy in scenes of breathtaking pastoral beauty. The rich greens of Italian farm land were pure Kodachrome. The first was in a field of hot peppers in the loveliest of hilly rural settings, just outside a picturesque Umbrian town. As the sun rose, peasants began working the soft earth nearby, paying us no attention as we sat up and rubbed our eyes. The second night we splurged on a big spaghetti dinner at a very comfortable country inn, had hot baths and sank into soft mattresses and clean sheets for the first time in what seemed like years. Money was the key to comfort in Italy, just like everywhere else - that's where the big advantages of bourgeois conformity and greed come in. The next morning, suffering under the peculiar Italian disdain for breakfast of any kind, and unable to face the grim prospect of more Italian hitchhiking, we took a train into southern France.

Chapter 49

LA FRANCE

The drive through the Pyrenees was very beautiful, and punctuated by a number of pleasant encounters with generous and friendly people. However, the thumbing was not really a lot better, so I invented a ruse which I was to employ many times afterward. I made a sign which proclaimed, "Quatrieme heure ici!" ("Fourth hour here!"), thereby shaming passing drivers into stopping (the use of "deep shaming" techniques had been a tradition in my family for many generations). Two or three times, it worked superbly. Charming French people pulled over immediately, aghast at the message ("*Mais non, mes enfants - c'est impossible! Permettez-nous ...*") as though some element of national pride was at stake. Gildas's nationality and good humour came in very handy during occasional moments when I lost all idea of what was being said. They would treat us to lunch in a country restaurant and then send us on our way with bundles of wine and cheese and their best wishes. This generosity was commonplace in France, a country I love. No doubt, my ability to speak the language affected my feelings about the place as well as my reception. But what a profound difference between France and Italy!

Somewhere in the western Pyrenees, I had a particularly important insight, concerning the tragic character of European history. When told that we were headed for Pamplona, our French driver nodded approvingly and said "Ah oui, Pampelune ..." *Pampelune*?!! I was shocked and hastened to correct him until Gildas nudged me with an "I'll never really understand Canadians" look that was to appear with increasing frequency as time passed. I pressed the point: "But Gildas, it's not Pampelune - it's "Pamplona"! Pampelune sounds like pantaloons and Loony Tunes and other things which might enrage the already pissed-off, sangria-drenched Iberian populace. At festival time, these people throw live goats out of church towers - more than understandable as a religious sacrament, of course - but they do it for fun! How will they react to ignoramus outsiders mispronouncing their names?" Leaving me to my rant, Gildas chatted nervously with the driver in some kind of Bretonne-Basque patois and ignored me. It burst upon me that I was surrounded by a continent of mad men who denied one another the right to call their native lands by the names they had chosen. Thus, the seductively lovely "München" became the effete "Munique", the romantic "Paree" the hum-drum "Paris", and, tit-for-tat, the sturdy "London", the drab and joyless "Londres" - *laundry* capital of Europe! One need hardly mention the British propensity for calling Nederland the saucy "Holland(aise)", and Deutschland the contagion-rife *Germ*any. This problem has plagued Europe for millennia, triggering countless wars, and my revelation is definitive proof that hashish deepens one's perceptions.

Chapter 50

PAMPLONA, SGT. PEPPER AND LSD

A series of bus and car rides got us to Pamplona on the 6th of July. We stayed at the camp ground near the centre of town, where there may have been Spanish people but which was in reality, the first international hippie love-in, attended by young people from all over Europe and North America. It was a joyful, wacky, stoned reunion with our best friends in the world, reunited here by some kind of miracle. Daisy, Joy and a new friend, Amy Benson, arrived, Daisy and Joy fresh from a gruelling hitch across North Africa, Amy fresh from months of "heroin addiction" in Istanbul. The addiction was more pretension than fact, I think. Amy was from New York and had a lot invested in becoming a tragically-addicted type interesting person. She carried a lump of opium with her which she showed to people when her credentials were in question. Amy's father was an American art house film distributor. Through him, she and Daisy had stayed with Pier Paolo Pasolini at his apartment in Rome the previous fall, an identity-booster if ever there was one. I would see all of Pasolini's films at the National Film Theatre in London, two years later. You're probably wildly curious about my favourite Pasolini films. To be honest, I'm not much of a fan: appreciation requires the earnest cinephile's high tolerance for tedium. His *Gospel According to St. Mathew* and *Salo* are his best; Pasolini's personal obsessions ruin most of his films. Only Salo transcends them, but, with its scenes of high-ranking fascists forcing coprophagia on helpless young peasants, it's not a good date movie, nor the kind of film one sees twice for the pleasure of it.

Pamplona also featured the first examples I'd seen of families of British tourists on "the Continent", with their trunks full of English food: cans of corned beef, Spam and rice pudding, packets of tea and jars of Marmite. Why did they travel? If you eavesdropped, you could actually hear them talking in hushed tones about the horrors of garlic and olive oil, not to mention their revulsion for long-haired hitch hikers. I also suspected that they were the exception that proves the rule regarding sex and travel.

The Beatles' latest album, *Sgt. Pepper's Lonely Hearts Club Band*, was released on June 1st, 1967. However, none of the places I frequented regarded the event as sufficiently important to blare it 24 hours a day as demanded when members of Beatnik Empire were near. Rumours about its availability prompted me to ask a Pamplona record shop owner to play it on his loudspeaker system. I sat on the curb and listened while reading a copy of LIFE magazine which had pictures of the Watts riots in Los Angeles (the vicious oppression of life in Watts included a complete absence of public transport. There was no getting out of Watts, literally or figuratively. How long would it take *you* to riot? Of course, you, dear reader, would surely have shown some initiative, pulled yourself up by your bootstraps, got an education and made something of yourself). In truth, most music sounded trite when I was high on acid. Enough has been written about *Sgt. Pepper*'s brilliance. I hear it sold quite well. My response was more heretical. It was a little too self-conscious and finely controlled, compared to the groundbreaking Revolver. In fact, it struck me as a re-make of *Revolver*, with a bigger budget. Not that it isn't one of the greatest pop albums ever made. But I think that, after *Revolver*, my expectations for it were too high. A gust of cool wind blew along the pavement as *A Day In The Life*'s long final chord faded away: the Summer of Love would soon give way to fall. High on hash one evening, I heard *The Doors* for the first time. Jim Morrison's brooding, haunted music signalled the souring of the psychedelic revolution in America long before the murders at Altamont. The baroque tumult of *Light My Fire* wrenched the listener free of romantic illusions about love and sex - death infused our very genes, yet we could not escape the "mire", the primitive impulse to fuck and procreate. C'mon baby, light the primal fires of my lust. The sodden weariness of the music contrasted sharply with the bright optimism of the Beatles – of course, I OD'd and vomited as usual. Its ominous pall has hovered over American life ever since, presaging the culture's free-fall into cynicism, class war against the weakest, and despair - the fabulous Internet, i-Things, social networking and the trickling down of all those heroic entrepreneurs notwithstanding. Its ugliness is forever threatening, like a storm front that won't blow away - a perpetual Weimar: no matter how bad things get, we're burdened with the realization that they could be much, much worse.

*****

John, Peter and Tom arrived, from England, to accolades - John with $1000 worth of LSD, ostensibly from the same hippie chemists who supplied the Beatles (how many times was that claim made in 1967? And who *really* made all that stuff? And why?). The feeling in the campground was one of joyful anticipation. My psychedelic baptism was fast approaching. Each hit of John's LSD ("250 micrograms") was delivered, quaintly, on a sugar cube. As the deep acid tremor began to shake my soul, I took out my diary and wrote, slowly, that I was afraid to look up from the safe haven of the page. I was with Gail, Gildas, the Aussies and a few others. When I finally raised my sight, the world and my friends had the look of 8-millimetre colour film, not silent but in full stereo. Voices echoed. Shadows were deep purple and everything had a

Drawing by the author, summer, 1967.

207

grainy, bursting-with-life quality. I felt intensely *present*. On closer examination, Gail's face was a microscopically pulsating map of many colours, the skin semi-transparent, each cell vibrating like an amoeba. Her eyes were sky blue but painted with odd circles of mascara, her hair was streaked with gold. She avoided my piercing gaze - she had not taken the drug. Beside everyone else, she was hung with sadness and caked with artificiality - stuck in the waifish, anti-hippie, Carnaby Street posture that was *de rigueur* for obedient young women at that historical moment, but still very pretty in her incongruous pink dress. I could have been kinder to her, I suppose. The grass on which we sat was a crushed mass of life, thrusting tragically up towards heaven and not making it very far ... Eventually, I got up and wandered around the camp ground. Acid slows one's pace to a spiritual shuffle. I looked down at my bare feet stumbling slowly through the dust - the sight was somehow beautiful and elemental - like a sustained cutaway in a Jesus movie, illustrating Christ's long soul-searching wanderings in the desert. Then I sat by the path and watched beautiful humanity float by. I had a feeling of perfect harmony with the world as well as a serene detachment. Before my eyes, human life seemed to unfold in a loving, aesthetically complete... inevitability.

After a few hours, Gildas and I wandered into town. The streets were filled with happy crowds. We were invisible. There were no police – we'd scared them off with hatless threats of free love and

Drawing by the author, summer, 1967.

LSD. No rain of goats from clock towers. We traded understanding looks as strange sights and beautiful women passed by – what a pleasure life was. We stopped in a park, the Plaza de La Cruz, at the centre of which was a shaded square where an enormous wrought iron cross stood in a shaft of sky light. It was made from industrial scraps of metal combined in a transcendent work - extremely ornate, almost grotesque - raw and exciting, like a crucifix crossed with a porcupine. It dominated the square with its dark presence, seemingly infused with the belief of most of the people who gazed upon it. The artist had triumphed - even as a non-Christian I could look at it and be fascinated by its impact - a power that overwhelmed the Christian meaning and surpassed it. However, in later researching the thing, I discovered that it was a relic of the fascist 1930s, and is widely despised as a symbol of domination.

I noticed a little three-year-old boy run around the square and was touched by the energy and interest with which he met the world. A few minutes later, as we watched the bulls thunder through the streets, smearing tourists and locals against the rough wooden hoardings like Spanish flies, his young mother asked me to hold him on my shoulders, so that he might see over the wall. She was a lovely, dark-haired Spanish woman who must have thought I was a native. We Welsh Swedes can pass for anything. I imagined that the boy was my son, and felt, for the first time in my life, that I wanted a son and a daughter some day.

Gildas and I shared a frugal but outrageously wonderful supper in a nice restaurant - of rough bread, red wine and green beans with peppers and corn. On acid, the fact that it was a side dish seemed irrelevant to me, and after the waiter left I boldly set it directly in front of myself. Back at the camp ground, we watched a fiery sunset and the quicksilver movement of the clouds. I was attempting to seduce Joy (she was the only female in our original group whom I hadn't slept with) when Gail rushed in and broke up the proceedings.

Chapter 51

ENCORE UNE FOIS,
LA FRANCE

We left Pamplona on July 11th and started north - Amy and Joy with Gildas and Daisy with me, two groups hitching separately. Gildas had invited the four of us to his home in Brittany. In Bordeaux, in high summer, road side tents invite passersby to freely sample the local wines - can you imagine Ontario vintners doing this? And its not leading to drunken carnage on the province's highways? It was very hot and Daisy and I partook as often as possible, always ordering the champagne. Champagne, I discovered, is a beverage which makes the rigours of hitchhiking far less stressful – I highly recommend it. Close to the source, one wine costs much the same as another I guess, but, steeped as we were in the mercenary traditions of North Amerika, the generosity of the wine-growers of Bordeaux astonished us. Daisy tended to be bubbly anyway and the champagne made her cheerfully delirious.

One evening, we found ourselves near the edge of a town - Quimperle (not to be confused with Quimper) - on a narrow street lined by what we would call tenements, but sans front stoops - so close were the buildings to the street. Traffic was fairly heavy, but we were stranded, luckless, and as the sun sank and the roar of cars subsided, a young woman holding a baby opened the shutters just above our heads and smiled down at us. They made a sublime picture in the setting sunlight. We smiled and saluted her and continued our attempts to hail a ride. As she watched, I got out my "Sixieme Heure Ici!" sign and held it up for her amusement. She laughed. A few

Daisy, Amy and Joy, summer, 1967. Photo by Gildas Failler.

minutes later, her husband appeared at the door and invited us in. They spoke no English – but motioned us to join them for supper in their modest kitchen. They were workers - he was the mechanic from *The Umbrellas of Cherbourg*, if I recall correctly. We ate a simple meal and, without much to say - given my limited French and their taciturn but friendly manner - I felt embarrassed by their generosity. The meal came to an end and, as Daisy and I exchanged looks that wondered where we would stay that night, the husband rose and led us up two flights of stairs to a high-ceiling attic room. It contained a dozen large cages housing a collection of live exotic birds, a parrot, and a large four-poster bed. Madame brought up clean sheets and pillows and Daisy and I settled into one of the most pleasing nights we spent together. When we were far down the road the next day, I realized that I had left my Albert College ring there, on the bedside table. It was the 16th of July. I wonder where my ring is now. Perhaps it lies there still, in a blanket of dust, the bird cages silent now, the spirit beings who were our hosts long since returned to the ether.

I spent over a month in Brittany. On arrival, we camped under the stars outside Benodet, an idyllic seaside village surrounded by farms with ancient hedgerows and wild ponies, while Gildas made fragile peace with his family.

Before dawn on the morning of the 17th of July, Gildas, Daisy, Amy, Joy, and I built a roaring fire on the sand and dropped acid together on the beach. It was the best trip I ever had, starting as the sun rose and the fog lifted off the water. Although acid tripping is often a rather private and inward affair, shared experience can be powerful. In the beginning, we huddled together around the blaze in the cool morning air. As the drug's effects began to take hold, we became aware of a faint sound, like the buzzing of a bee, drawing nearer. A mile down the beach, a tiny figure appeared - a guy on a mo-ped creeping slowly along the water's edge. For what seemed like hours, he grew larger, then larger, buzzing louder and finally towering over us, suspended in the air. He wore a trench coat, goggles and cap, and the stony expression of one engaged in high speed travel. At the last second, he shrank to normal size and buzzed past, small, silly and faintly mysterious. Everyone had seen and felt the same thing: we laughed at the overwhelming beauty of our surroundings and the comic absurdity of human life. Mo-Ped Man was a Zen messenger signalling the beginning of our journey through hours of stoned reflection and mild hallucination. Gildas had chosen a perfect setting: ancient farm land beside the ocean. Horses frolicked in a nearby field, and dozens of wild rabbits - as though scattered around by unseen hands for our amusement - danced and leapt and ruminated in the long grass, unafraid of us. The drug seemed to make us One with our surroundings, connecting us with an Eden-like sensibility. We wandered away in private reverie and reunited at sunset around a storybook site we dubbed "The Alice Tree." An angel brought wine and food and we celebrated life until the stars were reflected in the sea.

Eventually, we moved to Gildas's family home in Quimper. Despite offering many pleasures, it was a wrenching return to civilization. Gildas's father owned a fish store in Les Halles and was head of a solidly middle class family who sat and watched television every evening (just like the folks in Kingsville) and ate like kings every day (unlike the folks in Kingsville). His mother was a formidable cook. Each noon-time, she set gigantic bowls of steaming langoustines before us, with homemade garlicky mayonnaise - aioli, I would later learn. This would be the opening salvo in a lunch that included melon, pate, steak, frites, salad, fruit and cheese, cakes, coffee. The Faillers seemed amazed by my enthusiasm for the food. Given our wealth of resources, North Americans could eat so well. Yet, MacDonald's and Subway are king. Why? Really, why? Why does the North American population expect so little of its table?

Chapter 52

FRENCH WINE/WOMEN/SONG

Daisy, Joy and Amy departed for London after a week or so, and I stayed on. A couple of weeks later, Gil and I went to a large family wedding of some Failler cousins in Dijon. I sent for my good church suit from home - the expense and complexity of packing and mailing it from Kingsville all the way to France was a trial from which my mother never quite recovered. I was an old hand at wine-drinking, now, and there was nothing like a French wedding to complete the process which had begun with that free Icelandic Airways half-bottle some ten months previous. Gildas's mustard-country cousins were owners of a large vineyard and winery - we enjoyed a taste-tour of *les caves du patron*. The tasting provided a well-lubricated segue into the next day's festivity. "Catherine et Jean" were married on the 5th August, 1967. The wedding feast was a high-point of my *tour de France*. Melon au porto began the meal, which then proceeded through Terrine du Chef, Turbot Sauce Hollandaise, Gigot Vert Pre, Haricots Maitre D'Hotel, Salade, Plateau de Fromages, Peche Melba and Liqueurs. Sounds prosaic by the standards of today's jaded "foodie" industry, with its martinet chefs and their blow torch animal foam nightmares, but give me real food any day. Vive la France!

Following the dinner, a traditional sing-song was held. To the great pleasure of the guests, each man (myself included) rose and sang a solo of his choice. Audience reaction, borne along on a river of fine drink, ranged from gales of laughter to mock outrage to wild applause at the musical revelation of each performer. I sang my Jerry Lewis/Jean Paul Sartre version of *I'll Go My Way By Myself* (a guaranteed French crowd-pleaser). It was a flawless performance, complete with the bowed head of faux humility at the end: "*I'm by myself... alone!*" - and the crowd went wild. I reaped my reward, one enjoyed by each performer: following each song, all the women lined up to kiss the singer. The hilarity and kissing went on for hours, and was, as you may imagine, dear reader, a mixed blessing: I can lay claim to having

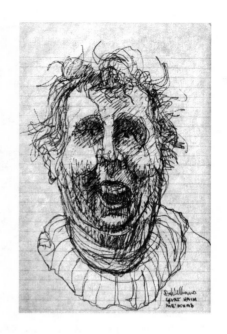

Drawing by the author, summer, 1967.

kissed more of the belle daughters of La France - and their mothers and grandmothers and great grandmothers - than anyone I know. Hippies are all about love, after all.

As if I wasn't drunk enough by the end of this warm and memorable August evening, I was accosted, as the crowd drifted out into the night air, by Claude - a classic *vieux patriot*, in beret with watch chain - and challenged to a drinking contest. The banquet tables had been arranged in a large "U" shape, seating over two hundred guests. Grand-Pere Claude bade me start at one of the "U"'s prong-ends and drain the glasses of wine that had been left by the diners. It wasn't a bad selection: a 1964 Gewurztraminer, a 1963 Champigny "Les Hospices", a Patriarche 1957 and a Faye D'Anjou 1947, and, although I wasn't, by any stretch of the imagination, *thirsty*, having kissed half the people in the place, I wasn't about to beg off for fear of contagion. Gamely, blindly, I took up the challenge, proceeded along my half of the "U", finally

Gildas's charming cousin, Annie, summer, 1967.
Photo by Gildas Failler.

meeting - some seventy or eighty quaffs later - what appeared to be octogenarian triplets, all named Claude, at the half-way point. I will lower the curtain on this dissolute tableau - as we linked arms the old man and I, swaying visibly, burst into a bizarre medley of ancient songs that I didn't know I knew - perhaps raising it again only for a brief flashback to an earlier but no less intoxicating moment, when I kissed Gildas's charming cousin, Annie. I had sung my song, and kissed a few dozen eager, well-dressed French women of all ages. The banquet hall seemed to fall silent when Annie stepped forward. She was a slender pretty twenty-nine-year-old brunette who lived in farm country outside the town in a converted school house with her *commerce-voyageur* husband and their one year old son. I was seized with desire. But here, in front of hundreds of sharp-eyed wives, mothers, aunts and daughters, I chose discretion, kissed her lightly and braced for my oscular commitment to a line of French women including fifteen grinning crones who brought up the rear. But Annie's kiss stayed with me. Happily, she invited Gildas and me to stay *chez elle* following the wedding.

At her home, Annie and I sat across the table from each other late that evening, at first touching our sock feet by accident, then resting them, one upon the other, as the cool air of the August night

Gildas Failler, Quimper, France, July, 1967.
Photo by author, courtesy of Gildas Failler.

crept along the stone floor. The heat began to rise as I proceeded
along her calf and then up her thighs with furtive toe, she doing
likewise, till our feet nestled like bi-lateral love birds. My arousal
was almost unbearable. Annie's husband was away on business, and
Gildas didn't mind, but we were hampered by Annie's watchdog
brother-in-law, Georges, a terse and colourless presence crouched
in a corner, peering at us un-self-consciously from behind a book.
Annie whispered that she would come to me in the night (Gildas
and I, addicted to sleeping under the stars, camped out in the tall
grass of the schoolyard, next to a field of cows), but after hours of
delicious anticipation became abject torment, I rose from my bed
and knocked softly on the door of her room. She had fallen asleep
and fell apologetically into my arms, groaning with reticence and
lust as I held her. I urged her towards the bed, but her little son
was sleeping in the room. Her cunt was drenched with desire, but
she resisted when I pulled her towards the moonlight. In growing
desperation, I backed her against the kitchen table, lifted her nightie
over her head, kissed her breasts and jammed my cock urgently
against her. But despite my efforts, Annie stayed technically true to
her husband. It was the 6th of August, 1967.

Annie and her family would soon depart for a new life in Tunisia. She wrote me a year later in London, inviting me to visit her, proffering the earthy trinity of "le boire, le manger et l'amitié" (Annie seems to have grasped my character and interests well), but her belated offer and the lure of the North African drug culture lay behind me now. I felt sad for her and her thwarted desire, as well as mine.

Back in Quimper, Gildas and I watched a festival parade in which ancient Bretons marched through the streets playing bagpipes and wearing costumes from our common Celtic heritage. The women dress in black and wear tall phallic bonnets made of lace. Later in Benodet, Gil and I took more acid, danced to *Ruby Tuesday* with teenaged *Parisiennes en vacance*, grew tired of Brittany, bought a battered 1951 Citroën 2CV "Camionette" or "Fourgonnette" furniture van (labelled "*Les Meubles Kernouat de Concarneau*") and loaded it up with all our stuff. The little truck was old and grey, and her tiny engine was so tired that, on some mountain roads in Switzerland, I had to walk along beside her, speaking softly and stroking the roof, to keep her going. It was my first car.

During final days in Brittany, Gildas and I had formulated a number of plans. We had heard that one could find casual work in Garmisch, Germany, at the American forces base or in the service industries nearby. For a day or two, we were going to drive to Afghanistan and buy better versions of those stinky Istanbul sheepskin coats and sell them in London for fantastic profits. Then to northern Europe and across Siberia, to Berkeley, California, the

Le deux chevaux, Quimper, 1967. Drawing by author.

western centre of the Beatnik Empire. Our Citroen was mandated to take us a long way. The little truck whimpered softly when we spoke of these plans in her presence. She was like one of those tiny, pathetic Welsh ponies that were bred for work in the coal mines and trained to live on hope. Old, frail, blind, good, trusting, brought to the surface after decades of toil - having more than earned, in a just world, the greenest pastures in a perpetual Maytime - she's confronted instead with gloomy, rain-swept streets leading to nowhere but the knacker's yard. Of the original *deux chevaux*, there was little more than perhaps a *demi-cheval* remaining, and most of that power went towards the production of noise and exhaust fumes. She carried us as far as Geneva, and quietly expired.

Chapter 53

GENEVA AND MIRJAM

Land-locked Switzerland borders on five countries – France, Germany, Italy, Austria and Lichtenstein – and the paralyzing anxiety that results from being thus surrounded may explain why she never developed a language of her own. Her people were habitually silent prior to 1534 when a band of German monks seeking the formula for absinthe stumbled upon her lush and verdant low country. Exhausted and half-starved, these brave soldiers of enlightenment beheld an agrarian paradise populated entirely by attractive young farm girls who passed their days making milk chocolate and tending vast gold reserves. Soon, delegations from Italy and France offered assistance, and her well-meaning neighbours divided the country into three fiefdoms, each reflecting distinct cultural and financial concerns. Despite the potential friction rising from this diversity, La Suisse has remained entirely neutral since 1815. Gildas's nationality and my mother's having been a French teacher combined to make French speaking Geneva our destination. It was the only place where we had significant contacts, namely two Indonesian sisters named Mirjam and Rehanna Udin, whom we had met at the Milk Bar in Plaka.

The Udin sisters' father, Sam Udin, worked for the UN at the International Labour Organization. He was a highly-educated and very conservative man whose ancestors hailed from Yemen. Paralleling the genealogical claims of the Williams dynasty, the Udins boasted having royal relatives in Bali, and Mirjam had been a

Balinese temple dancer during her adolescence. Sam, having turned down an offer of the Indonesian ambassadorship to Italy, had risen as high as most doctorate-holding five foot tall brown men might hope to in a white world. He married a Dutch woman of Jewish descent who, after bearing him three girls and two boys, became a Quaker. Sam girded himself with a gloomy intellectualism characterized (as far as I could discern) by contempt for almost everything. He was indifferent to my growing interest in the cinema, and told me that his favorite film was Henri Clouzot's documentary *The Mystery of Picasso*, in which the artist paints a work on camera: "It allows us to see a great artist fail," he said.

Rehanna was an opera singer who eventually opened a music school in Burgundy. Mouna, the youngest girl, had married Boudu Marcuse, son of the journalist Jacques Marcuse (cousin of Herbert Marcuse, the radical leftist intellectual and theoretician of the New Left). The old man had authored *The Peking Papers*, a sardonic denunciation of Chinese communism, with accounts of murder and drugs in the underbelly of a revolution then embraced by a substantial portion of the Western left-liberal intelligentsia. A scathing critique, utterly unimpressed by the noble ideological declarations of the Maoist regime, it's from an old China hand who had seen too many good intentions drowned in blood ever to be a believer. Jacques was married to a slender melancholic French woman who spoke only in whispers.

Mirjam, a nurse, was the oldest of the five kids – twenty-five when I met her. She spoke six languages and lived in a modest apartment a stone's throw from the Rhone River, which flows through Geneva. She was in the final stage of a long-term affair with a truck driver whose main distinction was ownership of a sloop that he sailed on Lac Léman. Following my arrival, Sloopy hung on no longer.

Gildas promptly found work and lodging(!) with a Swiss family who (like most Swiss) owned a watch company, and I embarked on a search for employment, too. One supper time, Mirjam and I went for fondue in the old city. Its pristine winding streets were unusually busy on that warm fall evening, and it emerged that a film shoot was taking place at a restaurant near our destination. I walked gamely through the crowd and soon stood face-to-face with

221

Alain Delon and Marianne Faithful who were starring in a faux-art (soft porn) film called *Girl On A Motorcycle*, known to its core audience of British wankers as *Naked Under Leather*. Its writer/director/cinematographer was Jack Cardiff, a star cameraman who had shot *The Red Shoes*, *Under Capricorn* and *The African Queen*, and I guess he had earned the right to realize some of his personal preoccupations on film. In the restaurant scene, Delon and Faithful share a Swiss fondue (the sequence starts with an overhead shot that zooms back from a bubbling pot of Gruyère), and I'm uncertain if Marianne was naked underneath her leather outfit or not, although if you think about it, she had to have been. Pale and emaciated, looking like a heroin addict, and famous for hobnobbing with Mick Jagger, off camera Marianne was actually too scrawny to be attractive, and I briefly felt concern for the choices Mick was making in his private life. However, although the film was critically trashed, I rather liked it, despite the cheesy whiff that rose from its non-Gruyère scenes. Cardiff saturates the film with deep gloomy colours and creates imagery that telegraphs the story's tragic ending. In homage to Hitchcock, Cardiff renders her apparent death wish by unleashing flocks of black birds that flicker across the screen during moments of passion. In its best-remembered sequence, Delon makes brutal love to Faithful on a pile of logs with the sound of chain saws in the background, while she whips his backside with a fistful of long-stemmed red roses.

As a country bumpkin from Canada, I found all this very European and exciting. Mirjam's extended family inhabited large book-filled apartments with high ceilings where they smoked Gauloises and had what I assumed were deep Existentialist conversations. They were very nice to me and, through a Marcuse connection, I was offered a *film* job! However, before you decide that I'm some kind of fancy toff whose class and social connections made for easy segue into the glamorous world of international cinema, the post was about as far from *Naked Under Leather* as could be. I was to microfilm the index card catalogue system of the Geneva Public Library, a task which would earn me two hundred dollars for a month's work. The refrigerator-sized apparatus I wheeled into the catalogue room each morning made a loud roar, used cassettes of 16mm film, and recorded one frame for each index card. As you may have guessed,

Mirjam and friends, Geneva, Switzerland, August, 1967.

the Geneva Public Library held zillions of drawers full of trillions of cards and it was far and away the most boring film I ever worked on. To break the monotony, I inserted dozens of joke cards with fake book titles, my photograph, dirty jokes and anti-war slogans into the mix, but at over twenty-seven hours running time, the GPL card index microfilm made Sergei Bondarchuk's 10-hour *War and Peace* play like a music video, and I don't think any human being but me has ever sat through the whole thing. However, should you ever find yourself in the Geneva Public Library, look under "Williams, Douglas G. L.", "hippies", "hashish" and "LSD" for lots of books they don't actually have.

*****

Geneva is an elegant, very wealthy city with spectacular shops and beautiful cafes. Signs embedded in the sidewalk warn pedestrians: *Défense De Cracher Sur Le Trottoir (Don't Spit On The Sidewalk)*, and at Christmas time, despite widespread belief that the Swiss have no sense of humour, butchers hang slaughtered pigs in their shop windows dressed in top hats and tuxedoes. As a neutral country, Switzerland's been home to many historical figures and exiles down on their luck. *In My Life*, Leon Trotsky writes about revolutionary meetings with Lenin and other Russian emigrés in the Café Landolt, where I often stopped for espresso on my way to the library.

Shortly after arriving, Gildas and I visited the *centre ville* cafe area in hopes of scoring some hashish. It had been a long dry spell and we were eager to experience anew the heightened levels of consciousness, transcendent spirituality, and projectile vomiting that only cannabis can provide. A Swedish kibbutz friend had sent a tiny quantity of hash in letter form, ironed flat between sheets of aluminum foil, but it hadn't lasted long. Now, as we sat outside in the balmy evening and watched the passing parade of Mercedes Benzes and richly-attired citizens, our gaze lit upon two obvious fellow travelers in a cafe on the other side. Dressed in expensive hippie duds – the girl had a spectacular head of cropped curly hair and wore an embroidered Afghani sheepskin coat; he a fringed leather jacket, aviators and scarf – their eyes presently met ours across the square. If anyone had dope, it was these two. After a longish wait, I got up, crossed the road and approached them. Of course, as with scoring dope in Toronto, Istanbul or a remote Syrian village, there was no telling who might be a drug cop, so my foray was a bit paranoia-inducing for everyone. I greeted them with sly circumspection, and asked if they had any hash to sell. They said "No" and I shrugged and smiled and retreated to the other side. We sat for a long time, sipping hot chocolate, chatting and eyeing our friends across the way. When they rose to go, our hopes faded - until they turned and headed straight towards us. They were handsome, intelligent-looking people. "Hello, nice to see you" they said a little too loudly, shaking our hands with European formality. It felt like we were spies in Nazi Germany, involved in a diversionary charade while secretly trading information. With a hidden gesture, the young man dropped a matchbox on our table and they quickly walked away. It was full of hash. The moment confirmed our belief in a universal underground of hip people who would change the world with generosity and love. Gildas was particularly wowed by this kind of moment. He was saving his money for a trip to Berkeley, California where he was sure that "hippie utopia" had begun. In fact, the Digger community in San Francisco would declare the *Death of Hippie* in a mass mock funeral at sunrise in Buena Vista Park on October 6th. Even then, our views were beginning to diverge. While I saw an unfolding police state, a hybrid of 1984 and Brave New World, hovering ominously over us - what I called a "perpetual Weimar" with fascism waiting in the wings - Gildas idolized America as a land of opportunity that would soon endorse drugs and free love and allow anyone to become rich. He was a budding libertarian, on a rightward path that ultimately led him to embrace the French demagogue Le Pen and neo-fascism.

A local cinema hosted a Francois Truffaut retrospective, and it was there, at Mirjam's suggestion, that I began my art film education. Not surprisingly, I had seen only two French films in Kingsville. Their unexpected appearance on the Roxy's rural screen may be explained in seven words: *Brigitte Bardot's bum and Elsa Martinelli's breasts*. Despite annual screenings of *Mom and Dad*, many Kingsville movie-goers were hungry for images of female body parts, and European producers occasionally met their needs with mildly titillating films such as Roger Vadim's *Et Mourir de Plaisir (Blood and Roses)* and Jean Luc Godard's *Le Mepris (Contempt)*. Both films were serious efforts – Vadim's a voluptuous exercise in vampire eroticism, and Godard's an exploration of self-hatred among the Parisian left intelligentsia of the early 1960s – but Kingsville's dearth of beautiful vampires and self-hating Parisian intellectuals made the films somewhat baffling for all but the most single-minded ticket holders.

Truffaut is seldom called a misogynist, but *Jules et Jim* stands today as transparently pessimistic about male-female relationships and mostly blames it on the alluring mystery and seeming irrationality of women. But, with its message hidden in a rich rendering of historical period and a beguiling performance by Jeanne Moreau, it's one of Truffaut's undisputed masterpieces, and emblematic of a vanished era when films were often personal works worth analyzing. We emerged from the cinema into a cool Geneva night with a crowd of people who were moved, disturbed and enchanted by a great work of art – an audience aware of history and deserving of a popular art form that reflected their thoughtfulness and sensitivity. The experience contrasts sadly with a contemporary cinema that leaves one diminished and enervated, that has more in common with attending football games or bull fights than a worthwhile cultural event. Cinema, the greatest art form ever created, continues to be squandered and degraded by the rulers of capital. Jules et Jim's ambiguity and beauty astonished me, and bolstered my determination to enroll in film school in London.

I was drawn into the Udin circle and spent many days with the family. We often ate supper together. Once, a *fondue Bourgignon* was announced; in the afternoon, dipping sauces were prepared and one of the girls was dispatched to the *chevaline* to buy the meat which would be cooked by each diner in a communal pot of hot oil in the middle of the dining table. When I asked what a *chevaline* was, I was told that it was a horse butcher. I was about to eat horse meat, something never done in Kingsville - or Canada - as far as I knew. Mirjam and I smoked a lot of hashish before attending, an act which did little to unravel the nonsense of cultural prejudice regarding human consumption of animals, and laughingly reaffirmed my habitual bad trip. In a typically lively discussion at the Udin table, it was noted that the Chinese eat dogs; the Koreans eat living monkeys' brains; pigs are highly intelligent – North America alone kills one hundred million a year for food. Trained cows traditionally perform in Russian circuses. Horses are more beautiful than pigs, but less loyal than dogs. "Pork," "poultry," "venison" and "beef" are euphemisms that mask the origins of our food. Much of childhood entertainment is devoted to anthropomorphizing animals ... As glistening platters of tender horse meat and a score of bowls of flavoured mayonnaise (tomato, herbed, mustard, curry, chopped pickled vegetable, onion, caper, cornichon), whipped crème fraiche, Bearnaise, Hollandaise in a variety of flavors, were set before me, the ghost of Bambi stood looking over my shoulder, gently mocking: - *"Some Lassie sausage, perhaps? How about a kilo of Trigger and 200 grams of Flipper? All who eat will someday be eaten..."*. Despite the unsavoury vision whirling in my mind, the meat was tender, the meal delicious, and humanity has devoured trillions of animals since that evening in Geneva.

On occasion we visited friends in the hill community of Servion, notably an architect who had built his family's home in breathtaking view of lake and mountain, and who seemed to have the perfect life. The interior was designed for functionality and constant creation – from cooking meals to production of art and design projects. The spectacle of these people's complex, interesting lives both fascinated me and made me increasingly anxious about what I was doing with mine. I began to focus concretely on London. Daisy was there, and Ned Logan had urged me to look him up when I arrived, with promises of a NATKE card and union work in West End theatre. But I was also loath to stop travelling. I had hated school all my life, and feared that a return – in whatever context – would be disastrous.

Youthful desire was the engine of my relationship with Mirjam, and she made it very easy to interpret my feelings as "love." She was beautiful, sophisticated, well-read and worldly. But, at nearly five years older than me, she had a clearer idea about what she wanted than I. "Our song" was Rodrigo's passionate and romantic *Concerto D'Aranjuez* in all the forms available: in Miles Davis's popular 1960 album, *Sketches of Spain*, in its symphonic versions, and in Richard Anthony's pop-hit rendition, *Aranjuez, Mon Amour*. But Mirjam had another theme song that signaled a perspective that I didn't share: Nina Simone's moving rendition of Jacques Brel's *Ne Me Quitte Pas – Don't Leave Me* – whose message I would ignore and which has echoed solemnly down the corridors of my life for nearly fifty years since.

My son Sam has said that he can't imagine his mother and me together, that we were so different in outlook and energy. Through the romantic, erotic, hash-induced haze of my Geneva days, I perceived the same. Mirjam and I were opposed in every way – she was cynical and conservative in political, artistic and social outlook – and I was rarin' to change the world and everything that came with it. It irritated me that she withdrew and stuck her nose in a book at every opportunity. She read Simone de Beauvoir, but rejected the burgeoning feminist movement. She liked making provocative statements, tinged with contempt for humanistic values, such as "If I ever get raped, I'll just lean back and enjoy it." Such remarks were indicative of an obtuse defiance that I sensed was aimed at me, and which became more pronounced as time passed. But we had good times too – she sang and played the guitar, made great food and taught me to cook, and I believed for a while that our differences could be overcome. But when we saw a Japanese film, Hiroshi Teshagahara's *Woman In The Dunes*, one of the Sixties' great art-house movie parables, my confidence was shaken. In a surreal, comic and ultimately chilling production, the film tells of a contemporary Everyman – an amateur entomologist - who falls into a sand pit while vacationing in remote wilderness, and is trapped. At the bottom of the pit lives a peasant woman who spends her days digging out from the relentless flow of sand that threatens to engulf her home. She welcomes him in every way her circumstance allows. Despite strong attachment to his urban existence and career, and many attempts to escape, the man eventually gives in to the simple life embodied by the woman, and, when offered the chance to leave at the film's conclusion, he decides to stay. The director deepens the film's atmosphere of eerie profundity with repeated shots of rivulets of the sands (which will eventually bury them - and us all), relentlessly flowing into the pit. I read the writing on the wall: women would trap you, and once you let that happen, there was nothing to be done but shelve your silly dreams and give in to the timeless rituals of survival and procreation. Mirjam seemed to agree with this view, but given that she was woman and I man, the film's message put us in opposing camps. I knew I had to get out. There were lots of women to love, and lots of new things to see and do before I succumbed to the spell of lunar madness that was Mirjam.

Chapter 54

FROM GENEVA TO LONDON

I left Geneva on the October 24th, 1967. The fastidious city's gutters were briefly strewn with dead leaves. I'd got used to regular food, sex, and lodging, and could microfilm a library drawer of index cards with style and panache as impressive as any man's. But I needed new challenges. Gildas had headed for Denmark, where he would live with my strange-eyed lady of Copenhagen, Lene Jürgensen. But, when I bid Mirjam "Adieu," she heard "Au revoir". It was a failure to make myself clear which would return to haunt me.

It was sunny and warm as I stood on the outskirts of town, like I'd done so many times. Leaving Mirjam was not wholly a relief – our love had been real, and I wondered if I would live to regret her loss. As years passed, would she achieve some kind of super-romantic status – iconic and irretrievable? Or would I forget her when the next beautiful woman came along? It was a gamble I was willing to take. This rather pleasant self-interrogation was interrupted by gloomier questions. Why the hell London? Did Mediterranean Doug really want to live in this expensive, cold, rainy and inhospitable city? Was I willing to work in a slave-job to survive? Was acceptance by a snotty British film school a realistic goal? When would I ever again be able to sleep under the stars? What the hell was I doing?

The truth was, almost everyone I knew on the road had gone home, or embarked on a less escapist, more productive stage of their development. The Summer of Love was over. Sure, I could have headed south alone through autumnal France, wintered in Crete or the hippie colony in Ibiza, or got really serious and swum to Morocco. There, I would find fellow travelers who had turned their backs definitively on the straight world, and were now in the throes of living out predictable fates. They would stay for years in North Africa, slowly go native, spend increasingly meaningless lives trying to impress newcomers with cynical erudition about life in their adopted country, while remaining perpetual outsiders despised by a local community with whom exotic mutual attraction had eventually worn thin. Finally they'd become drug addicts murdered by street thieves, or die of hepatitis and malnutrition in a Maghreb jail, forgotten and alone. Attractive as this vision was, if you had no money in those places, you were casting your fate to the wind, and sooner or later, you'd never be able to go home. Why? Because the world you had rebelled against all those years ago would have vanished. Returning like Rip van Winkle, you'd find your parents sick, senile or dead, everyone else having moved on. The culture itself would have changed: no one would be impressed by the little-remembered worldly bloke with bad teeth and graying beard who told alarmingly downscale travel stories in slightly halting English with a faraway look in his eyes. Back in Canada years later, I encountered such guys who'd stayed too long at the fair, and now drifted - rootless and friendless - through a world where they didn't connect and no longer counted. Later, I ran into guys - now men - whom I'd known on the road years before, selling trinkets or pan-handling in downtown Toronto. Aside from these caveats, I was sorely tempted to stay free, but my nerve failed me and I set course for London.

The hitch to Calais was uneventful except for the night I spent with a Catherine Deneuve look-alike and her lesbian house mate. At sunset I found myself in Aix Noulette, one of those little French villages whose store fronts don't bother with signage: if you lived there, you knew where the butcher and baker were – their wares were displayed modestly in front windows for all to see. I was tired and hungry, and prospects for the evening looked dim. While eyeing some tantalizing *charcuterie* in one such window, I began wishing that a beautiful blonde in a *deux chevaux* would pick me up and take me home. A few seconds later, a beautiful blonde in a *deux chevaux* pulled up and asked me: "Voulez-vous manger les crepes?" She invited me aboard and we drove for all of sixty seconds to her house on a charming side street a block from the centre of town. Never had wish fulfillment arrived so swiftly and precisely, and *franchement*, I was a little thrown. I met her house mate, a brunette who bore a striking resemblance to Deneuve's sister, Francoise Dorleac, who had died the previous June in a fiery car crash. We three had supper in their kitchen. They said they were both high school teachers, and that the blonde's husband had died two years ago. They were friendly, very attractive but reserved, and I was so blinded by testosterone and coming-of-age movies that I kept pinching myself, unable to get a fix on what was going on here. I knew from dirty jokes and Kingsville experience that school teachers – even female ones – were sometimes sexually attracted to their students. Surprisingly, one such sexual relationship – between two young men and their unmarried female teachers - had gone on in Kingsville High School for years, but like the Australian aboriginals who couldn't "see" Captain Cook's impossibly enormous (by aboriginal standards) ship when white men first arrived, the scandal was so huge and outrageous that the townsfolk were psychologically unable to acknowledge its existence. Back here in Aix Noulette the situation seemed too good to be true, and alarm bells were sounding in my head. Was I about to relive the scene in Sam Fuller's *Shock Corridor*, where the hero finds himself locked in the Nympho Ward of a state insane asylum? Well no, the doors weren't locked, but the strangeness of the situation and my lack of control over it unnerved me. My French wasn't as good with new people and I missed a lot of what they said, but they smiled as they conversed, and cast benign glances in my direction. The tension was somewhat relieved by Deneuve's suggestion that we go to a movie. A long-awaited production of *Le Grand Maulnes* was playing nearby, and they regarded it as a must-see. Based on the wildly-popular French novel, it's a bizarre, dream-like tale that ends in tragedy and despair. We were supposed to be impressed by Maulnes' purported greatness (which appeared to stem from a cretinous poetic commitment to a futile romantic quest) and my two companions were very moved by the experience. The book's qualities had translated well to film in the audience's view – I was surrounded by a flood of sniffling, weeping women (and stoic men) as we exited the theatre. But as far as I could see, director Jean-Gabriel Albicocco's chief aesthetic contribution was to smear the camera lens with Vaseline for every shot to create a smudgy, diffused image, rendering the events unfolding on screen ever more boring and obscure.

I had had sex with about a dozen women since leaving home, but I had always initiated the intimacies, and felt a degree of control which – while it may have been illusory – precluded the ambivalence I now felt. Was it theirs or mine? Both women were gorgeous, experienced, kind and liberated – this was the stuff of great erotic tales for books and movies. They made a bed for me on their sofa, and as I lay there, the blonde came and sat close beside me to say goodnight, giving me a final chance. But peering timorously into the gift horse's mouth, I leaned so far forward that I fell in and disappeared. Looking back, I think the problem between us was that they were grownups and I wasn't. They were at least thirty, and that in itself was enough to dissuade me: they were too old! A rather glum breakfast followed the next morning, followed by my swift departure.

The rest of the hitch to Calais really was uneventful. In the Dover ferry's vast public passenger room, I stretched out on one of the plentiful benches with my head on my knapsack. I noted that if this had been a Greek ferry, hundreds of us would have been crammed into a cargo container with chickens, goats and giant bricks of feta cheese, with real danger of sinking. But here there was plenty of room, pleasant snack bar, contented crowd and, with memories of the Titanic still fresh in everyone's mind, lots of lifeboats. I noticed an odd couple sitting a few rows away – a grizzled but hip-looking Caucasian guy and a younger, very attractive part-Asian woman. They had a relaxed, friendly demeanor, and smiled at me as I dropped off to sleep lulled by the gently rolling sea. Later, as I humped along the gang plank at Dover, they drove by in a Volvo sports car. The man leaned out and asked if I was going to London, and I climbed aboard. The young woman said her name was Stella, and that she was Indonesian – the mild coincidence of her and Mirjam's nationality was subsumed by her movie star looks. He was Bob, an American Vietnam vet. America was in its third year of murderous official involvement in South East Asia, so his discharge must have been relatively recent. I concluded that she and the car were the prizes he'd won for his services. Pretty impressive prizes, thought I, but when I asked him about his war experience, he darkened and didn't answer. Stella offered to share their room with me in a nice hotel on Russell Square, and for the second night in a row, I found myself with the prospect of a seemingly available and very attractive sexual partner accompanied by an ambiguous second fiddle whose role was not yet clear. Bob had worked as a radio announcer in Los Angeles and was a funny loquacious guy. They were less open about Stella's past. We smoked some hash and I was shocked when Bob revealed (and removed) an artificial leg. Maybe his disability explained the luxurious state in which he lived – did vets get big pay-offs for lost limbs? I didn't ask. Bob began caressing and kissing Stella, and she responded un-self-consciously. I'd fallen into the less-attractive version of the classic "threesome" situation – *the two-guys-and-one-girl* scenario – the gender ratio now ironically counterposed to the missed opportunities of the previous night's fiasco. They evinced no concern for their privacy. The three of us lay on the large bed together, Stella in the middle. She was spectacularly beautiful from head to toe, and Bob descended to her thighs to unzip her jeans. I unbuttoned her blouse and revealed her perfect breasts. I felt something which I assumed was her hand caressing my erect penis, and continued on my quest to arouse her, but when I glanced down, I saw that Bob was engaged in sucking my cock. I'm a generally calm person, cool-headed in emergencies for example, but in this instance, I promptly sat up and blurted something to the effect that there was "still time for the girl." A shortage of time didn't seem to be uppermost in anyone's mind, but it was the best I could come up with off the cuff. Still, some guys might have got hysterical, pulled out a .45, shot everyone, set the room on fire, crawled out on a ledge and threatened to jump. But although I had never desired sex with a male, the feelings of homophobia I experienced from time to time were not so powerful that I found Bob's indiscretion unforgivable. Who knew what he had been through in Vietnam? As previously discussed, sex in foxholes seldom involved women, sex with Third World prostitutes was soul-destroying, and military gang rapes of indigenous people almost never ended happily, so I kept my head. To his credit, Bob promptly backed off, and I watched as he mounted his dazzling companion and fucked her with considerable relish. When it was over, he flopped down in a chair in the corner and Stella repaired to the bathroom leaving the door ajar, and sat on the toilet with her head in her hands. Feelings of male entitlement kicked in, and I stood at the door and begged her to come back to the bed so that I could fuck her too. She didn't want to, but my pleadings triggered brotherly sympathies in Bob, and he more or less demanded that she do as I asked, which in retrospect, sheds revealing light on their relationship. Wearily, she rose and returned to the bed and let me have my way. Following this, neither of them showed the slightest interest in a feminist analysis of what had just transpired, and eventually we all fell asleep. Ours was a rather curt and disinterested parting the next morning. Obviously I didn't grasp something important, but over forty years have passed, interpretations may now vary, and everyone but I may have long forgotten these details of my first night in London.

Chapter 55

BRITISH CULTURE I

My twenty-first birthday, October 26th, was warm and sunny in Russell Square as I looked the wrong way and stepped into the path of a car hurtling along on the wrong side of the road. I was aware of the British proclivity for doing things their way, but it took me a few near-fatalities to absorb the subtler implications of the culture. Luckily the vehicle swerved, burst through a hoarding and plunged into the Thames, but it was a signal that acclimatizing myself to the bulwark of peculiar habits that form British life was fraught with varying degrees of peril. I had survived crossing the street, but the second hurdle – one of lasting importance – was the food. My chosen lifestyle thrust me into working men's steamy cafes where I was confronted with menus of appalling crumminess. In *Down and Out in Paris and London*, George Orwell vividly describes the nutritional regimen of "tea and two slices" on which the British working population hobbled, consumptive and toothless, through life in the twentieth century. Grease-soaked tubes of breadcrumbs ("bangers"), fatty rashers of bacon, Marmite, fried eggs, pork pie, beans on toast, tasteless cakes drowned in cold custard punctuated with festive red blobs of "jam", constitute a national diet boasting an infantile level of invention and a dearth of good ingredients that – along with an educational system, pro-monarchy propaganda, rampant alcoholism, and housing standards all designed to secure great privilege for an extreme few - indicts the British ruling class for crimes against humanity with no further elaboration necessary. However, if you require further justification, look at the cuisine of the republic only a few kilometers east, across the channel.

I found Daisy's bed-sitter in one of those grey rainy sections of London called Chutney or Flapham or Piveltwitch – evocative names of ancient origin now signifying crumbling row houses and council flats of mind-numbing sameness. Yet everyone I met was thankful for what they had, and respectful of their betters. Daisy welcomed me with open arms and we coasted pleasantly for a few days on the momentum of our recently-shared past in Israel, Spain and Brittany. She had started teaching primary school and spoke enthusiastically about her little charges while imitating their London accents with hilarious skill. I got in touch with Ned Logan in Nottingham, and he gave me the name of his friend Phillip, who had a bed sitter in Notting Hill Gate, an attractive area that was handy to London's West End. I stayed with Daisy for a few days, but my plans were too unfocused for permanent arrangements, and I decided to move on.

Ned's Notting Hill friends were a group of impoverished bohemian intellectuals who spent their days chasing the ephemera of shelter from the rain, roll-up cigarettes, briefly borrowed cars, impecunious Brighton weekends, short spells of employment, occasional trade in grey market merchandise, attenuated afternoons in the Coffee Mill, cheap Indo-Pak curry dinners, a gnawing envy of those with money, and grand schemes for the future. A few years older than me, they post-dated the "angry young men" of the fifties, but missed out on the youth rebellion and were too conservative to reject the values of the "straight" life. Women were a foreign land for these penniless Englishmen, and their alienation combined intense longing with resentment bordering on misogyny. To me their oddest characteristic was a rejection of any leftist ideas or views. Each had had a few years of college, but (ridiculous as this sounds) ideas of rebellion seemed to have been drummed out of them by carefully constructed curricula designed to bolster the status quo. "The system" was never blamed for their problems, only themselves. They were the kind of people one encounters everywhere, who vote against their own interests, identify with their oppressors, and support electoral candidates who utter remarks indicative of a commonly-held sentiment or prejudice.

Ned urged me to read the disillusioned former Stalinist, Arthur Koestler, and Phil loved the tormented Catholicism of Graham Greene. Phil, who resembled Laurence Harvey, was a frantic, threadbare aristocrat who lived on belief that an enormous inheritance would come his way when the legal profession had resolved some minor contradictions in the wording of his legacy's documentation. I suspect that he may not have read *Bleak House*. He'd already waited five years for his due, and the dreams that his elusive fortune afforded him would prove to be greater than what was finally delivered. His blatant victimization never prompted him to summon the police nor hire another lawyer, for, despite the system's reverence for inheritance, helping people like Phil is not what the gentlemen of those professions do. Phil kindly let me sleep on his floor for many weeks. When I asked Ned about him some twenty years later, he said that Phil's entire fortune had been consumed by lawyers employed on his behalf: he never got a penny.

Richard was a moth-eaten duffel-coated literature student who eventually attained a teaching post at London University. He was rather like John Hurt in *Midnight Express*: long greasy hair, glasses taped together, dirty fingernails, mustache and beard, rotten teeth, good brain and a sly sense of humour. Richard haunted the Coffee Mill during times when Phil and Ned were nowhere to be seen, and could always be counted on for a friendly greeting and a coffee.

Chapter 56

A WEEKEND IN NOTTINGHAM

After Israel, Ned had retreated to his parents' home in Old Lenton, Nottingham, a tree-filled enclave surrounded by high rises and council flats. Their home, named "The Cottage," was extremely charming, living up to all the chintzy clichés about the brighter side of "the Englishman's castle." Ned's mother had worked with Ann Jellicoe and Joan Littlewood in children's theatre and his kindly father was an automotive light bulb salesman who typed his wife's plays in the evening. You don't encounter many bulb salesmen now – men of a distinct British caste who drove from town to town proffering little packets of bulbs to snooty motor traders – their memorized trivia of brands, model numbers and buyers' first names having been replaced by slick, computerized product delivery systems. The Lewises' faces all bore traces of the sad anxiety that comes with awareness of mortality's looming menace.

The looming menace was felt by all that night. The weather had turned cold when I arrived, and the warmth of my reception at The Cottage did little to dispel the shock of Britain's lack of central heating among the upper-lower-middle class. A small coal fire in the sitting room, augmented by cups of hot tea and buttered toast, was faint comfort by the time I slid under the shockingly icy sheets in the upstairs guest bedroom.

The weekend's highlight was a pint of bitter at *Ye Olde Trip to Jerusalem*, the oldest pub in England, where it's said that Catholic Crusaders stopped for hot chocolate on their way to spread Christian love in a manner far superior to the bloody and reviled methods of Islam. The dust on the rafters above our heads was, astonishingly, nearly two feet thick, giving the upper reaches of the room a cave-like appearance. It was also troubling confirmation of the British reputation – among European and American travelers - for uncleanliness. For example, I often heard that British girls seldom wash their brassieres. In 1967, refusing to wear brassieres – and even threatening to burn them - had become fashionable, and I charitably participated in their removal whenever possible, but I must confess that, in the moment, careful examination of such items of apparel for hygenic misdemeanors always took a back seat to more pressing concerns. Still, the sight of those rafters - piled high with the dark sedimentary accumulation of nearly a thousand years of horse dander, animal hair, dust mites and their feces, all held in firm suspension by the gluey effluent of a billion consumptive sneezes - did little to dissuade me of the veracity of foreign suspicions regarding British sanitation. The British class system had created bitter social relations stretching back to feudal times and the medieval char-woman's disinclination to climb a ladder to dust the rafters may have been triggered by the drunken attempts of lords, knights, squires, vassals and retainers to look up her skirts from below. So, as we stood in that ancient place, I lowered my gaze from the ceiling and quietly slipped my hand over the top of my glass. However, the shoal of filth above our heads was cause for further speculation: a stratigraphic core sample of the thickest layer would arguably contain within itself a fascinating and potent DNA history of the Nottingham community. Science tells us that a human sneeze may produce up to 40000 droplets sized between 5 and 100 microns, jettisoning them at speeds of up to 200 miles per hour. These floating spheres of mucus may contain, not only viral bodies, but remnants of DNA torn loose from the sneezer's bronchia, nasal passages and mouth by the convulsive expulsion of air. Heavy droplets are pulled down by gravity; lighter ones may remain airborne, lifted high on drafts from open doors, ensuing sneezes or warm bursts of flatulence and, in the case of this oldest pub in England, alight on the mounting layers of dust, above. Somewhere, buried in that biorganic heap of flotsam and jetsam, might be found evidence of a brief scuffle, say, between the Sheriff of Nottingham and Robin Hood, during which there was more than one involuntary expectoration of DNA. Using the enhanced tools of microbiology, entrepreneurial biologists with a flair for showmanship may one day clone both the despised sheriff and beloved outlaw for all the world to see. I hope Robin escapes the inevitable side show and resumes his legendary activities: it would be great to see the rich robbed by the poor for a change. Until then, I'll keep one hand over my pint of bitter and the other poised for loosening brassieres, English or otherwise.

Nottingham's cultural attractions notwithstanding, Ned was about to leave home once more, but not for London. He announced that he had enrolled in Sussex University's playwriting course. I was on my own again.

Chapter 57

BRITISH CULTURE II

Language is as prey to fashion as clothing, and may reflect deeper currents in the culture. At time of writing, a favorite pundit word is "recuse," which means "to reject or challenge (a judge or juror) as disqualified to act, especially because of interest or bias." Its popularity reflects a growing recognition of corruption in public life, and the notion that leaders and appointees frequently have agendas that conflict with the public good. However, it's rare for buzzwords to reflect progressive aspects. The promotion of the phrase "Life's not fair," in the wake of Ronald Reagan's discredited "trickle down economics" and his vicious assault on unions, now sounds utterly Orwellian in its propagandistic intentions, the way Nike's "Just do it!" implicitly encouraged people not to think so much (as they had in the Sixties). Recently, the word "robust" was rescued from obscurity, where it languished as a favored descriptor for ground coffee. Suddenly Dick Cheney and the U.S. State Department were using "robust" to describe American response to terrorism, and it's been employed frequently to signify the lively spirit behind handing of billions of public dollars to needy financial institutions. Imperialism had already taught us a host of new words in the Bush years: "redacted," "embedded," and colorful expressions such as "clawback," "shock and awe" and "paradigm shift." In late Sixties London, "beleaguered" was a favorite term, used to describe, not the Vietnamese, nor the rural poor in the American south, but powerful social groups. Police faced with incomprehensible (and infuriating!)

anti-war demonstrations, politicians accused of corruption or sexual naughtiness, religious leaders grappling with growing public contempt for their proffered fairy tales, university chancellors wringing their hands at student occupations, union leaders attempting to quell worker militancy, even the poor Royal family's confronting disrespect and contempt – all combined in a frenzy of *beleaguered-ness* on the part of the ruling class and their toads. In newspapers and magazines, managers and bosses of all kinds were frequently photographed from above, huddled together, looking up at camera, vulnerable, humble and confused, just following orders and earnestly trying their best to please us all. Terms like "beleaguered" were hallmarks of a media campaign to garner sympathy for society's oppressive governing institutions, and, by extension, to make their victims into criminals who were doing the vicious and insensitive beleaguering. A relentless barrage of propaganda portrayed society's critics as naïve, unkempt, uncouth, uneducated, un-white, and worthy of contempt by the beleaguered middle class, who, after all, were the main beneficiaries of institutional benevolence.

Employment.

Manpower is a privately owned chain of hiring halls for near-slave or "casual" labour. My first job required appearance at an east London warehouse at 7:00 am. My new mates and I were met by a man driving a sparkling Jaguar XK-E who told us to call him "Mr. Jimmy." Inside the warehouse were piles of rotting rolls of carpet, which we were to move to another area. Mr. Jimmy was rich and told us that he was going to get even richer. I think we were all very happy for him. But the casual labour scene paid barely enough for supper, so I soon sought employment at a firm more in keeping with my tastes and abilities: Harrods department store. To my astonishment, I was hired to wrap newly-framed paintings and pictures in their art gallery. I worked for Mr. Delbert Bragg, he of the remarkable warm-fruit-pie-on-tilted-sill cranial features mentioned in the pogo stick incident, earlier, and I became one of the foot soldiers of the British work force. In the 1960s, Harrods was very old school, and its employees regarded working there as a privilege, which indeed it was. Hundreds of minor human variations on Bob

242

Cratchit moved purposefully to and fro, the pro-Tory newspaper of their particular cast tucked under arm, their tatty suits and frayed collars constituting the uniform of millions of malnourished folks who knew their place and loved the Queen. Each lunch time, I rode the clattering employee lift to the top floor's staff dining room - a bright airy space with large windows and decent English fare – Dover sole, steak and kidney pie, and paper-thin slices of roast beef with mushy peas. At night, in the dark, I emerged with hundreds of others from the staff entrance at the rear of the vast building.

Chapter 58

A REVEALING ANECDOTE

In an effort to avoid wearying the reader with statistics or clichés that may obscure larger truths (all of which I would have just made up anyway), I present, here, the following experience, which may shed some light on British life in the late 1960s. One day, I lost my umbrella in the London Underground. Of course, an umbrella is a necessity there, and, being broke, I went to Her Royal Highness's Lost Property Office (HRH-LPO) in Baker Street, to see if mine could be retrieved. It was raining when I arrived. I filled out a small form proffered by a forlorn-looking man who regarded me with unconcealed melancholy. His thin hair was swept back and his watery eyes bulged slightly: he looked like someone facing a strong wind. He motioned me to follow him through a door at the rear of the office, to an area where, I assumed, lost things had been saved. I was surprised, then, to be led along a dimly-lit passage, to a second door among many, marked "UM10/47." My guide removed a large set of keys from his pocket - old keys of a kind seldom seen now - and rattled one of them in the lock, all the while murmuring to himself about I knew-not-what. He stepped inside and in the shadows I saw him throw a large switch. There was a flood of pale yellow light, and a faint rush of echoing sound which seemed to come from a great distance. He turned, waited for me to enter, and in a moment, I stood at the edge of a vast room, like an oversized cathedral. To my astonishment, it was filled with countless millions of umbrellas, stacked up on long high shelves, stretching into what

I can only describe as "infinity". Above us were other levels filled with umbrellas and connected by catwalks. "When did you say you lost it?" my companion asked, looking down at my application. His hands trembled slightly.

"Last Tuesday," I replied.

"Morning or afternoon?" he asked, squinting at me in the wind.

"Afternoon, about 3:30."

He calculated for a moment, moving his lips, and finally: "That would be Aisle M912 in Sector D," he said, pointing into the distance. Eventually, we reached our destination. I gazed up at the wall of umbrellas. There were, perhaps, one hundred thousand umbrellas in M912, Sector D, and they looked identical. The little man was standing close to me now, as though he feared I might try to pull a fast one. "These won't be properly labeled for another fortnight," he muttered wearily, and pointed to a man in the distance who was seated atop an enormous library ladder. He was writing on a portable tablet and wearing a miner's lamp which cast a hot beam of light onto a stack of labels in front of him. I sneezed. The man on the ladder looked up, fumbled, and a little cloud of yellow labels fluttered down through the stillness. "And, of course, in a few years they say that the filing system will be computerized – what a shambles that will be!" My companion shook his head weakly, as though the gesture was adequate substitute for fuller explanation. "We had hoped to finish filing the 1940s by March, 1980, but it'll never happen now. I'm glad I won't be here to see that mess!" He didn't look glad, and I wondered if he'd found his career fulfilling. It was possible that they were planning an interim microfilming of all the IPO's records, but I hesitated to ask. He blew his nose and I pulled an umbrella from the shelf. It looked approximately like the one I had lost, but unlike mine, it had a spring-loaded opening device which would release at the push of a button. Phillip, my aristocratic friend in Notting Hill, had one just like it. "Three times the price of mine," I thought. "This is it," I said, not too loudly, unsnapping the strap. I held it out like a duelist, my thumb on the button, ready to test. The little man sprang to life: "NOT INSIDE! IT'S BAD LUCK!" he shouted, grabbed my hand and looked around fearfully, as though my gesture might have started a chain-reaction - a billion blooming umbrellas under one roof - spawning enough ill fortune to summon up the Antichrist, bring down an Empire, and make it rain forever.

A few minutes later, lost in thought, I emerged into the street. It had stopped raining, and the sun was making a rare London appearance. Strangers sang and birds smiled at one another. I was curious to see if my new umbrella would open, but just as I was about to try, I noticed the little man locking the front door. For a moment, I stood on the teeming pavement, while he looked at me through the glass. He gave no sign of recognition, yet I felt he was watching me, waiting to see if I'd open it. I refused to offer him the satisfaction. It was then that I noticed the label that was attached to it. It was stamped with the letters HRH-LPO, and written on it: "*Marble Arch Station, Bench 7, September 4th, 1936, 11:43 am.*" Without looking at him, I turned abruptly and walked away.

It has been over forty years since I visited the LPO at Baker Street. I have never opened the umbrella - not once. I live in another country where no one cares about rain. The umbrella sits at the top of my closet, a sombre memento of times past. Occasionally, when it catches my eye, I think of mailing it back to HRH-LPO in England, with a long hand-written letter confessing how I claimed the thing in error. It's an option worth considering.

Chapter 59

AN UNEXPECTED VISITOR

The weeks and months at Harrods dragged on. People happily spent their whole lives here – who was I to champ at the bit? But then, who was I to leave Kingsville in disgust? Who was I to take a year-long holiday, fucking lots of attractive young women while enjoying illegal drugs? Who was I to travel carefree around Europe and the Middle East? Who was I to be trapped in a war zone, where the fight was not mine? Who was I to rebel against society, or criticize the war? Who was I to go to a fancy film school in fancy London? Who was I to break my mother's heart, both now and long ago? I'd get my comeuppance. I would pay for all the things I'd done. The question was, who would demand payment? I was free.

Ned, who visited occasionally from school, his older brother Bob, Phil, and Richard were my friends in the winter of 1967-68. Although they called themselves The Wasters, they had little to waste but their lives. Despite their conservatism, they espoused an iconoclasm that made them suspicious of virtually everything. Everything – be it idea, observation or feeling – was a "hook", a devious form of manipulation by obvious or unnamed forces. They sometimes referred to a person named "Doister" at "the Castle" and implied that they were members of a cabal. I later learned that *Ralph Roister Doister* is a comedic play, a milestone on the historical transition from medieval mystery plays to modern theatre. Doister is described as a "ridiculous pretender to gayety and love (who) is betrayed into all sorts of absurd and humiliating scrapes" which accurately describes how the Wasters viewed themselves. It all meant little to me, however, but functioned as a device to keep simple-minded colonials confused, an apparent source of amusement to all but me.

The Wasters and their world suddenly became irrelevant in late February when work at Harrods ended for the day and I stepped into a typically foggy London night. It was the kind of life-altering moment that occurs in books or movies, but seldom in real life, particularly among actuarial accountants. Having sex with St. Tammy of the Mangers was one, leaving for Europe another. It frequently involves a choice to be made, with stakes whose enormous importance is clear only in retrospect. There, under a street lamp, was Mirjam,

Portrait of Mirjam, London, England, April, 1968. Photo by author.

waiting for me. It was a moment when I could have steered my life firmly in another direction. And I didn't. I was lonely, hungry, cold, and lacking direction. She was lonely, hungry and cold too, though perhaps not lacking in direction as much as I. Although I had mixed feelings at seeing her, her affection and warmth were irresistible. She was the *Woman in the Dunes*, and my fate was sealed. I was not the first man in history to take refuge in a woman's bosom. We hugged and kissed and walked, arm in arm, into the dark city.

I had rented the smallest room in Notting Hill Gate, a triangle-shaped former closet, barely bigger than a manger, that couldn't quite accommodate the small cot that came with it. One corner, jammed against the wall, was elevated slightly to fit, and the bed was skewed at a needless-to-say uncomfortable angle, compounding the challenge of sharing the thing with one's mate. Fucking on the cot required hanging on to the edge of the bed simultaneously with one's partner. But despite this impediment, biology triumphed, and Mirjam and I managed to resume our sex life. So great was that inestimable force, and so oblivious to our circumstances, that, as far as It was concerned, we might well have settled in and raised eight or ten children in our little room. It didn't care.

We soon found a better place near Portobello Road, where its famous outdoor market was only steps away. Our single room sat above a laundromat, whose twenty-four hour thrum lent a nostalgic Greek-shipping atmosphere to our new home. Hotplate for cooking, electric penny-meter for heat, and window sill for cooling milk and butter – these were the highlights of a luxurious new chapter of our life together. Mirjam, who had taken nurse's training at Hammersmith Hospital, found employment there. She introduced me to the writings of Elizabeth David, an imperious crusader against the preposterous dreariness of English cuisine, whose book *Mediterranean Food* became our gastronomic bible. We bonded around the unholy trinity of non-English cooking: olive oil, garlic and wine, augmented by hot peppers, tomatoes, brown rice, aubergines, courgettes, sun-dried olives and *herbes de Provence*.

Chapter 60

BRITISH CULTURE III

From lines of barrows stretching for blocks in both directions, the Portobello market sold everything from onions to furniture. In springtime, her sombre tones were emblazoned by bouquets of fiery yellow daffodils. But the buying of tomatoes afforded me insight to the British caste system and its sharp contrast with the "democratized" consumption of North America, where the customer is (theoretically) always right. Buyers were not allowed to pick and choose which tomatoes they preferred; rather, one ordered a pound and the barrow man would pick your tomatoes himself, placing them in a shallow paper bag for weighing. His choice always included a rotten one, and the buyer had no say in the matter. It was posh and uppity to object, and this was not a market for the posh. You took your fair share of the rotten ones – same as everyone else – the way the poor had taken their fair share of Hitler's bombs, conscription, rationing and generalized poverty since the start of WW2. After arguing a few times without success, I accepted my rotten tomato and silently blessed the Queen and the House of Lords for maintaining order where the authority of the vendor trumps that of the buyer in this nation of shopkeepers.

Lawrence Durrell wrote: "I am just a refugee from the long slow toothache of English life." At first I was merely shocked at London's living conditions. But the shock gave way to revulsion, not only at the poverty, but at the denial, acceptance and defense of its misery everywhere I turned. I noted in my journal, that on

250

BBC radio a "lyrical upper class female voice" read a letter from a pensioner: *"After paying my rent, I realized that I had only one shilling per day for food. By careful buying, I managed to get through the week successfully. I wonder how many of our well-paid workers' wives know the satisfaction of economical housekeeping!"* This is the mindset that happily obeys the Queen and has no need for a dictator, in the England that exasperated George Orwell. I'm not alone in detesting British life. Apparently, in spite of the neo-con entrepreneurial excitement of the Thatcher years, the squalor I encountered is now greater than ever. Christopher Hitchens wrote shortly before his death in 2011: *"This is the world of wretched, tasteless food and watery drinks, dreary and crowded lodgings, outrageous plumbing, surly cynicism, long queues, shocking hygiene, and dismal, rain-lashed holidays, continually punctuated by rudeness and philistinism. A neglected aspect of the general misery, but very central once you come to notice it, is this: we are in a mean and chilly and cheerless place, where it is extraordinarily difficult to have sex, let alone to feel yourself in love."* That last comment may seem merely fanciful, until you look hard at the specious culture of "hope" proffered year after year by the Royals, Lords and Commons. The U.K. has boasted the world's sixth largest economy since World War II, yet her Human Development Index (HDI is a standard means of measuring well-being, especially child welfare, utilizing a comparative measure of life expectancy, literacy, education and standards of living for countries worldwide) puts her (in 2009) in 26th place, behind Spain, Greece and South Korea, among others. The glittering pomp and circumstance of Britain's ruling class becomes even more despicable in this light. And in a hopeless world, what role is there for love?

We befriended our upstairs neighbours, a couple who typified the optimism and impoverishment of the British working class. I had grown up around mal-nourished kids, and these two were good examples of the adults produced by deprivation. Alan was a kindly forty-year-old motorcycle messenger in The City, London's financial district. With the appearance of a man twice his age - a gnarled face, toothless smile and body twisted by cold, rain and arthritis - Alan lived for his twin passions of wine making and sailing. He had bought an old ketch and had spent years outfitting it. One day, he

251

said, he and his wife Patricia would sail down the Thames to the open sea and freedom in the warm south. Pat, who was in her late thirties, wore thick glasses, cropped hair and exuded an emaciated sexlessness that was the either the cause or result of her childless womanhood. His dreams were hers. Their hopes for the future were bolstered by Alan's winery, an enterprise that included nary a drop of viticulture. His vineyards lurked in the evening shadows of Portobello Road after the market's closing, where the rotten fruit that her swaggering vendors had failed to sell to grateful customers was gathered by scavengers who had accepted their place in the great pecking order of British life. Alan made every kind of fruit wine you never want to taste from the stuff. Their single room was filled with vats of fruit mash in various stages of fermentation, demijohns, jugs of all sizes, filters, bubbling plastic tubes and glass bottles gathered over years of garbage-picking. The odor of rotting fruit filled the air, cut only by smoke from Alan's roll-up cigarettes. He explained the intricacies of wine making and their plans for the future to Mirjam and me, while Patricia tottered about the room with a fixed smile, silently refilling our glasses with Alan's late vintage Portabelloise. A contemporary wine reviewer might write of Alan's wines: "*bursts of hazy sunlight laced with diesel fumes and downpours, bitter wages and bosses' bum-kiss essences lingering on the nose, late harvest motorcycle leathers and harsh tannins greet the prandial tippler with over-ripe tangerine, apricot, saltwater taffy notes and a delightful bilgewater finish.*" Hangovers from his dubious brews were unusually severe, and I feared that his grasp of organic chemistry wasn't as firm as it might have been. In fact, I attribute my first migraine – and the "aura" which has appeared regularly since - to permanent brain damage inflicted by Alan's poisonous potables. He and Patricia "beat the system" by making their own alcohol and using the pub money saved to create the vehicle for their getaway. But old habits die hard. I pictured them riding high seas, lashed to mast and wheel, their tiny cabin crammed with vats of rotten fruit, a hedge against the voyage's unanticipated length, and determined to beat the system even in southern climes where wine was cheaper than water. Just before I left London in April 1970, I went round to visit Alan and Pat near Portobello. They'd disappeared without a trace.

"Swinging London" was the business world's interpretation of the Sixties youth rebellion. Its marketing involved a layer of entrepreneurs and shop girls in Carnaby Street and London's fashionable West End who were vigorously committed to acting out the corporate media's instructions in a robust manner. But as spring arrived, London's parks were filled with young people high on mind-expanding drugs, playing guitars and having fun. Mary Quant and Twiggy notwithstanding, there was a sense that an important layer of the intelligentsia in America and U.K. were siding with the youthful zeitgeist. The hip international glitterati included pop groups - The Beatles, Bob Dylan, Donovan, The Rolling Stones, Incredible String Band, Pink Floyd, Cream - and popular intellectuals - Herbert Marcuse, Tariq Ali, Tim Leary, Paul Krassner, R.D. Laing — while an outer circle of establishment pundits such as Bertrand Russell, Malcolm Muggeridge and David Frost earnestly tried to make sense of the whole thing for an outraged suburban television audience. Avant garde theatre, "happenings" and exhibits were staged at the Round House and the Arts Lab, and radical theatre groups sprang up everywhere, led by visionaries like Joe Orton and visiting gurus such as Julian Beck of New York's Living Theatre. Underground newspapers such as International Times (where I was janitor for six months during school) publicized alternative lifestyles and helped stoke rage against London's beloved British bobbies, whose kindly masks slipped revealingly when confronting anti-war protesters. But the joy and optimism of the counter culture was undercut by men like Enoch Powell, the openly racist politician and sometime Member of Parliament whose rightward trajectory led him from the Tories to the neo-Nazi National Front. He terrorized the immigrant Asian and West Indian populations with racist speeches. The Tories called him a "renegade" but in fact, he was used to sound the depths of racial tensions and distract people from the true authors of British poverty.

Chapter 61

FILM SCHOOL AND THE TROTS: THEIR MORALS AND OURS

Films such as Richard Lester's *The Knack, And How To Get It*, declared a new aesthetic for the Sixties generation: a character paints his flat – floors, walls, ceiling, furniture – in pure white, expressing a desire to shake off the old ways and failures of the past. The two most important films of the era were Stanley Kubrick's *2001, A Space Odyssey* and Michelangelo Antonioni's *Blow Up*, both of which reflected many questions raised by the counter culture: Kubrick was doubtful about technology's promise to liberate humanity; Antonioni was preoccupied with the nihilism of pop culture, and - seldom acknowledged - the mystery of the JFK assassination. Without the American president's murder – and those of Dr. King, Malcolm X and RFK - there might never have been a "Sixties" as we've come to know it. In *Blow Up*'s most haunting sequence, its protagonist attempts to make sense of a series of photographs he's taken, inadvertently, of a man's murder in broad daylight, the ambiguous involvement of the victim's female companion, and a slow reveal of a gunman hidden in the grassy knoll nearby. This dream-like realization of the most scandalous murder of the twentieth century, framed in the absurd rituals of Swinging London, thumbed its nose at official interpretations of the Zapruder footage of JFK's assassination, and invaded the screen like a repressed memory rising up from official history's subconscious. It was in this context that I dreamed of becoming a student again, but it wasn't until Mirjam and I moved into a house with an American couple named Vern and Diane in Shepherd's Bush that fate took charge. Vern was a student at the London School of Film Technique, and he claimed that enrollment was easy. He showed me a paper he'd written called *The Films of Joseph Losey*. One could actually study and think about film! How they'd howl in Kingsville! My plans fell into place: I would become The Student Prince, 60s style: radical activist, dangerous intellectual, budding artist filmmaker, heading off to an anti-war demonstration with a joint in one hand and a pint of bitter in the other. Somehow, none of my dreams included Mirjam.

I got an interview with the school's founder, Bob Dunbar, who had been a colleague of Eisenstein and other notables, and showed him my antiwar film script with a storyboard about a lethal snowball fight between gangs of children. Brilliant as it was, I sensed that the payment of my tuition was the deciding factor in my acceptance. The school was housed in a decrepit warehouse in Covent Garden; the student body was a politically- and racially-mixed collection of British and foreign students from Iran, Belgium, Switzerland, France, Greece, Italy, Brazil, Canada and USA, who invariably went on strike by the second term because so little – no film making, few lectures - was happening. The place was a breeding ground for insurrection.

The London School of Economics (LSE) was a stone's throw from LSFT (now the London Film School, headed by Mike Leigh) and the film school was visited by LSE Trotskyists who gathered under the banner of the Socialist Labour League and the notorious Gerry Healy. Vanessa Redgrave joined the "Healyites" and along with Tariq Ali, became an outspoken socialist revolutionary. Trotskyism had the answer for radicals who were tormented by communism's failure and the twenty million deaths attributed to Stalin's rule. Revolution's bitter fruit might make any reasonable person flee from politics altogether, but Trotsky's anti-Stalin manifesto, *The Revolution Betrayed*, his broad-ranging intellect and writings on art, literature and morality, and his martyrdom at the hands of a Stalinist assassin, made him a seductive read for young men whose personal experiences or astrological leanings (Trotsky's birth date and mine are the same) had primed them for an off-beat view of the world. Capitalism had unleashed a genocidal war on the Vietnamese people, a massive crime that most people ignored or blandly accepted as "part of life." (Why not take a Vietnam refresher: Google *My Lai* or *Pinkville Massacre*, and read about one of the numberless atrocities committed by American troops.) Could a system that did such things be supported? Vietnam wasn't an aberration: if you looked closer, capitalist forces waged war on dozens of fronts around the world, proclaiming "freedom" as their cause. Meanwhile, the communist world – for all its failures – had eliminated the profit compulsion that was the chief motive for war - the "military-industrial complex" that General and President Dwight Eisenhower had warned the West about. A convincing case was made that the real aggressors in the world were the capitalist countries, led by America. Outside the Sixties anti-war movement, such views were rare, but they're commonplace today, because communism's gone and war is a thriving industry.

On arriving in England, my strongest impression was the universal acknowledgement of the class system. How clever the American and Canadian ruling classes were to deny the very existence of a class system for so long. The American ruling class bought two centuries of relatively unopposed dominance by teaching school children that theirs was a "classless society" despite overwhelming evidence to the contrary, and a significant majority of people spent their lives believing it. For those who didn't, "class consciousness" was a form of deviance, denounced from both pulpit and Hollywood movie screen, lying somewhere between criminality and mental illness (or "thought crime," to quote Orwell). What astonished me was the widespread *acceptance* of the British class structure: most people loved the Queen and the traditional instruments of their own oppression. Feeling no such obligation, I became increasingly preoccupied with left politics, the war, and Marxism. I read *The Communist Manifesto* and Trotsky's *Their Morals and Ours*, because, as my Israel experience had illustrated, when push came to shove, pacifists like me were going to have to choose sides. But, the moral issues arising from class conflict – i.e, class war and *killing* - were a major stumbling block in my embrace of socialism. As I thought and read about the world, it became increasingly apparent that changing the system – in this case wrenching power, wealth and privilege from the ruling class – might cost so many lives that any sane man would have to question the project's worth. When they wheeled the guillotine into the public square, or lined the Maoists' "class enemy" up against the wall, would I blandly drop the blade or pull the trigger? As a career choice, it certainly wasn't what I'd envisioned. But worse than that, wasn't it wrong to kill? And if not, how many deaths could be justified? If we assume, for the moment, that substantial numbers of people are able to grasp that socialism is a sane way to organize our lives, that still leaves a lot of people who will fight to the death defending class privilege, either through irrational identification with the Royal Family, or in the faint hope that, one day, they might get rich themselves.

I had wrestled with the psychological hold the church had on me for years. Today's generation has less torment about god (and sex) because of decline in religion's authority. Although I no longer openly subscribed to those views, small but robust demonstrations in their favor kept waving placards in the back of my head: Church and State were united in defending "eternal verities" - moral standards which were unshakeable and true in the eyes of God. But Trotsky wrote of the governing double standard:

> *"In so far as the state is concerned, in peaceful times it limits itself to individual cases of legalized murder* (i.e. capital punishment) *so that in time of war it may transform the "obligatory" commandment, "Thou shalt not kill!" into its opposite. The most "humane" governments, which in peaceful times "detest" war, proclaim during war that the highest duty of their armies is the extermination of the greatest possible number of people."*

Governmental war-mongers' compulsion for extermination got a bad rap following the World Wars, and cries for ending capital punishment (the *reserved right* - the exception to the rule *Thou shalt not kill* - mentioned by Trotsky) gained ever-widening support. Public revulsion for state-led murder was a powerful ingredient in the antiwar movement of the 1960s, so powerful that for the next four decades, Western military aggression usually wore a mask called "peace keeping" in order to garner public support. Further erosion of public support has forced America to use mercenary armies and electronic warfare, while decrying the loss of spirit amongst the population's erstwhile cannon fodder. Fighting for American "democracy" ain't what it used to be. But she clings desperately to capital punishment - along with the world's most corrupt and oppressive regimes. Its political function – the reserved right to kill – is clear.

Governments and their moralizing support teams instructed their populations never to resort to violence on pain of hellfire (in this life, or the one after), while using violence freely at home and abroad when they saw fit. Meanwhile, God's spokesmen reminded us that "The meek shall inherit the earth." I began to suspect that they said that because The Meek were extremely unlikely to make a revolution. Their use of the word "inherit" was particularly cynical.

In the absence of peaceful opportunity for moral debate, the Vietnamese liberation fighters - the Viet Cong and its NLF – defended their own country and defeated U.S. imperialism by killing. While pacifists would solemnly wag their fingers at all those who committed violence, Trotsky had written some thirty years earlier that the violence of the oppressed is not the same as the violence of the oppressor. His example was the American Civil War:

> *"The question is not which of the warring camps caused or suffered the greatest number of victims. History has different yardsticks for the cruelty of the Northerners and the cruelty of the Southerners in the Civil War. A slave-owner who through cunning and violence shackles a slave in chains, and a slave who through cunning or violence breaks the chains—let not the contemptible eunuchs tell us that they are equals before a court of morality!"*

"*Contemptible eunuchs!*" Trotsky was talking my language: he wrote of emasculated philistines spewing "moral effluvia" in defence of class rule and their own privileges. I was hooked. His was a level-headed, morally defensible revolution. But Trotskyists were not bomb-throwing crazies. Lenin had written that such "revolutionary adventurism" - the violent spectacle of "left-wing infantilism" in the person of anarchist hot-heads (e.g. Weatherman, or today's Black Bloc) - achieved nothing but making the socialist movement vulnerable to victimization and repression by the state, as well as alienating the population. Failing, as always, to spark the masses into revolutionary motion, such violence was a sign of weakness, because it substituted "revolutionary heroics" for the sane, measured and difficult process of revolutionary movement-building. It also grievously underestimated the ability of the capitalist state to retaliate. Meanwhile, pacifism continued to argue that no violence was justified, whether the state was hypocritical about it or not. But the continuing obscenity of America's Vietnam slaughter urged a less passive philosophical response.

Chapter 62

ANDREW SARRIS, AUTEURS AND HITCHCOCK

My friends at film school included David I., a serious Iranian Marxist in exile who had been arrested in a Teheran cinema at age twelve for not jumping to his feet when the national anthem was played. Trained as an architect, he was distantly related to the westernized Pahlavi family (of the Shah), but the connection never did him any good, and, under the ensuing theocratic regimes, he grew up in ever-greater jeopardy; Tim H., a talented and melancholic English music student whose father was a bus conductor; Nikos K., an Athenian possessed of intelligent good humour, and his attractive German girl friend named Anna Maria, both of whom brought needed levity to our group; and Joe K., an earnest history student from Edmonton, Alberta. The rest of our classmates were aesthetes who adored European "art" films - Bergman and Fellini - and detested Hollywood; technophiles (the school produced many fine cameramen); guys with no particular interest in anything except getting drunk and having a "larf"; and guys who dreamed of producing pornography. The would-be pornographers were the most hostile to our left-wing politics. (I'm no prude, but the flood of pornography – now triumphantly gone "mainstream" – isn't progress for anyone but libertarians, who want to extend the tentacles of exploitation as far as possible. They are the ideologues of bourgeois morality for the demographic layers that capitalism targets with its ideas: "populism's little man", "main street", "the beltway", "905", etc.) and sooner or later come out of the closet as fascists.

My London School of Film Technique friends, L-R: Josepfh K., Nikos K., author, David I., spring 1969. Photo by Vasilis Pagonis.

Together, we "Trots" haunted the dingy LFS canteen, drawing the line between us and the other students, debating Marxist theory and assessing the films we saw each night at the National Film Theatre. The NFT featured a massive program of world cinema, with regular directorial retrospectives. Beguiled by notions of theory and methodology, we sought a coherent way of looking at films and embraced the *auteur theory* as expressed by the brilliant American critic, Andrew Sarris. His book, *THE AMERICAN CINEMA, Directors and Directions, 1929-1968*, defined our critical approach with an astonishingly accurate summation of the careers of great

My battered copy of The American Cinema, 1929 - 1968, by Andrew Sarris. Cover design by Milton Glaser.

(and not-so-great) directors. The auteur theory's main contribution was a sympathetic (in some cases hagiographic) re-evaluation of Hollywood directors whose output – along with the cinema itself – had been critically neglected at best or, at worst, condemned by snobs and philistines for pandering to commercial pressures and mass taste. In addition to Charlie Chaplin, John Ford, D.W. Griffith, Fritz Lang, Jean Renoir and Orson Welles, a prime beneficiary of the auteur theory was Alfred Hitchcock. His supporters (Canada's Robin Wood, for one) declared his films equal to or better than those of, say, Ingmar Bergman, the 1960s art house darling whose films are, today, considerably less watchable than Hitch's. The auteur theory was soon replaced by semiotics and deconstructionism and, while having established a permanent mode of respect for directorial oeuvres, it's now largely forgotten except as a Hollywood marketing tool whereby masses of drooling film buffs, trivia collectors and people desperately in need of genuine life experience regurgitate comparative box office totals while invoking the names of Lucas, Tarantino, Spielberg and Scorsese. However, I defy anyone attuned to the arts to read Sarris's Introduction to *The American Cinema* and not be profoundly impressed by his leadership in a cultural campaign that redefined cinema criticism and gave the Hollywood studio system its due.

Among the LSFT student body, we regarded ourselves as the only ones genuinely interested in world cinema. In 1968-70, many great directors visited the school or NFT screenings of their work: Jean-Luc Godard, Francois Truffaut, Sam Peckinpah, Milos Foreman, Ivan Passer, Abe Polonski, Satyajit Ray, Budd Boetticher

The immortal Alfred Hitchcock.

and Sam Fuller, among many others. I shook many an auteur's hand, but the most memorable moment was my exchange with Hitchcock. After decades in Hollywood, Hitch had shot a new film in his home town of London. He had returned at the age of seventy, both to acknowledge an NFT retrospective of his forty-eight films, and to promote the forty-ninth, *Frenzy*. The NFT audience was packed and my comrades and I sat in the front row, virtually at the feet of the Master of Suspense, who was now a member of Sarris's Pantheon of top directors. (I loved Hitchcock's films without reservation: *The Birds* and *Psycho* are still among my favourites.) Although he had seemed a little surprised by the worshipful stance of Francois Truffaut in his book-length dialogue about each of his films, Hitch's tone in public never varied from a glacial and taciturn response to questions – usually to the delight of onlookers - and he was no different with me. Following a long montage of clips from his films the audience was granted a question session, and I jumped to my feet, the first in line. A spontaneous instrument of his marketing campaign, I blurted out, "When is *Frenzy* opening?" Hitchcock turned his gaze in my direction and dead-panned, "November." Everyone laughed at my gormless enthusiasm and his one-word reply, but I can now say that I once spoke with the most famous film maker of all time, Alfred Hitchcock, and you can't.

Tantalizing as their ideas were, Trotsky's and Sarris's main appeal was that they were great polemicists. Sarris kept his political views to himself, but anyone who could write, at age thirty: *"Much of the sick, perverse, anti-humanistic humour sweeping through America today is an inevitable reaction to the sickening sentimentality of totalitarianism masquerading as all-encompassing humanism,"* was surely a fellow traveller.

Trotsky doesn't fall into the trap set by establishment critics for contemporary atheists who deny that belief in God is necessary for a code of ethics. In Trotsky's view, the world functions with ends justifying means – governments and the powerful base all their activities on this principle, invoking God's supposed values only when advantageous to their cause. Trotsky said that it was the *ends* which required justification, not the means. In response to the question of violence, which a revolution may inevitably entail,

Trotsky writes about how the "ruling class" or "bourgeoisie" uses the idea of "morality" as a tool of social control, to confuse the opposition with "eternal verities" to which they, themselves, don't subscribe:

> *"The ruling class* (in our day, the corporate plutocracy - DW) *forces its ends upon society and habituates it into considering all those means which contradict its ends as immoral. That is the chief function of official morality. It pursues the idea of the "greatest possible happiness" not for the majority but for a small and ever diminishing minority (*as per today's notorious CEOs - DW*). Such a regime could not have endured for even a week through force alone. It needs the cement of morality. The mixing of this cement constitutes the profession of the petty bourgeois theoretician, and moralists. They dabble in all colors of the rainbow but in the final instance remain apostles of slavery and submission."*

But it was the Marxist view of the material function of ideas that sold me on the whole schema. It stated that the ruling ideas of any epoch are the ideas of its ruling class. Stated in contemporary terms (Meredith Kolodner in the ISReview):

> *"Consider, for example, the major media corporations operating in the United States - ABC, CBS, CNN, and NBC. Who owns them? Capitalists. Who controls them? Managers working for capitalists. The result of concentration of the means of communication in the hands of a small number of families is that the ideas transmitted by the major media represent the interests of those families, with ideas such as - "Capitalism is the best social system ever," "Inequality is inevitable and natural and even useful because it motivates people to work harder," "Socialism is inefficient and*

oppressive," "Anything is possible for an individual living in the United States if he works hard enough and plays by the rules."

The deeper one looks at the perpetuation of class and racial divisions in America, the more offensive these ideas become. Noam Chomsky labels this process "Manufacturing Consent." I finally felt freed from the world view that I'd grown up with in Kingsville. And, if not yet interesting to other people, I at least interested myself.

Chapter 63

TRIUMPH OF THE DUNES

Mirjam seemed to be on perpetual night shift duties at Hammersmith, and my free evenings were taken up with NFT screenings and other extracurricular activities. Parties with eager girls in miniskirts were ubiquitous, and love was accessed at the cost of a smile. I remember lying on my back on a living room floor while a hundred girls in mini-skirts stepped across my upward gaze as though auditioning a private part. Hash, beer, wine and cigarettes were social lubricants and the birth control pill made things easier still. Friends of the kibbutz Danes arrived and contacted Ned, and an angel named Birthe fixed her sites on me. She and I attended a friend of a friend's party, and spent the entire evening in our nameless host's bedroom, where we ignored the intermittent enraged banging at the locked door. Birthe was a voluptuous vanilla ice cream cone in female form, as blond as any I'd beheld, and as sweet. At the beginning of our evening, she slowed the express train of my desire, saying we hardly knew each other. I took my time, and slowly, reverently removed her freshly-laundered brassiere, revealing creamy breasts with soft aureoles like circles of pink rose petals. Her scent was lovely, she tasted heavenly, and when I descended (slowly!) between her thighs, I drenched my face in love until hours later the gentle bucking of her hips finally ceased and she fell asleep. Later, we walked a furious gauntlet to the party's front door, smiling, shaking hands and saying goodnight as though we were honoured guests regrettably forced to depart early. In the hot bright street at dawn, I met Mirjam coming from work. We walked home together and slept most of the day.

Despite her gainful employment, Mirjam was ordered to leave Britain when her visitor's visa expired. I shed tears on the railway platform, and felt predictable rage at the Home Office or the Foreign Office or the Chancellor of the Exchequer or whatever it was, at their squandering of a perfectly good nurse and my perfectly good mate. She was obliged to apply for a work visa from Switzerland, and it would be a minimum of ninety days before she could return. However, my loneliness was assuaged by Birthe, Daisy, an English woman who lived next door to Daisy, and the heiress to a major Australian wine fortune famous for its Tawny Port. Her vast wealth failed to make her attractive – she was dumpy and unhappy and uninterested in anything but finding a man to love her. I met her in the street in Notting Hill Gate and realized we'd had a brief encounter in Israel the previous summer. She seemed to find our meeting fortuitous and lost little time in reminding me who she was. We went to her flat in Bayswater, drank some of her Tawny Port, and made rather hot love on a few occasions. But her glum aimlessness failed to spark genuine enthusiasm in me and, when I listed the virtues of nationalizing the Australian wine industry under workers' control, a subconscious impulse to terminate our relationship may have been at work.

Mirjam returned just as the spring term ended. I had blown an opportunity to write her a severance letter, and our life of *faux*-monogamy resumed. LSFT students had been invited by Clive Donner, a British director who sat on the school's board of governors, to come and be extras in his film *Alfred The Great*, starring David Hemmings, fresh from Blow-*Up*. Donner was a

TOWARDS the end of an evening of beating, shooting, gassing and mass arrests on the streets of Chicago, Hubert Humphrey was nominated as the Democratic candidate for the Presidency of the United States.

One of many horrific headlines from 1968.

terrible filmmaker but a summer on location in Galway, Ireland, promised to be fabulous drunken fun, especially since a group of my *drunk-not-interested-in-anything-but-a-larf* English buddies where definitely going. My comrades deigned to go – there was a Carl Theodore Dreyer retrospective at the NFT, featuring his little-seen masterpiece, *Ordet*, whose characters discuss death and stand around a coffin for much of the film's two hour running time – and, between their guilt-tripping and Mirjam's, I flexed the over-used idiot section of my brain and stayed in London.

Few people of my generation will forget 1968. Britain's fascination with and horror at the phenomenon of America reached near hysteria with the murders of Martin Luther King and Bobby Kennedy. The counter culture had shifted its emphasis from psychedelic love towards rebellion and protest. London's biggest antiwar demonstration culminated in a violent confrontation with the police in front of the American Embassy. The system was lashing out viciously at its critics, and hasn't ceased to this day.

*****

A typical stagehand job for ordinary productions in British theatre may involve as little as five or six minutes work per night. It consists of lightning-fast scenery and prop changes on a darkened stage between scenes and acts. Precise positioning of a different table, a hat stand, a bouquet of roses - all these combine in a clockwork–like ritual that strives for effortless illusion. You can't drink on the job. It's important to avoid collisions in the darkness – with each other and with the precious performers. You may spend hours in the wings, or drinking tea and smoking at the stage door, but when your cue comes, you have to show up and be dead accurate every time. Ned, true to his word, got me a job as a stagehand in London's West End at the Strand Theatre, where a revival of the popular 1938 comedy, *Dear Octopus*, starring Cicely Courtneidge and Richard Todd, was enjoying a successful run. I had little idea who Cicely Courtneidge was, but Richard Todd had played Robin Hood for Disney, and had starred in *A Man Called Peter*, which my mother took me to see in 1955. It's a well-regarded film about a famous preacher, Peter Marshall, who dies tragically at the end of the story. My father was hardly a man of God, but the film's sad conclusion, with an image of Peter's wife rowing alone out to sea and his last words *"See you in the morning, darling, see you in the morning"* repeated on the sound track, suddenly made my mother weep uncontrollably, shedding tears she had suppressed since my father's death. Now, each night at the Strand theatre, I encountered the face of Peter Marshall/Robin Hood in the shadows, slipping deftly past him while he straightened his cufflinks and stepped onto the stage. Our eyes met in friendly acknowledgement of each other's importance to the whole, but I never told him how cool he was as Robin Hood or how he finally made my mother cry.

Mirjam and I limped along, she proclaiming love, I veiling my indifference. Yet I couldn't manage to extricate myself. I've always been drawn to domesticity, and in a manner common to lovers everywhere, we made our little world. We talked about the future, and sometimes about children. Lying in bed after making love, I often looked at her face in the twilight of our room, its beauty reduced to an elemental graininess with a timeless aura – what the male hero of *Woman In The Dunes* saw during tender, sandy moments. Nothing better - this connection was what life was all about. If you wind back the giant voice recorder that God uses to keep everything we say for later prosecution, you'll find it: I said, in a voice heavy with fatalistic despair: "If you get pregnant, I guess we should get married." Mirjam later remarked that she "forgot" to take her pill the next day. Like a good Kingsville boy, I married my pregnant girlfriend at the Hammersmith Registry Office on the 19th of July, 1969. Sam Udin attended and we celebrated at an Indonesian restaurant afterwards.

On Saturday, 20th of September, 1969, I wrote in my journal, *"The crying of a baby, somewhere in the street below, un-nerves me so much that I can't organize my thoughts."* Although the baby below my window wasn't mine, the son Mirjam soon bore me was. Michael Sam Williams arrived on March 4th, 1970. I was twenty-three years old, Mirjam, twenty eight. A month before his birth I wrote: *"How I'd love to experience the sweet urgency of the chase again! And it's over for me! How absurd! I'm twenty-three! I should have a million women! And of course there's always guilt. Mirjam seems so devoted, so in love with me. Christ, if she only were as bored as I. She's tasted a good deal of loneliness in her time (Ne Me Quitte Pas) Now she's got me and won't let go. The tragic thing is she's still lonely in her marriage, and it seems to me it's going to get worse. One iota of honesty between us would make the whole thing crumble."* I had begun a phase of despair and uncertainty which I should have chosen not to share with wife and child. But it was too late. I was responsible for my own actions, but Mirjam was surely obtuse to have chosen so unlikely a mate.

I had little to show from my 2 years at LFS beyond a diploma sloppily rendered in Letraset by the LFS office staff and a ninety-second vampire movie, starring Mirjam and me. The British film industry was in a slump; her unions had closed doors to new membership. There was no doubt in my mind that Canada was where my future lay. I had graduated from a fancy British film school (as it turned out, no one in Canada had ever heard of London School of Film Technique. Ryerson had a primitive television course but there was no film school in Canada), my cousin Graham was a noted Toronto TV director who would help me get work. Joe K.

Mirjam and the author, London, 1968. Photo by Vasilis Pagonis.

was headed there, and Tim, Nikos and David spoke of emigrating. Canada's image was one of optimism and bounty. The NFT had shown the National Film Board of Canada's bombastic Academy Award-winning promotional film, *A Place To Stand*, which had been created for the Ontario Pavillion at Expo '67 – it was an embarrassing, full throttle proclamation that Ontario was the best place to live in the whole world. The NFT audience met the film with stunned silence followed by ripples of nervous and derisive laughter.

Lawrence Durrell declared that "Everyone loathes his own country and countrymen if he is any sort of artist." Being a "Canadian" was out of the question - a mild longing for maple syrup was hardly a definition of identity. But my father's failure to return from the dead, early disappointment in my cousin Graham, and my three years in London drove me to abandon "Englishness" as identity's mask, as well. I had waded too far into internationalism's waters to turn back. I believe that rejection of national identification is a moral obligation, no matter how virtuous such "patriotic" sentiments are said to be. Its embrace harbors too many opportunities for reactionary manipulation. I will never declare "My country, right or wrong," nor even "I Support Our Troops," which is a chicken-shit version of the former and our government's attempt to gain support for aggression while denying its political reality. I revere my right to define who I am, without qualification. I had some of the credentials I believed an interesting person might enjoy: cinematic immersion and my reading of film criticism had honed my aesthetic preferences – I believed that creative and artistic decisions were wholly within my abilities. But I had been bitten by the Marxist bug – even my Iranian friend, David, would refer to it as a "blood disease which has no cure." I felt moral obligation to help the oppressed "elaborate the morality of insurrection." Although on a gut level I wanted to be an artist, I was impatient with aesthetic concerns while the Vietnamese were being slaughtered. I read that the napalm America was dropping on Vietnam was a mixture of gasoline and polystyrene, designed to make the flaming stuff stick to human skin. Sam Peckinpah showed the opening 12 minutes of his *The Wild Bunch* at the NFT to a stunned audience: its Wild West slow motion carnage, including climactic self-annihilation, seemed to explain everything from the

Zapruder footage to American aggression in an audacious vision that left the audience speechless. Jean-Luc Godard signaled the end of the bourgeois world with his film, *Weekend* (prematurely, as it turned out). I began to counterpose aesthetic concerns and political consciousness, a formula guaranteed to make me hate anyone who hired me, despise the products of bourgeois production, and getting a job very complicated. And combined with a lust for quick gratification and personal freedom, I wasn't a leading candidate for 1970's *Husband And Father Of The Year* award.

In the London papers, I read about Ned's new play, performed at a national student drama competition: *"The afternoon dragged hard, grey and wearisome as the day outside through "Fortress" by Ned Logan – yet another variation on the obsessive theme of anonymous characters in limbo waiting to get out."* I felt sorry for Ned, but couldn't help think his nihilist vision reflected the politics of the middle class, who were dismissed by Lenin as a class with no historical future.

In my journal I wrote on March 27th, 1970: *"The sunlight falls through the branches and across this page in a beautiful, dappled pattern. Its gentle movement arouses joy, sadness and nostalgia in me. Then the light fades and these feelings are transposed to ones of a cooler, thoroughly melancholy tone. Life is an endless variation on the same theme."*

Mirjam, Sam and I took off from Gatwick on the 24th of April, 1970, Canada-bound. Sam never cried the whole way across the Atlantic. People were charmed by our baby. He was the most beautiful being I had ever seen.

THE END

CPSIA information can be obtained at www.ICGtesting.com
Printed in the USA
LVOW061226120812

293927LV00004B/38/P